SOVIET-AMERICAN RELATIONS

SOVIET–AMERICAN RELATIONS

Understanding Differences, Avoiding Conflicts

Edited by
Daniel N. Nelson and Roger B. Anderson

A Scholarly Resources Imprint
WILMINGTON, DELAWARE

The paper used in this publication meets the minimum requirements of the American National Standard for permanence of paper for printed library materials, Z39.48, 1984.

©1988 by Scholarly Resources Inc.
All rights reserved
First published 1988
Printed and bound in the United States of America

Scholarly Resources Inc.
104 Greenhill Avenue
Wilmington, Delaware 19805-1897

Library of Congress Cataloging-in-Publication Data

Soviet-American relations : understanding differences, avoiding
  conflicts / edited by Daniel N. Nelson and Roger B. Anderson.
      p.   cm.
  Papers originally presented at a symposium held Feb. 20–21,
1987, at the University of Kentucky in Lexington, sponsored
by the Dept. of Russian and Eastern Studies.
  Includes bibliographies and index.
  ISBN 0-8420-2300-3.   ISBN 0-8420-2326-7 (pbk.)
  1. United States—Relations—Soviet Union—Congresses.
2. Soviet Union—Relations—United States—Congresses. I. Nelson,
Daniel N., 1948–   . II. Anderson, Roger B. III. University of
Kentucky. Dept. of Russian and Eastern Studies.
E183.8.S65S577   1988
327.73047—dc19   88-19726
                                                                 CIP

About the Editors

DANIEL N. NELSON (Ph.D. Johns Hopkins University, 1975) is a professor of political science at the University of Kentucky. He is the author or editor of more than a dozen scholarly books concerning Communist party states. His recent works include *Elite-Mass Relations in Communist States* (1988) and *Alliance Behavior in the Warsaw Pact* (1986). His articles have appeared in such journals as *World Politics, Journal of Politics, Problems of Communism,* and *Soviet Studies.*

ROGER B. ANDERSON (Ph.D. Michigan State University, 1967) is professor and chairman of Russian and Eastern studies at the University of Kentucky. As a scholar of Russian literature, he has published books on Karamzin (*N. M. Karamzin: The Teller in the Tale*) and Dostoevsky (*Dostoevsky: Myths of Duality*). His articles range from Pushkin to Pasternak and treat particularly the interplay between important examples of Russian prose and theories of evolving Russian culture.

Contents

Preface

An extraordinarily successful two-day symposium on Soviet-American relations was held on February 20–21, 1987, at the University of Kentucky in Lexington. Its success was measured not only by the large attendance from campus and community, or by the considerable media coverage, but also by the substance of what was said and by the commitment of participants and audience to learn from one another. The high quality of the presentations and discussions, as well as the numerous requests to make the papers available to a wider public, has made this volume possible.

The University of Kentucky may not have been a likely site for an in-depth examination of Soviet-American relations; it does not have a graduate program in Soviet-East European studies and may lack the visibility for international programs that other institutions possess. However, the 1985–87 period saw the creation of a new and larger Department of Russian and Eastern Studies, a reinvigorated Office of International Affairs, and many other steps at our university that evinced greater commitment to studying "the world." We thought that it would be important for the university to become part of a critical debate regarding Americans' understanding of the Soviet Union, and how that understanding can play a role in avoiding conflict. We also thought, and are even more convinced today, that the issues of Soviet-American relations are made, not resolved, in Washington or Moscow. Only through a broadly informed debate about how best to recast U.S. relations with the Soviets can superpower conflict be managed and avoided.

Therefore, in the spring of 1986 it was decided by the Department of Russian and Eastern Studies to begin plans for a major symposium, to be held one year later. Professor Roger Anderson, as chairman of the department, assumed the principal role in this planning process. The cooperation received from numerous university and community sponsors was gratifying. We began to see that there was a strong reservoir of interest in, and concern about, the direction of Soviet-American relations. Financial support and enthusiasm for the project are evident in the list of contributors: the College of Arts and Sciences, the chancellor of the Lexington Campus, the chancellor of the Chandler Medical Center, the Graduate School, the Kentucky Humanities Council, the Sanders-Brown Center on Aging, the Department of Political Science, the Patterson School of Diplomacy, and the College of Law. Community involvement was assisted by the Bluegrass International Affairs Council. We were pleasantly surprised by the degree of interest and willingness to contribute financially to such a major symposium, and we are indebted to these sponsors.

Our gratitude also extends to Daniel Helmstadter and Richard Hopper at Scholarly Resources for their interest in this project, and to both Kim Hayden and Betty Pasley at the University of Kentucky whose expert word-processing skills were used many times by the editors.

From the outset we recognized that only the most pluralistic forum could hope to encompass our goal. Professor Anderson sought to bring together experts from a wide variety of disciplines and backgrounds—law, theology, economics, sociology, political science, arms control and security studies, and literature—to talk about their area of expertise and to bring that expertise to bear on the core issue of developing a deeper understanding of the Soviets in order to avoid conflicts with them.

"Understanding" can mean many things. Inherent to our concept of understanding is to further the perception and comprehension of differences between the United States and the Soviet Union in terms of culture, history, security, and values. Simultaneously, we see understanding in this context as meaning an enhanced recognition of similarities between the superpowers as they both confront parallel social and economic crises while endangering their own survival through spending for a nuclear war they must never fight.

Since the conference was held, changes in Soviet-American relations have been, in some ways, dramatic. The reevaluation of mutual perceptions advocated by several contributors in this volume already has begun. That such steps have been accelerated because of summit meetings between the leaders of the United States and the USSR is obvious. Equally clear is the long path ahead of the superpowers, in all domains of their interaction, toward cementing a new, less conflictual relationship. The contributors to this volume, although having written their papers in early 1987, nevertheless point to steps in that path toward a fundamental shift in Soviet-American relations, some of which we now know were taken by 1988.

The complex goals we set are obviously unachievable in one volume. However, the contributors have provided signposts for the reconsideration of Soviet-American relations. At the very least, we are certain that America's process of reconceptualizing its encounters with the Soviet Union must intensify in the late 1980s and into the 1990s. The Cold War and "New Cold War" have consumed so much of the world's resources, and so many lives (often through proxy wars and wars of intervention by both superpowers), that both the United States and the Soviet Union may suffer the ignominy of self-inflicted decline. Before the rest of the world might breathe a sigh of relief, it would be worthwhile to remember the penchant of the powerful to take others with them in defeat.

Daniel N. Nelson
Roger B. Anderson

Contributors

JANE L. CURRY is an associate professor of political science at Santa Clara University. She is the editor of a number of volumes on Eastern Europe, including the *Black Book of Polish Censorship, Dissent in Eastern Europe*, and *Press Control around the World*. She also has authored *Polish Journalists: Professional Action in a Political Cauldron* (1988) and has written and spoken frequently on issues of Soviet-American and American-East European relations. She received her M.A. from Indiana University and her Ph.D. from Columbia University.

MARK G. FIELD is professor of sociology at Boston University; a fellow in the Russian Research Center at Harvard; a lecturer, Department of Health Policy and Management, Harvard School of Public Health; and an assistant sociologist, Department of Psychiatry, Massachusetts General Hospital, Boston. Field was born in Switzerland and holds a Ph.D. in sociology. His interest in medical sociology and comparative health systems has taken him to the Soviet Union eleven times since 1956. He is the author, coauthor, or editor of five books and over one hundred articles in the professional literature.

JON HURWITZ received his B.A. from Indiana University in 1977 and his Ph.D. in political science from the University of Minnesota in 1984. After teaching at Grinnell College from 1982 to 1986, he joined the Political Science Department at the University of Pittsburgh, where he specializes in mass political behavior. He has published in journals such as the *American Journal of Political Science, American Politics Quarterly, American Political Science Review, Political Psychology*, and *Social Science Quarterly*. He is currently involved in an investigation with Mark Peffley of Americans' views of communism and the Soviet Union.

MICHAEL T. KLARE is director and associate professor of the Five College Program in Peace and World Security Studies, a joint endeavor of Amherst, Hampshire, Mount Holyoke, and Smith colleges and the University of Massachusetts at Amherst. He is also an associate fellow of the Institute for Policy Studies in Washington, DC, and the defense correspondent of *The Nation*. He received his B.A. and M.A. from

Columbia University and his Ph.D. from the Union Graduate School in 1976. Klare is the author of *War without End* (1972), *American Arms Supermarket* (1985), and *Low-Intensity Warfare* (1988). His articles on international affairs and defense policy have appeared in such journals as *Foreign Policy*, *International Security*, and *World Policy*.

JACK MENDELSOHN, a former senior foreign service officer, has been deputy director of the Arms Control Association since March 1985. From 1981 to 1983 he served in the U.S. Arms Control and Disarmament Agency as deputy assistant director of the Strategic Programs Bureau and as senior ACDA representative on the U.S. START delegation. He earlier served as special assistant to the chief negotiator of the SALT delegation (1972–75) and as U.S. representative on the Special Political Committee for MBFR at NATO headquarters in Brussels (1977–79). Mendelsohn received his B.A. from Dartmouth College and has graduate degrees from the University of Chicago and the Institute on East Central Europe at Columbia University. He has published widely on arms control and East-West relations.

JAMES R. MILLAR is professor of economics and project director for the Soviet Interview Project. His *The ABCs of Soviet Socialism* won the 1981 Society of Midland Authors Award in nonfiction (politics/economics). He is editor of *Politics, Work, and Daily Life in the USSR: A Survey of Former Soviet Citizens*, the first volume of studies drawn from the Soviet Interview Project. He also edited the *Slavic Review* (1975–80) and was a founding member of the Academic Council of the Kennan Institute for Advanced Russian Studies. Since 1984 he has served as director of International Programs and Studies and associate vice-chancellor for academic affairs at the University of Illinois at Champaign-Urbana.

MARK PEFFLEY is an assistant professor of political science at the University of Kentucky. He received his B.A. from Indiana University and his Ph.D. from the University of Minnesota in 1984. His articles on public opinion and voting behavior have appeared in such journals as *American Political Science Review*, *American Journal of Political Science*, *American Politics Quarterly*, and *Political Behavior*. He is currently involved in research with Jon Hurwitz to explore public images of Eastern bloc countries and models of mass political reasoning in foreign affairs.

DAVID E. POWELL received his Ph.D. in political science from Yale University. He is a research associate at the Russian Research Center, Harvard University and the author of *Antireligious Propaganda in the Soviet Union* (1975). Professor Powell also has written numerous articles on the political, economic, and social conditions in the USSR.

BRUCE RIGDON is an ordained minister with the United Presbyterian Church and professor of church history at McCormick Theological Seminary in Chicago. He is chair of the National Council of Churches Committee on U.S.-USSR Church Relations and is involved in other aspects of international church affairs as well. He has traveled frequently to the Soviet Union, Eastern Europe, and the Middle East.

BURNS H. WESTON is the Bessie Dutton Murray Professor of Law at the University of Iowa. He received his B.A. degree from Oberlin College in 1956 and his LL.B. and J.S.D. degrees from the Yale Law School in 1961 and 1970, respectively. His books include *International Law and World Order: A Problem-Oriented Coursebook* (1980) and *Toward Nuclear Disarmament and Global Security: A Search for Alternatives* (1984). Weston is a member of the board of editors of the *American Journal of International Law*, chairperson of the Independent Commission on Respect for International Law, and a member of the American Bar Association's Standing Committee on World Order under Law. He also is a senior fellow of the World Policy Institute, a fellow of the World Academy of Art and Science, and a member of the Council on Foreign Relations.

STEPHEN WHITE is a reader in politics and associate of the Institute of Soviet and East European Studies at the University of Glasgow, Scotland. He was educated at Dublin and holds doctorates from both Glasgow and Oxford universities. He is joint editor of *Coexistence* and a member of the editorial boards of *Soviet Studies* and the *Journal of Communist Studies*. His recent publications include *Communist Politics: A Reader* (coedited with Daniel N. Nelson, 1986) and *Ideology and Soviet Politics* (coedited with Alex Pravda, 1987).

Introduction: Encounters, Conflicts, and Superpower Relations

Roger B. Anderson

The Encounters of Superpowers

The United States and the Soviet Union are but two nations, no matter how powerful, among a host of nations. As such, we compete for advantage when our interests overlap, choose economic and political allies, and order our respective domestic politics in keeping with the cultural values by which we identify ourselves. However, we and our Soviet counterparts stand apart to occupy a unique, yet shared, category. As nuclear superpowers, we know, as does the rest of the world, that the safety of global life itself is at stake in the competition that preoccupies us. We each "enjoy" a role of responsibility that all other countries directly or indirectly acknowledge and take into account as they go about shaping their own national destinies. Americans and Soviets cannot avoid the problems that both separate and join them. As different as we are ideologically, we are also different as societies in our historical experiences, our cultural traditions, and in our definition of what constitutes an individual's identity vis-à-vis his society.

Since World War II the task of appraising and managing conflict between the United States and the Soviet Union has been based primarily on strategic-military considerations. In large measure that condition is unavoidable. The prospect of a nuclear war lies at the heart of our mutual fears, and we have both resorted to military criteria to model our respective notions of security. A renewed cold war, which started in the late 1970s, is still with us, one result of which is the paradox of frequent calls for and proposals about arms control even as more Soviet and American national wealth is spent on armed preparedness. Each country risks the economic and social health of its people through huge military outlays. Neither can spend the other into defeat, but that does not stop the process of expanding weapons systems, the overkill of which is increasingly redundant.

The prospects of anything like fundamental cooperation between the superpowers on questions of global nuclear disarmament or political antipathy are currently poor. Therefore, we must accept a more modest task in an effort to manage the conflicts now characterizing Soviet-American relations. That task is to explore and bring to light the broadest possible range of issues—social, political, and strategic—to which both we and our Soviet counterparts must necessarily respond. These include social issues such as priorities of public education and health care, retirement, and old age in differing versions of a postindustrial society. They range to the influence of religious beliefs and practices, and the subtle effect they have on our political institutions. They include the Third World, in which so much superpower competition is played out in tactical and symbolic forms. Additionally, these issues reflect our respective views of our allies in Europe as well as our differing attitudes toward international law. In each case the assumption is that such comparisons and contrasts add incrementally to a fuller picture of American and Soviet conceptions of the world and help clarify what each of us seeks from the world we perceive. At least in some areas, we define reality quite differently, and if that is indeed true, then it especially behooves us to discuss more openly the reasons for these differing conceptions. To do so reinforces the common ground on which we can exchange the rationale and historicocultural reasons for our dissimilarities.

In our encounter with the "other," both we and the Soviets are ready to see each other as the personalized embodiment of what we dislike or fear generally. Here communication is constantly occurring, but less on the level of information than on that of attitudes and emotion. When we examine Soviet and American visions of national security, or the Third World, or the laborious process of nuclear disarmament, we see the personalized outline of the other rather than the objective issues and options that might lead to solutions. Also, that other—our counterpart and opposite—can become the personification of what we wish to reject in ourselves. For example, the dirty tricks and duplicity of espionage and covert operations are common to both the KGB and the CIA. The justification on both sides for such activities is the shared assumption that the other engages, or would if it could, in just those nefarious activities. Fighting fire with fire, then, each uses the tactics it ascribes to the other and blames its opposite number for the deeds it factually commits. Seeing the outline of this dark other legitimates what is hard to justify in oneself.

It is ironic to contemplate the extent to which our perception of Soviet intentions and practices affects our own society and foreign policy. Clearly, U.S. military and foreign aid budgets have grown at the expense of environmental stewardship and medical research in such areas as nutrition, AIDS, and cancer. SDI research is funded heavily, while overall monies for the study of foreign affairs, including Sovietology, have dwindled. Our predetermined vision of Soviet global strategy influences the campaign platforms of national, and even state, officials. Thus, to some degree the full voice we give to condemnation of the Soviet version of reality restricts our stewardship of our own society. In other words, the traditional monolithic interpretation of Soviet rule and society pushes us toward an equally monolithic sense of America and our place in the world. We have long been prone to politicize Soviet studies in our own country, to subordinate a diversity of opinion to reigning preconceptions centered about a narrow understanding of national security. The Soviets have unquestionably done the same. Each superpower has put on a different pair of colored glasses that tints the world with a dominant hue and thereby restricts its vision of reality to the narrow range it is ready to see.

We would do well to examine with heightened effort what we reject in our enemy—and why. This order of knowledge helps us to avoid the blinding effects of fear and ready hate that all too often increase friction and diminish our respective national treasures of talent and goods. By focusing more attention on matters of daily life that separate us, in addition to matters of military strategy, we are more ready to perceive the presence of problems that confront us both. As never before, each superpower stands in need of an intelligent curiosity about the problems and options that we face together in an increasingly volatile world. It is incumbent on us to comprehend what our differences are, why they have arisen, and to find ways to live with them. To do so in no way condones our Soviet counterparts; it affirms, instead, our intellectual viability and pragmatism in a period of significant change. To condemn those different from ourselves without such understanding adds nothing to an effective American foreign policy. Such condemnation only tends to blind us to the growing number of problems facing our respective societies that are not ideologically driven.

The Rhetoric of Violence

With the settling in of the "New Cold War," the United States has tended to concentrate on questions of hostility and security, of implied threats and moral self-justification, as bases for international order. Together with these emphases, and perhaps because of them, we have witnessed an atmosphere of increased rhetorical simplification in America. That simplification affects our self-perception, superpower relations, and ultimately the working actualities of both American and Soviet society. It is perhaps predictable, therefore, that the specter of nuclear conflict has again moved to the forefront of the popular imagination. Whether or not we agree with this change in the tone of Soviet-American relations, the American public has grown increasingly aware of the ghost-dance of danger and hope that we and the Soviets constantly perform. That awareness frightens both partners, but it also has heightened curiosity and consciousness about each other.

Since 1979 we have seen a strange mixture of superpower relations. Military expenditures increased significantly during the first term of Ronald Reagan's presidency and continued at the level of 13 to 15 percent of the GNP in the USSR, but SALT I and SALT II have remained a reliable basis for predicting deployment and continued negotiation. Even as the rhetoric of ideological conflict has risen in volume, more Americans travel within the Soviet Union and participate in cooperative professional projects than ever before. Citizen exchanges abound even as our embassies shrink in size. Perhaps as never before, Americans and the Soviets are joined in matters of survival that transcend ideology. One of the most dramatic of these exchanges involves the monitoring of the Soviet nuclear weapons test moratorium by the National Resources Defense Council in July 1986. It presently may be the working assumption in Washington that Moscow is behind terrorism in the Middle East, Africa, the Philippines, and Central America, but, even so, Washington has cooperated with Moscow in creating a number of nuclear risk-reduction centers. These involve military and diplomatic personnel on both sides who maintain active communication aimed at keeping international incidents, including terrorism in far-flung "hot spots," from escalating into unanticipated levels of conflict.

The presence of the primal danger that nuclear war represents significantly raises our curiosity about how our Soviet counterparts view the bomb and terrorism, how they handle differences with their allies, what they value in a national leader, how they educate their children, and if they anticipate retirement with anything like the mixed feelings we observe in ourselves. The presence of mutually assured destruction has strangely sparked a sense of urgency in our daily lives that military might cannot satisfy. As the television miniseries *Amerika* raised the simplistic specter of Soviets running our national government at gunpoint, other stations showed feature-length films about the day-to-day existence of work and marriage in the USSR. At some level, deep fears and lively curiosity interweave within the larger framework of an acknowledged interdependency.

Some Americans accept the proposition that the accelerated expansion of our military, and a breakout of the existing ABM Treaty, assures peace through the strength of military hardware. Other Americans believe that international peace is better enhanced by achieving a broader knowledge of how and why our two peoples live and behave as we do. Social and psychological issues are starting to shoulder their way into diplomatic maneuvering and military technique to help explain the competition that marks Soviet-American relations. This emerging amalgam is healthy, for it brings to the surface the idea that historical and social forces cannot be separated from efficient management of international tension.

To Manage Conflict

To manage conflict, one must understand all the important forces behind it. To explore the connecting passages that open up thereby shifts the question of competition away from the rhetoric of violence to the more substantive issue of how each of us responds to the same problems. To quote Richard Nixon in an address to the Los Angeles World Affairs Council in March 1986, we and the Soviets must pursue "rules of engagement for living with our differences rather than dying over them. . . . We can never be friends but we cannot afford to be enemies." We have no choice but to accept the terms of competitive coexistence and rely on pragmatism to give ballast to the listings of ideological teleology heard from both superpowers.

About 15% of the Soviet GNP is devoted to the military, while our own economy's growth in the 1980s has revived an enhanced military-industrial infrastructure. Neither country is performing very well on the stage of international economic competition. We both run the risk of spending ourselves into diminished stature in the interests of a military-based security that, in fact, heightens the chances of a nuclear exchange.

To scale down the militarization of social wealth, there must be an accumulation of some measure of trust on both sides. Since governmental trust cannot precede public knowledge, it serves us well to explore what explicitly divides us from the Soviets and what implicit issues neither country can avoid contemplating. In a democratic society the dissemination of opinion and information about such issues is indispensable. It is fundamental in an academic setting in which specialists talk among themselves. It is no less fundamental to distill the issues and options that emerge from such discourse and to put them before the American public in a wide variety of forums.

We are entering a new period of Soviet-American relations. Paradoxically, it is a period wherein global importance imposes a variety of security obligations on both superpowers while making direct military conflict between us unthinkable. Vast sums of our respective productivity are devoted to preparing for a war, the occurrence of which could destroy the globe itself. Our mutual policy of nuclear posturing, however, is not the only dimension of our interdependence.

Both our societies are in the midst of realizing the opportunities and problems of a rapidly changing world economy. The United States and the Soviet Union are slipping in absolute terms. Mikhail Gorbachev has strived to make the Soviet economy more efficient, but with mixed results. The American economy, meanwhile, is beleaguered by the cheaper, high-quality goods produced, particularly by our Asian allies. Both superpowers have a troubled environmental picture to contemplate in the future—a costly proposition no matter who pays for it. We are both targets for the rising economic and nationalist expectations of traditionally powerless nation-states. The spread of terrorism as a form of foreign policy confronts the United States and the Soviet Union more immediately, and therefore more poignantly, than does the threat of war between us. Socialist or capitalist, we both need to refurbish our economies, reformulate educational policies for the next century, improve medical care for our peoples, and create a more farsighted attitude toward managing nationalist and religious hot spots in the Third World. A case can be made that to ignore such issues in the interests of narrowly defined national security itself adds to the atmosphere of hostility that both superpowers wish to alleviate.

Understanding Differences

The topics and range of opinion in the following chapters presume the presence of, first, a heterogeneous historical process—an evolution—that is at work in both the United States and the Soviet Union; and, second, the presence, in Russia as in America, of complex forces of thought and differing constituencies that organically affect domestic and foreign policy in both countries. If there is an argument advanced here it is that the Soviet Union is not a monolith, no more than is the United States, Israel, France, or any other nation-state. Our societies breathe and flex as tensive wholes. Russia is subject to evolution and experimentation, and we risk a limitation of ourselves if we ignore the nature and effects of the competing needs and aspirations at work in Soviet society, both now and in its past. As academics with professional interests in Soviet social and political structures, or informed citizens looking at another country, we would do well to examine the institutional and popular complexities operative in the Soviet Union. In turn, curiosity about how the Soviet people look at the world might reveal how they strive to interpret us amid our own complexities.

To repeat the reigning opinion that the broad spectrum of Soviet life is frozen in predictability and governed by the unchanging directives of an intransigent Party elite is simply inadequate. It suggests a narrowness in us that we would much prefer to consider to be the attitude of the Soviets themselves. It is simplistic and a disservice to ourselves to think that historical change happens to us but not to our Soviet counterparts. To act uncritically because of such assessments courts ineptitude and fortuitous mistakes. Social values and cultural definitions are not manufactured by power elites. To a large extent, these values and definitions establish parameters by which such elites gain a legitimacy that allows the formation of their agendas.

There is an assumption here that the line between official political apparatus and society is permeable in both the United States and the Soviet Union. Most certainly such permeability in our two countries is not identical, and it is no wiser to leap to the naive conclusion that Americans and Russians are really the same underneath. To do so in its own way ignores the distinct histories that have formed us and the cultural values by which we recognize ourselves. Our two cultures, our most basic assumptions and attitudes, have been formed through our respective national histories, necessarily yielding differing world views. The simplifications that result from intransigent hostility toward the Soviets, and uncritical assumptions of our homogeneity with the Soviets, end eventually in unrealistic ethnocentrism.

While it is the political and social dimensions of Soviet-American relations that are most readily apparent in the following chapters, together the contributors speak to an underlying anthropological principle: to comprehend the specific points of contention between groups one first must understand the structural assumptions on which the differences of choice and behavior are based. For one country to disparage another as an automatic response distorts self-affirmation into a dangerous antagonism. For any country to move from its own cultural givens to insistence on the universal applicability of those givens invites a powerful unconscious response of self-preservation from a competitor nation. In return, that response can itself be interpreted as hostility. The danger is that the cycle can escalate until the weaponry that both use as instruments of foreign policy becomes the overriding mutual reference point. The ultimate danger is that a loaded weapon eventually demands to be discharged. To explore the differences between the United States and the Soviet Union is fundamental to the management of the real and potential conflicts between us.

There is, then, a common thread running through the presentations here that lies outside matters of political preference or the assignment of blame. That thread is the presence of structural issues in the world at large to which we both must necessarily respond. These issues run from the question of health care for our respective societies to what characterizes our allies and our targets for projecting diplomatic and military influence around the world. The center of gravity is in that plastic, living amalgam of values that distinguishes our cultures, out of which our differing forms of problem-solving emerge. If we cannot understand each other by direct conversation, then we can at least glimpse the other contemplating the same problems and issues that we also must consider. This is a point that Howard Wiarda repeatedly has emphasized. He urges the United States to pursue "a more empathetic understanding of foreign cultures and institutions than before, an understanding of them in terms of their own cultural traditions and even language, rather than through the distorting. . .prism of Western social science."[1]

A society's continuous proximity to crisis carries serious hidden costs. The presence of assured crises does not so much foster prospects of real peace as does the polity's numbed acceptance of an endless series of short-term responses. The price we pay as a society is that of a foreshortened attention span and a narrowed sense of the world as dependent on the immediate rise and fall of American or Soviet interests. We too often assume that regional, and even global, issues are valid only as they refer to the myopic question of whether we or the Soviets benefit or lose at any given moment. Other parts of the world, notably the Middle East and Central America, seem important in terms of how they situationally help or hinder our metastruggle with the Soviets. This contributes to turning the Third World into a number of armed proxy or client states wherein the Cold War yields microcosmic hot wars seemingly without end or resolution. In a pointed remark, George Kennan has described the cost that a free society pays for such a simplification of the world and its fixation on antagonism with its ideological competitor:

> This endless series of distortions and oversimplifications; this systematic dehumanization of the leadership of another great country; this routine exaggeration of Moscow's military capabilities and of the supposed iniquity of Soviet intentions; this monotonous misrepresentation of the nature and the attitudes of another great people—and a long-suffering people at that, sorely tried by the vicissitudes of this past century. . .these, believe me, are not the marks of the maturity and discrimination one expects from the diplomacy of a great power; they are the

marks of an intellectual primitivism and naivete unpardonable in a great government.[2]

In a free society the reasons for difference, not just the results of difference, are considered open to public examination and interpretation. It is folly from our side, for example, to try to assess Soviet foreign policy without clarifying the Russians' historical obsession with securing national borders. Russia's invasion-filled past, most notably by Napoleon and Hitler, still deeply affects Soviet psychology and largely determines its relations with its allies. In contrast, America's borders have been inviolate, a condition that has shaped our popular imagination in its own way. To talk about Soviet-American relations we must add to the concepts of "right" and "wrong" the realism of a historical relativity that has made each nation distinctive. Add to such embedded differences certain military, economic, environmental, and social problems that we both must face and the central question of East-West relations shifts from the press of conflict to the comparing of historical definitions, without which coexistence is impossible.

Soviet citizens, for example, commonly find it hard to comprehend American-style advertising with its plethora of brand names and our penchant for constant comparison and choice. And those same Soviet citizens are unable to understand the reason for the adversarial relationship between executive and legislative branches of our government. While we celebrate "freedom" as the right to differ from those around us—to sing a solo part in society, as it were—"freedom" in the Russian experience is more likely to derive from one's sense of defined place within a larger whole, of being a part of the social chorus.

As a people, Americans are not inclined to study foreign languages or cultures. When such study does occur it is usually skewed toward the European traditions many of us share by heritage. Our sense of cultural pluralism runs to vigorous editorial differences in our communications media. We value the separation of power between different branches of government. These are different aspects of an individualism that we take for granted but that simply do not translate adequately into Russian society, either today or traditionally.

It is an egregious error on our part to assume that our social, cultural, or political values are normative in the world. We may not have private or public sympathy for Soviet society as a model to emulate, but it is proof of ethnocentric bias for us to judge Russian differentness from us as the measure of its illegitimacy. To do so ignores the complexity and versatility of the Soviets' reality on their own terms. It suggests an insularity and maladaptation unworthy of any great nation. To ignore the cultural values beneath an ideology different from ours is an issue that is larger than our interpretation of Soviet-American relations. It indicates a more general difficulty that Americans have with comprehending what other cultures want and how they go about getting it through social and political forms. As a people, we simply must acknowledge, and to a greater degree accept, what Islamic, Hindu, Confucian, or African values influence the aspirations and articulated policies of the world's various cultures. The growing strategic and economic integrality of the globe makes anything less a source of confusion and potential danger, to ourselves and to the continuation of our own values.

The pluralism that is the world does not require elimination of our competition with a country such as the Soviet Union. What pluralism does impose on us is the intelligent examination of our own values relative to those of other important peoples, both friend and foe, so we can live more realistically with such competition. For any country to seek the extirpation of such values, aspirations, and cultural perceptions different from its own isolates that country and makes difference itself the source of conflict. To understand that the Soviet Union is different from the United States is not enough. The "how" and "why" of difference need continuous public discussion in order to avoid the danger of equating such difference with an intolerable threat.

To study what the peoples of the Soviet Union want, of themselves and of the surrounding world, is far removed from endorsing the authority of the Communist party. It is more accurate to say that the study of those popular wants opens us to the working subtleties by which central authority after Joseph Stalin has been influenced by those masses. Such study has been slow to emerge, but James Millar (see Chapter 1) throws specific light on how recent Soviet émigrés view both the Soviet Union and the United States. He points out how complex are the assessments of the Soviet experience by those who choose to leave it. Millar also provides an exceptionally clear, although idiosyncratic, assessment of American life as interpreted by those recent Soviet arrivals. These émigrés give us much-needed insights into how Soviets view themselves and a unique perspective of how American habits, values, and behavior are perceived by our chief global competitor. By studying the factual complexities of Soviet society, we can also enrich our self-awareness.

Perceptions of Soviet Change

On the civilian scene we are witnessing the beginning of what could be revolutionary telecommunications contact between the United States

and the Soviet Union. Satellite broadcasts of Soviet television pro-
gramming (through the *Gorizont* and *Molniya* systems) are rapidly finding their way into American colleges as clips of Soviet newscasts are
beginning to filter into our news and documentary programs. Meanwhile, an uncensored President Reagan has spoken on Soviet television,
and, in 1986, representatives of the U.S. government, again without
censorship, received access to Latvian and pan-Soviet audiences through
the Chautauqua conference. On military and diplomatic levels, as on
the level of private citizens, the 1980s manifest a much more sophisticated and multifaceted set of contacts than the Cold War rhetoric at
first suggests.

The results of these many strands of contact are encouraging but
complex. Efforts by Gorbachev to restructure (*perestroika*) the Soviet
economy, including elements of private entrepreneurship, are widely
disseminated in the Soviet press. A more open airing of domestic political and cultural pluralism (*glasnost*) also has a high profile in Russia
and has clearly caught the popular American imagination. These are
serious, if still incomplete, steps toward evolutionary change in the
Soviet Union. The complexity for us in these new phenomena lies in
the fact that the evolution we observe is distinctively Russian and
collectivist; it differs markedly from our own model of change and individualism. At least to some in the United States, the presence of
change is uncritically synonymous with Western-style pluralism and our
own definitions of democracy. It is most important to keep in mind
Russia's traditional cultural values and psychology as we try to interpret
indications of evolution in Soviet society. It will benefit us little to
impose our own ethnocentric biases on others. In fact, as the Soviets
work out their own economic and social destiny, their policies will inevitably frustrate the expectations that we will be tempted to project
onto them.

The presence of change in Russia is thus something of a language
that Americans are ready to hear but must work to decipher. We are a
mobile people who appreciate newness and experimentation. The Gorbachev presence, at least potentially, suggests elements of a mobility
and experimentation that evoke a sense of concurrence between us
quite beyond ideology. The Soviet Russian life-style and popular opinion
will not coincide with ours, nor need they. Our curiosity is best tem-
pered with acknowledgment of cultural differentness as we formulate
the problems and options that face both nations.

The Soviet Union wants very much to occupy a position of parity
with the United States at some level. All too often such parity is posited
in terms of military clout—of atomic weaponry and the systems that
can deliver them. That wish for parity seems to stem largely from the
Soviets' demand for international legitimization of their own social

forms and values and from their own economic development in the future. Here, patriotic nationalism interlocks with an insistence on cultural self-determination. The wish for external acknowledgment of Soviet legitimacy actually bolsters the largely militarized Soviet economy as a way of guaranteeing some form of global prominence. It is wise for us to pay more attention to that drive for legitimization, and to use it as a lens through which to assess both Russia's domestic priorities and its foreign policy.

We have simply not devoted enough attention to this issue in the past. Too often we have seen the question of Russia's national self-determination, of its self-definition, as the simplified control by a small, powerful elite of ideologues that imposes its unchanging will on the powerless and passive Soviet masses. Stephen Cohen reminds us how unwise it is, both humanistically and tactically, to ignore another culture's inner dynamics or undervalue its influence on its own national policies.[3] To do so leads to a rigidity, the rhetoric of which flaws our own global policies.

That same simplification also carries the long-term risk of reinforcing a domestic political agenda in the United States that manipulates American public opinion in order to militarize further our own social and economic life, thereby risking an increased polarization of Third World alliances and reducing the quality of domestic discourse in our own country. This invites disruption and hostilities at home and abroad that can lose their reference points and thus gain an independent existence in history apart from their initial causes. This, in turn, threatens to heat up regional conflicts to the stage where superpower self-interest is tempted to exert itself. Additionally, we risk subverting indigenous regional aspirations to such superpower competition, a policy hardly leading to a more stable world.

Conclusion

In the following chapters, a variety of perspectives is used to consider superpower relations. Each essay includes the delineation of some issue or problem that both Americans and Soviets confront, for now and for the future. The result is a kaleidoscope of viewpoints, all rotating around the center of comparison as to how we each perceive and address those shared issues. One result is a sense of just how interdependent we and the Soviets are. The problems and issues we cannot ignore place us face to face, not to practice name-calling and fault-finding but to enhance problem-solving in functional ways.

Another result, and just as important in the long run, is a realistic appraisal of those distinctions between us that declare the obvious:

that our histories and cultural values often do not coincide, and that such differences do not nullify the legitimacy of each to the other. Understanding and studying the contrasts of our national experiences are requisite if competition between us is to be managed peacefully. It is of overriding importance not that we converge economically or socially but that both societies acknowledge the interaction that neither we nor the Soviets can avoid.

Notes

[1] Howard Wiarda, *Ethnocentrism in Foreign Policy: Can We Understand the Third World?* (Washington, DC: American Enterprise Institute for Public Policy Research, 1985), p. 35.

[2] George Kennan, *New York Review of Books*, January 21, 1982.

[3] Stephen Cohen, *Rethinking the Soviet Experience* (New York: Oxford University Press, 1985).

Part 1

UNDERSTANDING DIFFERENCES

1
Life in the USSR through the Eyes of Former Soviet Citizens

James R. Millar

Between 1970 and 1984 more than 125,000 former Soviet citizens emigrated from the Soviet Union to the United States. A comparable number emigrated to Israel, and somewhat more than 90,000 of Germanic stock emigrated to West Germany during the same period. The presence of this large and diverse living archive in the West offered a rare opportunity for Western students of Soviet society to learn firsthand about Soviet behavior and attitudes, information that until then was inaccessible. Little systematic survey research is allowed in the USSR, and even less is ever reported publicly, making inferences drawn from such sketchy data risky indeed.

The data on which the following analysis is based were collected by the Soviet Interview Project (SIP), which is a large project designed to discover from recent Russian emigrants how the Soviet system really operates and how Soviet citizens work the system for their own benefit. The data analyzed here were gathered in 1983 and 1984 by the General Survey of the SIP in which 2,793 individuals, or 79 percent of the sample, were interviewed for approximately three hours by means of a structured, Russian-language questionnaire. The sampling frame consisted of 33,624 individuals who arrived in the United States between January 1, 1979, and March 30, 1983, and who were 21 to 70 years of age (inclusive) at time of arrival. The sample was stratified on four background variables: nationality, educational attainment, region of last employment, and size of city in which last employed. Stratification was designed to maximize heterogeneity, and the referent population in the Soviet Union is defined operationally as the "adult, European population of large and medium-sized cities in the USSR."[1]

It is obvious even to people with little statistical sophistication that a survey of former Soviet citizens about their lives in the USSR must suffer from a number of potential biases. The respondents are emigrants, which *ipso facto* makes them different from their former countrymen who did not, or could not, leave and who, therefore, have not experienced life outside the Soviet Union.

In the case of the SIP, the overwhelming majority (about 86 percent) of the respondents were "Jewish" by some definition because most former Soviet citizens who have come to this country were able to leave only through invitation from a relative in Israel. Being Jewish represented the best ticket out of the Soviet Union, but there remained ways for non-Jews, such as non-Jewish spouses, to leave also, and an emigration based on family ties obviously produces a siphon effect that can generate a significant outflow of non-Jews and of Jews of varying degrees of "Jewishness."[2]

Since these individuals indeed did leave the Soviet Union, they were presumably unhappy about something there, which obviously is another potential source of bias in their responses about life in the USSR. However, as this was a family emigration for the most part, individuals left for various reasons, and not all left because they were unhappy with their lives in the USSR. Moreover, as will be seen, even among those whose memories were generally hostile to the Soviet Union, few rejected every aspect of Soviet life.

The problem of bias in the SIP sample has been treated extensively elsewhere.[3] Suffice it to say here that extensive efforts were made to minimize sources of bias and, subsequent to the survey, to test for the presence of various biases in order to evaluate the reliability of specific data subsets. I will show below how we have dealt with various problems of bias in the context of presentation of the data, for it is much easier to understand what the biases are and what can be done about them with concrete examples using the actual data.

For example, many of our technical consultants expected SIP to generate overwhelmingly negative views of life in the Soviet Union on the assumption that our respondents would be so embittered, or so anxious to please American interviewers, or so positively impressed with American life, that their responses would be highly distorted negatively. Our consultants were wrong. Certain Soviet scholarly commentators have predicted the same. My response to the latter is to challenge them to administer the questionnaire in the Soviet Union to a true probability sample. That would be a satisfying outcome for the project, but it raises the problem of potential bias in a new context. There are many questions that were asked in the SIP questionnaire that Soviet citizens might prefer not to answer, or might not answer candidly if they were still living as citizens of the USSR: whether they believed that senior officers in the KGB were "honest" and "competent," for example. No survey, of course, is ever completely free of bias. The main objective in the conduct of any survey is to minimize sources of bias and to identify and control for bias in the results. These have been SIP's methods.

Sources of Satisfaction and Dissatisfaction with Soviet Life

Although the overall assessment regarding life in the USSR by most former Soviet citizens who have emigrated to the United States is not in doubt, SIP respondents were able to differentiate between those aspects of the Soviet social system they repudiated and those about which they remained positive. Attitudes of SIP respondents also might have been affected negatively by any difficulties that they may have had in getting out of the USSR and by their experiences in the West. We sought in the survey to minimize these latter influences by asking respondents to base their answers on their experiences, attitudes, and beliefs during what we called the "last normal period of life" (LNP) in the Soviet Union, which was defined as a five-year period ending at the time the respondent's life changed as a result of the decision to emigrate.[4] The LNP ended for most respondents at the time they applied for permission to leave, which was, for the vast majority of the General Survey (G1) sample, 1978 or 1979. Interviewers were trained to remind respondents to focus on their LNP in formulating their answers and thus on a period in the respondents' lives before the decision was made to leave the USSR.

The SIP questionnaire contained a number of questions that called for self-evaluations by the respondents of the quality of life during the LNP. They were asked whether they had been "very satisfied," "somewhat satisfied," "somewhat dissatisfied" or "very dissatisfied" with their standard of living during their LNP in the Soviet Union (see Table 1-1). Approximately 11 percent, or 310 respondents, reported that they had been "very satisfied" with their standard of living; a total of 60.1 percent, or 1,653 individuals, reported that they had been either "very satisfied" or "somewhat satisfied"; and only 14.7 percent claimed that they had been "very dissatisfied" before deciding to leave. The remaining 25 percent were "somewhat dissatisfied."

Thus, even though our respondents had voted with their feet about whether to live in the USSR, they nonetheless represent a heterogeneous group with respect to their evaluations of their standard of living while they were Soviet citizens. This suggests that they can tell us something about the ultimate sources of both support for, and alienation from, various aspects of Soviet life. What is more, variation among our respondents may be used to analyze the characteristics that predispose Soviet citizens toward alienation or support with respect to specific

Soviet institutions and conditions of life. In many instances our respondents' answers reflect an explicit or implicit comparison of the United States and the Soviet Union.

Most Western observers of Soviet life have indicated surprise at the high proportion of former citizens who reported some degree of satisfaction with their standard of living. It is interesting to note in this connection that length of time since departure from the USSR had no significant impact upon reported satisfaction or dissatisfaction while in the Soviet Union.[5] We also know that the majority of respondents was satisfied with the incomes they were earning here, suggesting that the LNP concept was, in fact, successful in minimizing contamination subsequent to the decision to leave the USSR. Moreover, the response on standard of living is consistent with the proportion of respondents who reported an economic reason for leaving the USSR. We coded up to three answers for each respondent to the open-ended question: "What were your reasons for leaving the Soviet Union?" Only 27 percent gave an economic motive as either the first, second, or third reason, as opposed, for example, to totals of 46 percent who cited a

Table 1-1. Self-Assessed Satisfaction SIP General Survey (G1)

| | | How satisfied were you with: | | | | |
		Standard of Living	Housing	Goods	Job	Health Care
Very satisfied	N =	310	645	139	711	518
	% =	11.3	23.3	5.1	31.8	19.3
Somewhat satisfied	N =	1,343	1,213	488	1,054	1,142
	% =	48.8	43.8	17.8	47.1	42.6
Somewhat dissatisfied	N =	694	379	634	303	570
	% =	25.2	13.7	23.2	13.5	21.3
Very dissatisfied	N =	403	533	1,477	170	450
	% =	14.7	19.2	53.9	7.6	16.8
TOTAL	N =	2,750	2,770	2,738	2,238	2,680
	% =	100	100	100	100	100
Missing values	N =	43	23	55	555	113

Source: SIP General Survey Codebook. Release 3.1.

Revised 9/25/87

religious or ethnic reason and 43 percent who gave a political reason.[6] Economic discontent was clearly not the prime motive for emigration by SIP respondents.

In considering determinants of reported satisfaction with standard of living in the USSR, the degree of satisfaction with housing in the LNP was the single most important factor. About 23 percent of SIP respondents reported themselves to have been "very satisfied" with their housing during their LNP, and a total of 67.1 percent, or 1,858 respondents, reported themselves to have been either "very satisfied" or "somewhat satisfied." Only 19.2 percent were "very dissatisfied" with their Soviet housing (see Table 1-1).

Most knowledgeable students of Soviet society have found these statistics difficult to believe. Soviet living space per capita is sparse even by European standards, not to mention comparison with space available per household member in the United States, and the quality of much housing in the USSR is also visibly poor in terms of both maintenance and amenities.

It is possible to test the credibility of our respondents' subjective evaluations of their housing in the USSR with objective data that also were collected from each respondent. One expects on a priori grounds that satisfaction with housing would vary directly with square meters available per member of the family. In that regard our respondents were not exceptional. Living space per capita is the single most significant determinant of reported satisfaction with housing. Moreover, it is known on the basis of studies throughout the world that dwellers who own their own homes normally report themselves as more satisfied with their housing than renters do, and this is also true for the SIP respondents. About one third of them owned their own homes or apartments in the USSR, and they were significantly more satisfied than those who rented.

In the Soviet case, however, a more important determinant of satisfaction or dissatisfaction with housing than with ownership is the extent to which the respondent (and family) had been obliged to share facilities with members of other households. Soviet citizens have unambiguously rejected communal housing. The more they had to share— such as kitchens, toilets, and the like—the less likely they were to report satisfaction with their housing in the Soviet Union. The least satisfied were students living in dormitories or individuals living in "corners" of other peoples' homes and who were therefore obliged to share everything: kitchen, bath, living space, hallway, and entrance and exit ways. These results confirm the political wisdom of the extraordinary home-building and home-renovating program that has been under way for more than three decades in major Soviet cities and support arrangements by state, local, and economic enterprise authorities to develop and expand private condominia ownership.

As is clear from several independent sections of the questionnaire, housing is a highly salient factor in the lives of Soviet citizens. We asked, for example, whether the respondents had ever made contact about any matter (other than emigration) with an official or official agency during their LNP in the USSR. Nineteen percent had done so, and over one half of these had done so about housing. Interestingly, a majority of these respondents reported that their complaints (or requests) ultimately had been satisfied to some degree.[7] Another indication of the salience of housing is the fact that some 192 couples in the SIP sample who had lived together during the LNP in the Soviet Union, and who were still living together in the United States at the time of the interview, reported essentially identical totals for square meters of living space in the USSR, despite the fact that members of each pair were interviewed separately (either simultaneously or sequentially) and could not have known the other's answer.[8]

Additional confirmation is provided by the results of a parallel interview project by the Osteuropa Institut of Munich, modeled on SIP, that has been conducted in West Germany among former Soviet citizens of German extraction.[9] The German project worked with a sample substantially different in composition from the SIP sample in that it was mainly Protestant, blue collar, and less well educated than the SIP sample, and had a significant representation of rural and small-city population. Despite these differences, answers to the satisfaction questions correspond very closely to those received by SIP (see Table 1-2). Sixty-nine percent of the German-Russian sample reported that they had been either "very satisfied" or "somewhat satisfied" with their housing in the USSR, and 60.7 percent reported that they had been either "very satisfied" or "somewhat satisfied" with their standard of living, percentages that are essentially identical to SIP responses for the same categories (see Table 1-1). Moreover, dissatisfaction with economic life in the USSR clearly played an even smaller role in the decision of German-Russians to emigrate than for SIP respondents.[10]

The former Soviet citizens who responded to the SIP General Survey were far from satisfied with all aspects of Soviet economic life. Only 5 percent reported that they had been "very satisfied" with the availability of goods during their LNP in the Soviet Union (see Table 1-1). An overwhelming 77.1 percent had been either "very dissatisfied" or "somewhat dissatisfied" with goods availability. These two categories were also 77 percent in the German survey (see Table 1-2). This result

Table 1-2. Distribution of Answers to Questions about Satisfaction with
the Quality of Life

	Standard of Living (%)	Housing (%)	Goods (%)	Job (%)	Health Care (%)
GERMAN RESPONDENTS					
Very satisfied	9.8	19.0	1.6	21.8	10.3
Somewhat satisfied	50.9	50.9	21.8	54.9	48.7
Somewhat dissatisfied	23.6	13.8	33.2	16.2	23.5
Very dissatisfied	15.7	16.3	43.4	7.1	17.5
TOTAL (%)	100.0	100.0	100.0	100.0	100.0
N =	440	442	440	408	439

Source: Brian D. Silver, "Political Attitudes in the SIP General Survey and the German Interview Project," mimeographed.

is not surprising to anyone who has done any shopping in the Soviet Union. Queues are still ubiquitous for fresh foodstuffs and for quality merchandise of all types. In fact, the smart Soviet shopper will join a queue before looking at, or even learning, what is being sold because delay could cost several "places" in line. One can always check out the merchandise after establishing a place in the queue.

What is surprising about SIP findings regarding goods availability are the differences among shoppers in degree of dissatisfaction. Controlling for all other factors, older customers tend to have been less critical; and consumers from smaller cities, where supplies are definitely less adequate, were also noticeably less critical of supply availability. This will surprise anyone who has traveled by train, or even by air, from Moscow to a provincial Soviet city and who therefore has seen the extent to which Moscow is the "cash and carry" center of the Soviet Union. Fruit, meat, boots, clothing, and even heavy furniture fill the train compartments and block the aisles.

Also somewhat surprising in SIP findings is the fact that, according to our respondents, many goods that are scarce in state stores are nonetheless consumed frequently. Meat, for example, was reported as "usually" scarce by over 80 percent of SIP respondents. In fact, the phrase "there is no meat" is common even in major cities. Nevertheless, 62 percent of the SIP respondents claimed that they ate meat every day, and 91 percent claimed that they ate meat at least several times per week. Only about 8 percent reported that they ate meat only several times a month or less (see Table 1-3). Similar high weekly consumption rates were reported for cheese, kefir, milk, and eggs, suggesting that Soviet consumers are obtaining a significant portion of these products outside of the official state retail network. Special distribution of food products—for example, by place of work or for special social, political, or economic status—is more important than either unofficial markets (*nalevo*) or the black market as an alternative to the official retail network.

The dissatisfaction consumers felt about the availability of goods did not arise, therefore, from malnutrition or serious deprivation but from frustration with the system of production and distribution as a whole, based, in part, on thwarted expectations. Better-off consumers were the more dissatisfied. Contrary to what has been believed in the West, however, the dissatisfaction of the better-off citizens did not stem

Table 1-3. Dietary Frequencies: Meat, Cheese, Kefir, Milk, and Eggs

| | | How often did you eat/drink: | | | | |
		Meat	Cheese	Kefir	Milk	Eggs
FREQUENCY						
Daily	N =	575	738	635	672	514
	% =	62.4	80.0	68.9	72.9	55.7
Several times	N =	265	144	220	155	319
per week	% =	28.7	15.6	23.9	16.8	34.6
Several times	N =	16	14	21	25	40
per month	% =	1.7	1.5	2.3	2.7	4.3
Never	N =	56	19	35	63	32
	% =	6.1	2.1	3.8	6.8	3.5
Subtotal	N =	918	919	917	919	916
	% =	99.00	99.00	99.00	99.00	99.00
Missing values	N =	4	3	5	3	5
	% =	0.4	0.3	0.5	0.3	0.5
TOTAL	N =	922	922	922	922	922

Source: SIP General Survey Codebook. Release 3.1.

Revised 12/6/85

from an inability to spend their income, for they had lower saving rates than those who reported lesser degrees of dissatisfaction. For these citizens, dissatisfaction stemmed from an inability to purchase the assortment they preferred for their market baskets. The picture one obtains of better-off consumers is one of individuals who spent a disproportionate amount of working time for personal shopping, who also tended to spend disproportionately on the legal private market (*rynok*) and on unofficial markets, but who still failed to satisfy their preferences in an optimal way with respect to the composition and quality of their market baskets.[11]

It is important to note that our respondents differed in degree of satisfaction on demographic variables other than income. For example, older respondents tended to be less critical of shortages, presumably because of a longer reference period extending back to the years of extreme privation caused by the industrialization drive of the 1930s, World War II, and postwar reconstruction. Citizens from the largest cities and the better educated tended to be the most critical of availability of goods even though they were relatively better off according to objective measures, and even by their own evaluations of their own economic status. Their reference groups were perhaps outside the USSR, for they were the most likely to have been informed about life outside the Soviet Union through both foreign and domestic media.

Buying goods and services in the Soviet Union requires a time budget as well as a money budget. Those with proportionally more time than money benefit differentially from the fact that the best goods inevitably require queuing. Those with more money than time are likely to become angry and frustrated because they may be required to steal time from work to spend their incomes and because they are obliged to spend a disproportionate share of their incomes on private markets where prices are higher than in state retail stores, or on quasi-legal and even outright illegal channels, which puts them at a certain personal risk in addition to paying higher prices.

Interestingly, these better-off customers did not prefer shopping in private markets when they were living in the USSR, and very few respondents felt that higher prices ought to have been charged in state stores. What they seem to have wanted was supplies of goods as plentiful as those existing in private markets but at the low official state retail prices, prices that have required over a 50-billion ruble annual state subsidy in recent years. The SIP respondents blamed the shortages met with in the state stores on poor production and not on subsidized prices, while high prices on private goods were considered gouging by the peasantry. The most fortunate consumers would appear to have been those with relatively high household income and with several nonworking "shoppers" in the form of grandparents or other senior relatives.

All of this suggests that reform of the retail distribution network will prove difficult for Mikhail Gorbachev. SIP respondents did not agree that a policy of higher prices in state retail outlets would be acceptable as a solution to the problem of queues. What is more, although a large majority indicated a preference for private agricultural production, generally there was no indication of a similar preference for privatization of the economy. The preferred solution—increased quantities of products at existing subsidized prices—represents a desire to eat one's cake and have it too, which is not an encouraging outlook for Soviet leadership seeking to rationalize the economy. Things will not get better with the passage of time, according to SIP findings, because the most supportive population will diminish as years pass: the population is becoming more educated, more urban, and more cosmopolitan, and each of these characteristics yields less-satisfied citizens. Moreover, a significant majority of SIP respondents indicated that supply conditions had deteriorated over their LNP—that is, during the end of the 1970s and the early years of the 1980s.

Jobs represented a very different domain of satisfaction. In fact, SIP respondents recalled their jobs as the single most satisfying aspect of economic life in the USSR. Fully 78.9 percent reported themselves to have been either "very satisfied" or "somewhat satisfied" with their jobs during their LNP in the Soviet Union (the figure for the German survey is 76.7 percent); only 7.6 percent of SIP respondents represented themselves as having been "very dissatisfied" (see Table 1-1).

However, for all but professional workers, satisfaction with jobs depended only marginally on satisfaction with income earned on the job. When asked, for example, about low productivity in the workplace, over 60 percent of those who had been employed in their LNP put the blame on inadequate material incentives, and this included especially those who had been occupied on the workshop floor—that is, the regular workers and their foremen.[12]

Despite poor or poorly designed material incentives, however, people evidently still found a great deal of satisfaction with their work. The single most significant determinant of satisfaction or dissatisfaction was whether or not one was able to work in the specialty for which he or she was trained.[13] This was of particular importance to white-collar workers. Satisfaction or dissatisfaction with one's job overall also was associated with job security, with blue-collar workers listing it at 37 percent versus less than 1 percent for income as a main source of job satisfaction. Job conditions also proved important as a source of job satisfaction, especially whether one had the equipment and information required to do the job well. In fact, poor working conditions were mentioned by only about 1 percent as a significant cause of low productivity. It is ironic that workers who are considered unproductive actually appear to enjoy their jobs.[14] These conditions would seem to suggest that improving incentives, and that means consumer satisfaction in the end, would provide considerable leverage with respect to productivity increases.

It is striking to note in the SIP results that women reported even higher levels of satisfaction with their jobs than men did, despite the fact that women earn considerably less than men do. On average for the SIP sample, women earned about 71 percent as much as men,[15] which is only somewhat better than the situation in the United States. Of particular interest in this comparison is that the Soviet gender differential in earnings derived predominantly from differential pay for similar jobs, whereas in the United States job segregation has been the main factor, with jobs dominated by women paying significantly less than other types of employment. Only about 10 percent of the differential in the Soviet Union could be attributed to occupational segregation. Despite this large earnings differential, women reported greater job satisfaction than men did, and they registered one of the highest rates of labor-force participation in the world: 80 percent.

In fact, with the exception of dissatisfaction with goods availability, women in the SIP sample generally reported higher levels of satisfaction, or lower levels of dissatisfaction, along all dimensions than men did when recalling life during their LNP in the Soviet Union. It is not at all clear what this signifies, especially in the light of answers to the question: "Who has it better in the Soviet Union, men or women?" Three percent of the men and 2 percent of the women in the sample reported that "women have it better." This response no doubt reflects general awareness among men and women alike of the "double burden" Soviet women carry for family as well as work responsibilities, a burden that can be measured in part by its impact on leisure time. For example, women spent much more time shopping per day on average than men did, and women participated in leisure activities only half as much on average per day as men. The relatively greater sense of satisfaction female members of the sample expressed about their lives in the Soviet Union does not appear to be supported by the objective data SIP has collected about their experiences. It derives perhaps from subjective evaluations rooted in the very significant role women played in family life in Soviet society. Or it could be an artifact reflecting a differential impact of emigration on men and women.

It is possible that the high rating respondents gave for their jobs in the USSR reflects disappointment with the jobs they have found in the United States. Sixty-seven percent (1,780 respondents) said "yes" in response to the question: "Suppose someone like you were considering leaving the Soviet Union to come to the United States. Would (he/she) be disappointed by the availability of jobs in this country that are suited to (his/her) speciality?" Interestingly, however, almost 90 percent said that such a person would not be disappointed with "the income (he/she) can earn" in the United States.

Health care in the contemporary Soviet Union has been the subject of considerable study and concern in the West in recent years. Two Western scholars, Murray Feshbach and Christopher Davis, have speculated that the Soviet medical care system is on the brink of collapse, judging by recent adverse trends in mortality and life expectancy data. However, SIP results suggest widespread satisfaction with health care in the Soviet Union and implicit relative dissatisfaction with medical care in the United States. Over 19 percent of the sample stated that they had been "very satisfied" with free public health care during their LNP in the Soviet Union, and more than 60 percent reported having been either "very satisfied" or "somewhat satisfied" (see Table 1-1). A comparable response was obtained in the survey of German Russians. Consequently, if there is a health-care crisis in the USSR, our respondents were unaware of it. They are not experts, but it remains significant that they did not perceive a crisis in health services.[16]

What is more, elsewhere in the questionnaire we asked several questions that provide indirect support for the conclusion that there is genuine and wide acceptance of socialized medicine among citizens in the USSR. For example, we asked respondents: "In what ways do you think that the United States could learn from the Soviet Union?" This was a completely open-ended question, and we coded up to three answers per respondent. About 17 percent said that there was "nothing" that could be learned, but the rest did give one or more positive responses (see Table 1-4). Control of crime was number one and mentioned as a first, second, or third "lesson" by a total of 50.9 percent of the sample. The educational system was number two at 47.5 percent, while health care ranked third (27.8 percent) as an area in which the United States could learn from the way things are done in the Soviet Union.

A random one third of the sample was also asked another question about what, if anything, they would keep if they had an opportunity to "create a system of government in the Soviet Union that is different from the one which currently exists." The Soviet medical care system was mentioned first, second, or third by almost 70 percent of those who agreed that something might be kept. Respondents also were asked at a different point in the questionnaire to evaluate by means of a

Table 1-4. In What Ways Do You Think that the United States Could Learn from the Soviet Union?

	1st Answer (%)	2nd Answer (%)	3rd Answer (%)	Total (%)
Crime; legal system	21.8	16.0	13.1	50.9
System of education; access to education	15.9	18.0	13.6	47.5
Health care	6.6	11.5	9.7	27.8
Military readiness	5.7	6.7	6.0	18.4
Childrearing/discipline	2.4	7.1	5.6	15.1
Upkeep of cities	2.6	5.2	6.4	14.3
Public transportation	1.7	3.0	5.6	10.3
Limit liberalism/freedom	3.4	2.1	1.9	7.4
Housing: price and quantity	1.4	2.1	2.9	6.4
Can learn nothing	16.8	0.1	—	16.9
Other answers; N.E.C.	21.7	28.2	35.2	85.1
TOTAL % =	100.0	100.0	100.0	
N =	2545	1344	662	4551
Missing values	248	1449	2131	3828

Source: SIP General Survey Codebook. Release 3.1.

seven-point scale where they stood in their LNP with respect to public versus private provision of medical care. As Brian Silver has reported: "Fifty-two percent of all respondents state the strongest possible concurrence with the statement that 'the state should provide free medical care for all citizens.'"[17] Thus, in a direct choice between private and public medical care, a substantial majority reported that they were in favor of public medical care. Overall, the survey establishes little room for doubt that there is substantial citizen support for free public medical care in the Soviet Union.

It is interesting to note in this connection that the former Soviet citizens we interviewed did not comprise two separate groups: those who used public medical services and those who availed themselves of private medical care. Private medical care was, at most, a supplement to public care, not a substitute. Those who reported themselves satisfied with public medical care in the USSR were much more likely to have made some use of private care than the dissatisfied; however, few, if any, appear to have relied exclusively upon private medicine.[18]

SIP respondents were asked to evaluate their own state of health during their LNP in the USSR. As is the case quite generally elsewhere in the world, older respondents and women reported relatively poorer health. Whether this perception was correct or not is not important. What is significant is that these two segments of the sample rated Soviet medical care higher than did those who reported generally better health.

These findings regarding Soviet medical care support those attained by the Harvard Refugee Project of the 1950s, in which the respondents also listed medical care, along with the educational system, as institutions worth preserving in any post-Bolshevik government.[19] The former Soviet citizens who have been interviewed in West Germany also have given a high ranking to both public health care and education.

General Patterns

As indicated earlier, SIP results do suggest the existence of significant gender differences. Women report themselves as having been either more satisfied or less dissatisfied in general than men do in every area tested except with respect to goods availability. Of particular salience is job satisfaction, where women report relatively high levels of satisfaction despite the fact that they earn less than men, are obliged to bear a disproportionate double burden represented by family responsibilities, and agree with the statement that "men have it better" in Soviet society. Women are also less likely to have participated in unconventional political activity, and they are less likely to have initiated the decision to leave the USSR. Relatively speaking, therefore, women represent a conservative force in Soviet society and, thus, a potential source of regime support.

The most striking demographic finding of SIP thus far, however, is the strength and pervasiveness of generational differences. Older respondents reported themselves as more satisfied or less dissatisfied along all dimensions of measurement, and this holds for almost any pair of age-differentiated segments. It is widely believed that older members of any society are likely to report higher levels of satisfaction, but this is not the case cross-nationally. In Western Europe, for example, in recent years it is the young who have reported higher levels of satisfaction. The older generations therefore represent another conservative force in Soviet society, but one that must be regarded as a "wasting asset."

There is other evidence to support the conclusion that the differences we have found are true generational differences, not merely life-cycle effects. For example, Donna Bahry has pointed out the contrast with the Harvard Refugee Project, in which it was the young who reported greater relative satisfaction with their earlier lives as Soviet citizens than the older generations did.[20] In fact, what one finds is that the current older SIP respondent generations were more satisfied as youths than is today's youth. This is supported further by the fact that when asked about brushes with the law and about participation in unconventional activities, members of older generations report such activities, if at all, as having occurred relatively recently in their lives, and, thus, at a later stage than for contemporary younger former citizens. According to Bahry: "The Soviet generation gap is indeed political.... In each case, the postwar and post-Stalin generations prove to be the most active: the most interested in public affairs, the most heavily engaged in 'mobilized participation,' but at the same time taking a greater part in unsanctioned study groups, protests, strikes, and other unconventional activities. Official Soviet ambivalence about the young would thus appear to be well founded."[21]

The dissatisfaction of youth with the economic, political, and cultural stagnation of the late Brezhnev years is offset for the senior members of Soviet society, presumably, by still vivid memories of industrialization and the purges, World War II and postwar reconstruction, and Stalinism in general. The enormous gains that have been accomplished since Joseph Stalin seem to have made them more tolerant of flattening trends, or even trend reversals, in the quality of economic, political, and cultural life in the late 1970s and early 1980s.

There is more than a little evidence for this view. We asked our respondents a series of questions that required them to compare the Stalin, Khrushchev, and Brezhnev eras. These questions sought to elicit, for example, in which era censorship was the most intrusive, and when the least. Similar questions were asked about economic inequality and privilege, nationality policy, and the role of the KGB. Let us divide the respondents into those who were born in 1940 or earlier (the Stalin generation) and those born in 1941 or later (the post-Stalin generation) on the assumption that the younger group would not have reached political and historical consciousness before Stalin died in 1953. What we find is that a majority of the older group rated the Khrushchev era as the best and the Stalin era as the worst. The younger group agreed on the Khrushchev period as a kind of "golden age," but voted Brezhnev's the worst in most cases. Even with respect to the power of the KGB a significant minority of the post-Stalin generation voted Brezhnev's era as the worst.

We also asked our respondents to review a set of statements about Soviet history during Stalin's time with the purpose of identifying those who were prepared to say something positive, however mild, about him. The majority of our respondents was unwilling to do so, and the only significant minority that would do so was found again among the youngest generations. Thus, if there is any significant neo-Stalinism in the Soviet Union today, it would be found among the young. This says something about the teaching, or nonteaching, of history in the Soviet Union, where prominent leaders can become "unpersons" for entire generations and where the past is controlled and manipulated officially for contemporary political purposes. Indeed, young people from families that had suffered from repression under Stalin were indistinguishable in their responses from older generations. The family, presumably, was the teacher of true Soviet history in these cases.[22]

As Bahry and Silver have shown, additional differences by age group may be seen in their evaluations of the competence and the honesty of regime leaders of eight key Soviet bureaucracies. Members of older generations were less likely than the younger to provide positive evaluations of either the competence or the honesty of middle-elite regime leaders. Fifty-seven percent of all respondents reported that "all" or "almost all" KGB leaders were competent (as opposed to 66 percent for the best regarded institution, the Academy of Sciences). With respect to honesty (or integrity), only 14 percent of all respondents said that most or all leaders of the KGB were honest (as opposed to 35 percent for the Academy of Sciences). It is striking that positive evaluations of leaders tend to be related inversely to educational attainment of the respondent and that perceptions of honesty decline with age. As Bahry and Silver report: "Younger cohorts rate the competence of Soviet leaders more highly than do older ones, even after educational differences are taken into account."[23]

Educational differences among SIP respondents are almost as striking as generational differences. The less well-educated respondents were more likely to report satisfaction with housing, jobs, medical care, and standard of living than were the better educated. They were less dissatisfied even with the availability of goods, and these differences persist even when other differences, such as age and region of origin, are controlled. This finding stands in contrast to the results of the Harvard Refugee Project, where those who had advanced their educational attainments under Soviet power tended to have been more satisfied and accepting of basic Soviet institutions such as public ownership of industry, or limitations on the right to strike. In fact, the strength of the positive relationship that was found by Harvard Refugee Project investigators between education and regime support led many contemporary observers to conclude that education could, and was being used to, shore up the regime, and the frightening long-run prospect was of a nation of educated, but brainwashed, regime supporters.

SIP results show just the opposite for the effect of education upon regime support. Holding material reward constant, every increase in educational attainment, even at the lowest levels of education, decreases regime support and relative satisfaction with life conditions as well. As educational attainment increases, so normally do material rewards in the Soviet system, but the subjective satisfaction SIP respondents extracted from material improvements did not keep pace.[24] Thus it is that former Soviet citizens who were in skilled blue-collar, white-collar, and other middle-elite positions requiring relatively higher educational levels were more likely to report themselves as dissatisfied and to question regime values and its policies despite the fact that today they represent the principal beneficiaries of the social system created by the Bolshevik Revolution.

Conclusion

Analysis of the first General Survey conducted by SIP reveals some striking patterns, patterns no Soviet specialist previously has had an opportunity to observe. Probably the most significant pattern in the short run for policies being proposed or implemented by Gorbachev is the strength and character of generational differences within the urban population. Whether for reasons of educational silence about the harsh, turbulent years under Stalin or merely from present-mindedness and sheer impatience with the relative backwardness of Soviet consumer and citizen comforts, the young are highly involved and highly critical, and thus reformist-minded. The young and well educated are more likely than other groups to participate in both conventional and unconventional social and political activities.[25] The older generation is, on the contrary, more cautious, cynical, and conservative in its evaluation of the system and its prospects, and it is more likely to be passive as well.

Educational influences reinforce this generational divergence, for the young are, in general, the better educated members of Soviet society. Similarly, women tend to be less critical than men, and they also are less well represented at the highest levels of attainment in the Soviet educational system as well as in top jobs. Finally, residents of small and medium-sized cities tend to be more supportive of regime institutions and less critical of life opportunities than those who were citizens of the largest Soviet cities, despite the fact that the latter offer, by common agreement, relatively many more amenities.

Respondents were asked an open-ended question designed to elicit the nature and strengths of their retrospective criticisms of Soviet society as of the date of the SIP interview: "Think for a moment about the Soviet system with its good and bad points. Suppose you could create a system of government in the Soviet Union that is different from the one which currently exists. What things would you want to keep in the new one?" The answers reinforced those given earlier in response to the question about what the United States could learn from the Soviet Union. Public health care, free public education, crime control, job security, and inexpensive housing top the list. Note that all of these represent activities of the Soviet state that subsidized the welfare of the individual household member of Soviet society.

Respondents also were asked: "What things in the present Soviet system would you be sure to change?" A list of their responses is presented in Table 1-5. Note that 40 percent of them gave "change the political system" as a first, second, or third answer, and another almost 17 percent recommended eliminating the one-party system. The answers in Table 1-5 point to a desire for more political and more economic diversity and for broader civil rights, but it is also clear that even after several years (on average) of life in the United States only a few SIP respondents were prepared to repudiate the Soviet political, economic, and social system entirely.

Although many were critical of specific aspects of American life, SIP respondents for the most part had succeeded in establishing themselves in the United States at the time of interview. Almost 61 percent were employed and another 6 percent (of adult immigrants) were attending school. Only 5.7 percent were unemployed, and the rest were either keeping house, on pension, or otherwise occupied.

SIP respondents were generally optimistic about their future in the United States. They were asked to place themselves at the time of the interview on a ten-point scale representing a range from the "worst possible life" to the "best possible life now." Approximately 38 percent of respondents ranked themselves above midpoint in quality of life in the United States, and 44 percent placed themselves on steps four and five. When asked "Where on the scale do you expect your life to be five years from now?" almost 82 percent placed themselves at step six or above, with 21.1 percent on step ten (as opposed to 8 percent now).

Table 1-5. What Things in the Soviet System Would You Be Sure to Change?

	1st Answer (%)	2nd Answer (%)	3rd Answer (%)	Total (%)
Political system	27.0	6.6	6.5	40.1
Allow private enterprise	9.3	10.5	9.8	29.6
Control of speech	3.5	8.8	13.6	25.9
Collective-farm system	9.4	9.3	7.1	25.8
Enforce rights	3.5	11.1	10.2	24.8
One-party system	6.3	6.0	4.4	16.7
Economic planning	2.4	3.3	3.8	9.5
Internal passports	1.3	3.6	3.1	8.0
Everything	6.5	0.5	—	7.0

Source: SIP General Survey Codebook. Release 3.1.

The former Soviet citizens we interviewed for SIP were obviously up-beat about their future in this country despite the reservations they expressed elsewhere in the interview about crime in the streets, job insecurity, health care, educational quality, and social isolation.

The criticism of the regime and the dissatisfaction with Soviet economic and political life in general during the LNP that we found hardly merits the title "dissent." The SIP respondents definitely were not revolutionaries, or even demonstrators. Over 50 percent (1,401) of the respondents were defined by Rasma Karklins as "non-critical passives," for they offered neither criticism nor overt acts of any sort that might have been construed as hostile to the regime during their LNP lives in the Soviet Union. "Critical passives" represented 26 percent (718) of the sample. They had held critical views but had not expressed criticism in even the mildest form, such as participating in an unofficial study group. Only 16 percent (445) were both critical and activist in any degree during their LNP, and of these no more than 2 percent might be considered to have been active enough to warrant the label "dissident." The implication is that the regime is under pressure from reformists, not revolutionists, and from individuals, not from any sort of *organized opposition*, whether loyal or not.[26]

Insofar as we can project SIP findings on to the Soviet urban population, we may conclude that Soviet citizens who live in the most desirable cities, such as Moscow, Leningrad, and Kiev, who have achieved the highest educational attainments, hold the most highly skilled jobs, earn the highest incomes, occupy the most comfortable housing, and who dominate consumption in all markets, private as well as public—in short, the "best and the brightest" of Soviet society—are the least satisfied members of that society, and that they are also the most ambiguous supporters of regime goals. This conclusion suggests that Gorbachev's pursuit of political reform and economic reconstruction is well founded in the desires and expectations of this critical mass of the young and the educated.

However, other SIP findings on specific attitudes, beliefs, and behaviors toward the essential ingredients of any such reforms—such as the negative relationship between education and regime support, the gradual diminution to be anticipated in the ranks of the more supportive older and less urbanized populations, the distaste for price adjustments in state stores, and the high premium workers place on job security—suggest that Gorbachev may find success for his reform program elusive. It also follows that failure of Gorbachev's reforms would entail continued economic stagnation and continued calls for reform, not political unrest. SIP results suggest that it is not regime stability that is at stake but, rather, the image that the Party has cultivated for itself as a force for progress and modernity and for successful competition with the advanced non-Communist world.

Notes

[1]For a description of the project design and of the technical details regarding sampling frame, sample, and questionnaire see James R. Millar, ed., *Politics, Work and Daily Life in the USSR: A Survey of Former Soviet Citizens* (New York: Cambridge University Press, 1987), esp. chap. 1 and app. A.

[2]For a discussion of "degrees of Jewishness" see Donna Bahry, "Surveying Soviet Emigrants: Political Attitudes and Ethnic Bias" (Manuscript, Department of Politics, New York University, 1985).

[3]James R. Millar, "History, Method, and the Problem of Bias," in Millar, *Politics*, pp. 18–24.

[4]The concept of the LNP was borrowed from a similar survey conducted with Soviet emigrants to Israel by Gur Ofer and Aaron Vinokur. See Gur Ofer, Aaron Vinokur, and Yechiel Bar-Chaim, "Family Budget Survey of Soviet Emigrants in the Soviet Union" (Research Paper no. 32, Soviet and East European Research Center, Hebrew University, Jerusalem, 1979).

[5]Michael Swafford et al., "Response Effects in SIP's General Survey of Soviet Emigrants," in Millar, *Politics*, pp. 372–405.

[6]The most frequently cited reason (48 percent) for leaving was to accompany family or friends.

[7]James R. Millar and Elizabeth Clayton, "Quality of Life: Subjective Measures of Relative Satisfaction," in Millar, *Politics*, pp. 39–40.

[8]Barbara Anderson and Brian D. Silver, "The Validity of Survey Responses: Insights from Interviews of Married Couples in a Survey of Soviet Emigrants," *Social Forces* (1988).

[9]For a description of this project see Barbara Dietz, "Interviews with Soviet German Emigrants as a Source of Information for Soviet Studies," University of Illinois SIP Working Paper no. G4, 1987.

[10]Based on one answer per respondent, the breakdown of reasons for emigration for the German-Russian sample is: ethnic or religious reasons, 63 percent; accompanying family, 22 percent; political or personal freedom, 13 percent; and economic, 3 percent. (Rounding brings the total above 100 percentage points.) Dietz, "Interviews with Soviet German Emigrants."

[11]Millar and Clayton, "Quality of Life," pp. 42–45.

[12]Paul R. Gregory, "Productivity, Slack and Time Theft in the Soviet Economy," in Millar, *Politics*, pp. 266–67.

[13]Millar and Clayton, "Quality of Life," p. 48.

[14]It should be noted that only 20 percent of SIP workforce respondents attributed low productivity to poor worker behavior in the form of alcoholism, apathy, or laziness, and that only about 8 percent cited poor management. See Gregory, "Productivity," pp. 248–50.

[15]Paul Gregory and Janet Kohlhase, "The Earnings of Soviet Workers: Human Capital, Loyalty and Privilege (Evidence from the Soviet Interview Project)," University of Illinois SIP Working Paper no. 13, rev. June 1986.

[16]The health care area is one, along with goods availability, however, in which SIP respondents perceived a significant decline in quality in recent years.

[17]Brian D. Silver, "Political Beliefs of the Soviet Citizen: Sources of Support for Regime Norms," in Millar, *Politics*, p. 111.

[18]Millar and Clayton, "Quality of Life," p. 49.

[19]Alex Inkeles and Raymond A. Bauer, *The Soviet Citizen. Daily Life in a Totalitarian Society*, (Cambridge: Harvard University Press, 1959), esp. chap. 10.

[20]Donna Bahry, "Politics, Generations and Change in the USSR," in Millar, *Politics*, pp. 91–94.

[21]Ibid., pp. 85–86.

[22]Rasma Karklins, "The Dissent/Coercion Nexus in the USSR," University of Illinois SIP Working Paper no. 36, 1987.

[23]Donna Bahry and Brian D. Silver, "The Intimidation Factor in Soviet Politics: The Symbolic Uses of Terror," University of Illinois SIP Working Paper no. 31, 1987.

[24]Brian D. Silver, "Political Beliefs of the Soviet Citizen: Sources of Support for Regime Norms," in Millar, *Politics*, pp. 116–25.

[25]William Zimmerman, "Mobilized Participation and the Nature of the Soviet Dictatorship," in Millar, *Politics*, pp. 332–53; Bahry, "Politics, Generations and Change," pp. 61–99.

[26]Karklins, "The Dissent/Coercion Nexus."

2
Fear and Loathing of the USSR: Public Images of Communism and the Soviet Union

Jon Hurwitz and Mark Peffley*

As a guest at a cocktail party, Joe is engaged in conversation when, far across the noisy room, another group begins a separate discussion. One of the participants in this distant group mentions Joe's name, whereupon Joe instantly tunes out of his own conversation and instead becomes attentive to the discussion on the other side of the room. Cognitive psychologists are fond of using this anecdote, now simply called the "cocktail party problem," to illustrate the power of certain stimuli—generally words or phrases—to capture and hold our attention like a strong magnet. Joe was indifferent toward the group across the room until the magic word, his name, caught his ear; thereafter, it was the only conversation that mattered to him.

In the domain of foreign relations there are doubtless exceedingly few of these key stimuli. The relative indifference of the American mass public to world politics has been amply documented (see, for example, Simon, 1974). Were Joe, our typical American, to hear phrases such as "foreign aid," "military preparedness," or "Reykjavik summit" from across the room, he would not be likely to shift his attention suddenly from a conversation in which he is engaged to a distant one.

Two closely related stimuli, however, clearly do have the power to attract and sustain our attention and interest: communism and the Soviet Union. Despite the tendency of many Americans to ignore matters of international relations, the mass public does seem to be attentive when either the Soviets or communism is on the agenda.

*The authors wish to acknowledge the financial support of the Office of Research, the Faculty of Arts and Sciences Faculty Research Grant, and the University Center for International Studies, all at the University of Pittsburgh. This research also was supported in part by a grant from the University of Kentucky.

The Chicago Council on Foreign Relations (CCFR), which provides valuable survey information on the American public and its views
of foreign policy, periodically asks its respondents to indicate the importance of assorted policy goals of the U.S. government. It is clear that
respondents to the 1983 CCFR survey were chiefly concerned with
domestic issues such as "protecting jobs of American workers." It is
equally clear that Americans' interest in international issues is usually
evident when policies are germane to communism, in general, or the
Soviet Union, in particular. "Containing communism" was judged to
be a "very important" or "somewhat important" goal for 85 percent of
the American public. About the same percentage considered "matching
Soviet military power" an important national goal for our country
(Reilly, 1983, p. 13). In short, the salient nature of communism and the
Soviet Union makes these topics an exception to the general tendency
of Americans to show little interest in politics abroad.

Consider, as well, the hostility that respondents to the CCFR survey vented toward the Soviets. Interviewers asked individuals to rate
twenty-four nations on a "feeling thermometer"—an instrument designed to measure the direction and intensity of affect that respondents
feel toward a stimulus such as the USSR. Possible ratings range from
100 degrees (the maximum favorable rating) to 0 degrees (the maximum
unfavorable rating). While individuals gave Canada a mean rating of 74
degrees, they assigned the Soviet Union a rating of only 26 degrees—
dead last among the nations listed (Reilly, 1983, p. 19). (Cuba, which is
seen as a puppet of the Soviet government by many people, received a
rating of 27 degrees.) Respondents seem to have the same contempt
for the then leader of the Soviet Union, as Communist party General
Secretary Leonid Brezhnev was given an average rating of 31 degrees;
only Palestine Liberation Organization leader Yassir Arafat and Iran's
Ayatollah Khomeini were viewed less charitably among world leaders.

The Chicago data thus offer some valuable preliminary insights
into American public opinion concerning communism and the Soviet
Union. It seems clear that, when foreign affairs do occupy our thoughts,
the Eastern bloc is often the center of our attention. Countries such as
the USSR (and other states associated with the Soviet Union) are,
without a doubt, viewed with more than a little disfavor and derision
by most Americans.

These findings are not particularly surprising and, indeed, lie at
the heart of U.S. postwar foreign policy. For more than forty years the
Soviet Union has been the central actor on the world stage to which
our government has responded. Virtually all postwar entanglements

have been launched either to respond directly to a Communist threat (such as in Korea and Vietnam) or to preserve environments that are hostile to a Communist takeover (exemplified most recently by U.S. support for the shah of Iran and the Marcos regime in the Philippines). Important postwar foreign policy doctrines—the Truman Doctrine, containment, détente—have been offered in response to a perceived Communist threat, as well.

In short, the Soviet Union, together with its system of government, has been the principal antagonist of American foreign policy. Both the American people and their leaders have displayed a fear and loathing of the Soviets that is unmistakable. Because a hostile reaction to the USSR is such a strong component of our political culture, it may seem that citizens and leaders of the United States merely are expressing a "natural" bias against an alternative governmental system and its chief practitioner. Such a bias, however, does not exist in all democracies, at least not to the extreme degree that it is found in this country. Communist political parties receive far more support in other democratic polities than they do in the United States (Epstein, 1980). More revealing, attitude surveys conducted in European democracies during 1986 and 1987 found that levels of support for, and trust of, General Secretary Mikhail Gorbachev run higher than for President Ronald Reagan.

Extreme anti-Soviet and anti-Communist sentiments, therefore, are largely, if not exclusively, a property of the American culture of opinion. What is it about communism, in general, and the Soviet Union, in particular, that frightens so many citizens of this country? What are our attitudes—our fundamental assumptions, beliefs, and perceptions—of the Eastern bloc? And what threat does the Soviet Union pose to Americans? Our first concern here is to answer these questions and to portray the anxiety felt by Americans when they look beyond their own borders to the outside world. A second aim is to examine the characteristics of American society that may engender such negative images of Communist countries. We close the chapter by considering some of the consequences of anticommunism for the making of foreign policy in the United States.

To gauge public opinion we interviewed a probability sample of 612 adults in the Lexington, Kentucky, area between June 8 and 18, 1987.[1] While our respondents are not necessarily representative of those who might appear in a national sample, we maintain that local surveys can provide invaluable insights into the process by which individuals arrive at their feelings and opinions about Communist countries.

Orientations toward Communism

The feeling thermometer is a useful device to assess respondents' affective orientations, or general feelings, toward another person or nation. In Table 2-1 we present the mean thermometer ratings pertaining to the United States, the Soviet Union, China, Poland, and "communism as a form of government." The Soviet Union, China, and Poland were identified clearly in the survey question as Communist nations. Unlike the thermometer scales described earlier, which range from 0 degrees to 100 degrees, our respondents used a scale that ranges from a low of 0, representing extremely unfavorable feelings toward the country, to a high of 10, which represents extremely favorable feelings toward the country.

The most striking pattern in the thermometer ratings in Table 2-1 is the polarization of affect toward the United States versus all three of the Communist countries. Almost everyone used the positive end of the scale to describe their feelings toward the United States (to yield a

Table 2-1. Feelings toward the Government of the United States and Three Communist Nations (Percentage of Respondents at Each Position on "Feeling Thermometers")

Scale Rating	United States	USSR	China	Poland	Communist Governments
Extremely unfavorable					
0	0.5%	13.2%	5.1%	8.6%	40.9%
1	0.3	7.8	3.4	4.9	9.7
2	0.0	9.6	6.8	12.2	11.7
3	0.5	19.4	13.0	15.9	11.2
4	1.0	18.9	15.0	21.0	9.1
5	2.3	19.1	29.4	21.2	10.7
6	3.8	6.2	15.0	8.8	3.2
7	11.1	3.7	7.2	4.4	1.3
8	34.8	1.7	3.6	1.9	0.5
9	20.5	0.5	1.2	0.7	0.7
10	25.2	0.0	0.3	0.4	0.8
Extremely favorable					
Mean rating	8.3%	3.4%	4.5%	3.8%	2.0%

Source: 1987 Foreign Policy Attitudes Survey, Lexington, Kentucky.

Table 2-2. Attitudes toward Communism (Percentage of Respondents Agreeing and Disagreeing with Each Statement)

Strongly Agree	*Agree*	*Neutral*	*Disagree*	*Strongly Disagree*
Communism destroys any trace of private initiative.				
42.4%	29.3%	0.3%	20.2%	7.7%
Any time a country goes Communist, it should be considered a threat to the vital interests and security of the United States.				
39.4	30.4	0.8	18.5	10.9
Communist countries won't be satisfied until people everywhere live under Communist rule.				
38.4	29.9	0.3	19.5	11.9
The United States should do everything it can to prevent the spread of communism to any other part of the world.				
42.9	34.7	0.5	15.0	6.9
As far as I'm concerned, all Communist countries are pretty much alike.				
26.0	28.6	0.5	21.9	22.9

Source: 1987 Foreign Policy Attitudes Survey, Lexington, Kentucky.

high average rating of 8.3). Feelings toward Communist countries, on the other hand, are very unfavorable: only about one fourth of the sample assigned a positive rating (that is, between 6 and 10) to China (our "favorite" Communist country). The Soviet Union and Poland garnered only a handful of favorable ratings. As in the CCFR survey, the Soviet Union clearly generates more negative feelings than any other nation in our study (mean rating = 3.4).

It is also notable that "communism as a form of government" is viewed with even more derision (at 2.0 degrees) than any individual state governed by such a system. In an effort to find out why individuals find communism so objectionable, we asked our respondents to agree or disagree with a series of statements about that system of government. These opinions are presented in Table 2-2.

As indicated by responses to the first item in Table 2-2, there is a prevailing consensus that a major liability of communism is that it "destroys any trace of private initiative" and therefore runs counter to the American values of freedom of choice and the work ethic—that is, economic individualism. However, hostility toward communism is based on more than just a clash of cultural values. As Table 2-2 reveals, there is widespread agreement (70 percent of the sample) that any Communist country should be considered a threat to the "vital interests and security of the United States." The threat posed by Communist countries is, no doubt, related to Americans' perception of communism as an inherently expansionistic system: about two thirds agree that Iron Curtain nations "won't be satisfied until people everywhere live under Communist rule." As a result, an even greater proportion of respondents (78 percent) endorse the goal of containing communism, agreeing that our government "should do everything it can to prevent the spread of communism to any other part of the world."

We found much less agreement with the last item in Table 2-2: "All Communist countries are pretty much alike." Apparently, many individuals believe that meaningful differences exist among Communist nations. In an effort to probe more deeply into the variegated beliefs people hold about Eastern bloc countries, we asked our respondents to indicate how well the words "aggressive" and "warlike" describe the Soviet Union, China, and Poland. We also asked them how much freedom they thought the people in these three nations have. The responses are presented in Table 2-3.

An interesting pattern emerges from Table 2-3. Although our respondents perceive a relatively monolithic Communist world when it comes to the individual freedoms such states permit, they acknowledge fundamental differences in the ways in which the three countries relate to the external world. Individuals do regard the Soviet Union as slightly less free than Poland and, especially, China. Thus, most respondents believe that the citizens of the USSR have "only a little" freedom or "none at all"; fewer than two thirds believe this to be true of China. Yet, these differences pale in comparison to the remarkable diversity of opinion on how aggressive and warlike the three Communist nations are thought to be. Three times as many individuals believe the USSR to be "extremely" or "very" aggressive than believe these words apply to China or Poland. Respondents are also much more likely—again by a three-to-one ratio—to describe the Soviet Union as "extremely" or "very" warlike than to apply this description to China or Poland.

Taken together, the data in Tables 2-2 and 2-3 suggest strongly that Americans tend to regard the Communist world as homogeneous in its *internal* characteristics; we see all Iron Curtain nations as restricting the freedoms of its citizens and as creating disincentives for private initiative. The Communist bloc is perceived as anything but homogeneous, however, when it comes to the *external* styles of the nations.

Table 2-3. **Traits Assigned to Communist Countries (Percentage of Respondents)**

How well does the word "aggressive" describe the government of:

	USSR	China	Poland
Extremely well	23.7%	4.6%	5.4%
Very well	46.2	17.3	11.5
Somewhat well	26.2	52.3	35.0
Not well at all	3.8	25.7	48.1

How well does the word "warlike" describe the government of:

	USSR	China	Poland
Extremely well	19.3%	6.5%	7.8%
Very well	35.0	10.1	9.9
Somewhat well	37.0	49.4	32.1
Not well at all	8.7	34.1	50.2

How much freedom do the people have in:

	USSR	China	Poland
A great deal	0.7%	3.4%	1.7%
A fair amount	18.1	31.7	23.2
Only a little	60.3	56.1	54.9
None at all	20.9	8.8	20.2

Source: 1987 Foreign Policy Attitudes Survey, Lexington, Kentucky.

Clearly, we tend to regard the Soviet Union as far more belligerent than other countries in the Communist world. Thus, without much information on the internal workings of individual Communist countries, people resort to simple stereotypes in assuming that communism operates much the same in all three nations. Aided by more information on the international behaviors of these countries, however, most respondents make important distinctions in making attributions about the external characteristics of Communist countries.

Attitudes toward the Soviet Union

The CCFR asked a cross section of Americans to assign a "thermometer rating" to numerous nations. Significantly, the mean temperature assigned to Poland (52 degrees) is closer to that of Canada (74 degrees) than that of the Soviet Union (26 degrees). The general dislike of communism exhibited by Americans is thus distinguished from the genuine hatred and suspicion that are reserved for the Soviet Union and its closest allies (the mean temperature of Cuba, recall, is 27 degrees).

It is apparent that Americans respond to the Soviet Union in strongly visceral, passionate terms. In Table 2-4 we present responses to a battery of questions designed to assess emotional reactions toward the USSR. By large majorities, the Soviet government makes people both "angry" and "uneasy" (Item A). This unease is understandable in light of the feeling of more than one half the sample (52 percent) that the USSR presents more than a little threat to the "vital interests and security" of the United States (Item B), and the belief by an even larger majority (70 percent) that the Soviet military "presents a real and immediate danger to the United States" (Item C). Most revealing, perhaps, are the responses to Item D, where, by a sizable margin (57 percent), people believe that we "should be willing to risk the destruction of the United States rather than to be dominated by the Russians." Obviously, the "better dead than red" mentality is still a large part of the American political culture.

It is worth exploring in greater detail the underpinnings of these strongly emotional, and consistently negative, orientations expressed by

Table 2-4. Emotional Responses to the Soviet Union (Percentage of Respondents)

A. Has the Soviet government—because of the kind of government it is or because of something it has done—made you feel:

	Yes	No
Angry	61.5%	38.5%
Uneasy	75.7	24.3
Fearful	56.1	43.9

B. How much of a threat do you think Russia is to the vital interests and security of the United States?

A Great Deal	A Fair Amount	Only a Little	Not at All
21.6%	30.3%	43.6%	4.5%

C. The military power of the Soviet Union presents a real and immediate danger to the United States.

Agree Strongly	Agree Somewhat	Uncertain	Disagree Somewhat	Disagree Strongly
30.9%	38.8%	0.3%	21.0%	9.0%

D. Americans should be willing to risk the destruction of the United States rather than to be dominated by the Russians.

Agree Strongly	Agree Somewhat	Uncertain	Disagree Somewhat	Disagree Strongly
32.6%	23.9%	2.2%	20.2%	21.2%

Source: 1987 Foreign Policy Attitudes Survey, Lexington, Kentucky.

Table 2-5. Respondents' Images of the Soviet Union (Percentage of Respondents)

How well do the following words (or phrases) describe the Soviet government?

	Extremely Well	Very Well	Somewhat Well	Not Well at All
A. Deceitful	20.5%	28.7%	42.3%	8.5%
B. Dishonest	19.4	22.5	46.5	11.6
C. Sincere	3.3	5.9	40.5	50.3
D. Powerful	36.4	43.0	18.1	2.5
E. Seeks to dominate other countries	30.7	31.7	30.8	6.8
F. Enslaves the people under its rule	26.7	25.5	36.7	11.0

G. If the United States and the Soviet Union were to reach a nuclear arms control agreement, how much do you think the Soviets could be trusted to keep their word without cheating on the agreement?

A Great Deal	A Fair Amount	Only a Little	Not at All
5.7%	36.5%	37.3%	20.5%

H. Most Communist countries are pretty much under the control of the Soviet Union.

Agree Strongly	Agree Somewhat	Uncertain	Disagree Somewhat	Disagree Strongly
34.2%	36.7%	1.7%	16.7%	10.8%

I. It is probably true that the Communists in Central America are puppets of the Soviet Union.

Agree Strongly	Agree Somewhat	Uncertain	Disagree Somewhat	Disagree Strongly
41.4%	39.4%	0.5%	13.7%	5.1%

J. One of the worst things about the Soviet government is that it prevents the Soviet people from worshipping God.

Agree Strongly	Agree Somewhat	Uncertain	Disagree Somewhat	Disagree Strongly
49.1%	21.3%	0.9%	17.1%	11.7%

Source: 1987 Foreign Policy Attitudes Survey, Lexington, Kentucky.

our respondents. Table 2-5 reports beliefs about the characteristics of the Soviet Union, enabling us to fill in the picture of the USSR that Americans carry in their minds.

Several themes stand out in Table 2-5, the first of which reveals an important stumbling block to any effort to reduce tension between the United States and the Soviet Union. Improved relations between the two countries would require some degree of trust; yet, an overwhelming majority of respondents describes the Soviet Union as at least somewhat "deceitful," "dishonest," and "not sincere." This deep suspicion of Soviet motives has a rather unfortunate consequence for public acceptance of future arms control agreements between the two superpowers. As indicated by responses to Item G, a majority (58 percent) maintains that the Soviets can be trusted "only a little" or "not at all" to keep their word on an arms control agreement.

Another common theme running through the responses in Table 2-5 is the tendency to view the Soviet Union as a strong, monolithic force in world affairs. People perceive the Soviet Union to be a very powerful nation (Item D) that seeks to dominate other countries in the world (Item E). Moreover, the Soviets are seen to have a controlling influence over most other Communist countries (Item H) and are perceived to be pulling the strings of Communist "puppets" in Central America (Item I). In short, individuals unambiguously regard the USSR as a potent world power.

There is also a general tendency to view the Soviet Union as a totalitarian state, as a majority of individuals believes the phrase "enslaves the people under its rule" (Item F) applies either extremely or very well to the Soviet government. More revealing, perhaps, is the widespread perception that basic religious freedoms are absent in the USSR (Item J). Agreement with this statement is telling not only because it demonstrates the assumption that the Soviet government prohibits religious worship but also because this practice represents "one of the worst" of their transgressions.

Many of these same sentiments were expressed in a different form when respondents were asked, in an open-ended format, whether there was anything in particular that they thought was "bad" about the government of the Soviet Union or that they "disliked" about it. One individual spoke for many of our respondents: "I don't like anything about it. I hate their lack of freedom to go places and say things and the fact that communism keeps them from worshipping God. I just hate communism."

Judgments about Soviet Policies and Leaders

In what sense do these perceptions of the Soviet Union—as an aggressive, often belligerent nation that frightens a good many Americans—affect the way individuals evaluate Soviet leaders and policies? Does the strongly negative view render our respondents cynical about the

USSR's rulers, or can citizens evaluate them in a fashion that is relatively divorced from their personal feelings about the country? By the
same token, does this negativism extend to judgments about the ability
of the Soviet system to take care of its internal problems?

Table 2-6 contains responses to a battery of survey questions concerning perceptions of the aims and goals of Gorbachev and the Soviet
government. Answers to the first four questions indicate that, by large
majorities, our respondents see the Soviet government as driven by
aggressive, power-seeking motives. Almost three out of four individuals
view the USSR as an aggressive rather than as a peace-loving country
(Item A). Large majorities believe that Russia seeks to dominate the
world (Item B) by gaining military superiority over the United States
(Item C) and by gaining control over smaller countries (Item D).

In the open-ended portion of the survey, similar assessments of
Soviet motives were found in many of the reasons that people cited for
disliking the USSR. Several individuals tied the expansionist goals of
the Soviet Union to their view of the philosophy of communism. In
the words of one respondent: "Communism works like a cancer—it
keeps eating away until it gets the whole." Another indicated dislike
for the Soviets "because of their philosophy. . .that they want to control the whole world and force their views on other people." The
comments of two other respondents reflected the widespread suspicion
that the Soviets' aggressiveness was directed more narrowly toward the
United States. One individual confided that "I'm just afraid they'll
take us over one day," and another respondent registered concern by
saying that "they are going to be the first ones to fire nuclear weapons."

Interestingly, the almost universal suspicion toward the USSR's
motives does not always translate into a suspicion about the intentions
of the Soviet leadership. Gorbachev has gained a reputation as a re-
former by advocating economic decentralization, a more open atmosphere for public discussion of socioeconomic issues, and modest political
reforms. In Items E through G, respondents were asked to evaluate the
sincerity of three of Gorbachev's major proposals: an arms control
agreement with the United States, a loosening of censorship, and the
introduction of competitive elections on a limited scale. In each instance individuals were asked to judge whether the proposals have been
offered sincerely or, instead, that the Soviet leader has been motivated
by more devious considerations.

We found that a substantial majority (58 percent) believes that
Gorbachev is *not* sincere in his electoral reform proposals, perhaps because for so many years a lack of political freedom has been one of the
most salient characteristics of the Communist world (Item G in Table
2-6). Yet, there is no agreement regarding the other two proposals. Our

Table 2-6. Beliefs about Soviet Intentions and Leaders (Percentage of Respondents)

A. Generally speaking, would you describe Russia as a peace-loving nation that would fight only if it had to defend itself, or as an aggressive nation that would start a war to get something it wants?

Peace-Loving	Uncertain	Aggressive
20.5%	7.3%	72.2%

B. Do you think that Russia seeks to dominate the world, or do you think that Russia only seeks to protect itself from attack by other countries?

Dominate World	Uncertain	Protect Itself
60.8%	5.0%	34.2%

C. A major goal of the Soviet government is to gain military superiority over the United States.

Agree Strongly	Agree Somewhat	Uncertain	Disagree Somewhat	Disagree Strongly
51.5%	32.8%	0.2%	9.4%	6.1%

D. A major goal of the Soviet government is to gain control over smaller countries in the world.

Agree Strongly	Agree Somewhat	Uncertain	Disagree Somewhat	Disagree Strongly
50.2%	36.0%	0.5%	8.8%	4.5%

E. Why do you think Mikhail Gorbachev has advocated an arms reduction agreement between the United States and Russia? Do you think he is sincerely interested in reducing levels of nuclear weapons in the world, or do you think he's just trying to get an agreement that gives the Soviets an advantage over the United States?

Sincerely Interested	Uncertain	Gain Advantage
48.6%	6.3%	45.3%

F. Why do you think Mikhail Gorbachev has proposed loosening censorship? Do you think he is sincerely interested in giving the Soviet citizens more freedoms, or that he is only trying to create the impression that the Soviet Union is becoming more open, when it actually isn't?

Sincerely Interested	Uncertain	Create Impression
48.4%	2.4%	49.2%

G. Why do you think Mikhail Gorbachev has proposed holding competitive elections? Do you think he sincerely wants to give Soviet citizens a greater say in politics, or that he is trying to create the impression that the Soviet Union is becoming more democratic when it really isn't?

Sincerely Interested	Uncertain	Create Impression
40.5%	1.5%	58.0%

H. It really doesn't make any difference who is in charge of the Soviet Union—all their leaders are basically the same.

Agree Strongly	Agree Somewhat	Uncertain	Disagree Somewhat	Disagree Strongly
24.8%	24.3%	0.2%	27.6%	23.1%

I. Compared to previous Soviet leaders, would you say that Gorbachev is more cooperative with the United States, less cooperative, or equally cooperative as previous Soviet leaders?

More	Equally	Less
68.4%	25.2%	6.4%

J. Compared to previous Soviet leaders, would you say that Gorbachev is more interested in keeping world peace, less interested, or about equally interested in keeping peace?

More	Equally	Less
61.0%	34.8%	4.2%

K. Do you feel Gorbachev is more interested in making the Soviet Union a freer society, less interested, or about equally interested in making the Soviet Union a freer society as previous Soviet leaders?

More	Equally	Less
53.3%	38.0%	8.7%

L. Do you feel Gorbachev is more interested in raising the standard of living for the Soviet people, less interested, or about equally interested in raising the standard of living for the Soviet people?

More	Equally	Less
58.0%	36.5%	5.4%

M. And compared to previous Soviet leaders, do you feel Gorbachev is more trustworthy in dealing with the United States, less trustworthy, or about equally trustworthy?

More	Equally	Less
34.1%	58.0%	7.9%

N. Which country is better at making sure that everyone has a job—the Soviet Union or the United States?

Soviet Union	Both Equal	United States
65.0%	1.3%	33.8%

O. Which country has a better public education system, through high school—the Soviet Union or the United States?

Soviet Union	Both Equal	United States
44.0%	1.5%	54.5%

P. Which country is better at taking care of its poor—the Soviet Union or the United States?

Soviet Union	Both Equal	United States
41.2%	2.7%	56.2%

Source: 1987 Foreign Policy Attitudes Survey, Lexington, Kentucky.

respondents are split evenly about the sincerity of Gorbachev's arms control overture as well as his position on censorship. Thus, even while most Americans appear to be quite cynical about the motivations of the Soviet nation, many are willing to give the current leadership the benefit of the doubt.

One possible reason for this apparent contradiction is suggested by responses to Items H through M in Table 2-6: there is impressive evidence to suggest that the American public sees important differences between Gorbachev and his predecessors. Slightly more than one half of our sample disagrees with the proposition that "all [Soviet] leaders are basically the same." More important, rather large majorities believe that Gorbachev is "more cooperative with the United States" (Item I) and "more interested in keeping world peace" (Item J) than previous Soviet leaders. Apparently, the general secretary's worldwide public relations campaign to publicize the goals of *glasnost* (openness) have not fallen on deaf ears in the United States. At least in terms of his international image, Gorbachev is differentiated from prior Soviet leaders.

Somewhat smaller majorities perceive Gorbachev to be more concerned with domestic reforms than his predecessors. Still, a plurality believes that, compared with others, Gorbachev is more concerned with "making the Soviet Union a freer society" (Item K) and "raising the standard of living" (Item L). This is not to say that our respondents are ready to embrace Gorbachev with open arms. Only about one third of our respondents believe him to be more trustworthy than previous Soviet leaders. Apparently, despite his other virtues, Gorbachev cannot shake the profound distrust of Americans toward Soviet officials.

We have seen, then, a strong suspicion of Soviet motives in general, although Gorbachev is differentiated somewhat from past distrust of the USSR's leadership. In what sense do Americans evaluate the policies of the Soviet government? We asked respondents to compare the effectiveness of the United States and the USSR in three areas: securing employment (Item N), public education (Item O), and taking care of the poor (Item P). It is important to keep in mind that very few individuals have much information about public policy in the USSR. Thus, most respondents can be expected to infer their evaluations of Soviet policies from their more general impressions of Soviet society and communism.

Perhaps because of the widespread impression that the Soviet economy ensures employment to all citizens, two thirds believe that the USSR has the advantage in the area of employment. It is revealing, nonetheless, that in two other areas that generally are regarded as strengths of the Soviet system—education and caring for the poor—majorities still see the United States as superior in performance. Even though poverty and the distribution of educational opportunities remain problematic in the USSR by objective standards, the Soviet Union compares favorably with the United States in these policy areas (McAuley, 1977; Lane, 1985, pp. 299–304). Thus, our national distaste for the Soviet Union appears not only to affect our perception of Soviet motives but also to lower our evaluations of the effectiveness of their system.

Further evidence on this point comes from the open-ended portion of the survey where we asked people what they thought were the good points about the government of the Soviet Union, or what they liked about it. The relative silence that this question elicited was striking. Most responses fell into one of two categories: either individuals reported there was nothing at all they liked about the Soviet government, or they indicated they were simply unable to think of any good attributes. The handful of positive comments primarily referred to the Soviet people (for example, nice, hard-working, clean) or Soviet culture (architecture, music) but not the Soviet government (social welfare programs). This suggests not only that images of the Soviet Union are consistently bleak, but also that information about the positive attributes of Soviet society is much more scarce than information about the deficiencies of their system. When asked to name something they liked about the Soviet government, several individuals were quick to admit that their knowledge was lacking when it came to more positive aspects of Soviet society, responding in the following manner:

I don't know much about them. There's bound to be something [good] if we knew them better.

No, I've never been there.

They're probably not so bad, but that's all we hear about them over here.

It is worth noting that, consistently, those who have the greatest amount of information about the Soviet Union are also most willing to give the Soviet leadership the benefit of the doubt and, moreover, to believe that there are legitimate differences between their rulers. In Table 2-7 we present responses to three of the items included in Table 2-6, broken down by the amount of attention that respondents pay to media accounts of Soviet reforms: the sincerity of Gorbachev's proposal of competitive elections (Item G), the amount of similarity among Soviet leaders (Item H), and the concern Gorbachev exhibits for making the USSR a freer society relative to past leaders (Item K).[2]

Table 2-7. Relationship between Attitudes toward the Soviet Union and Attention to Soviet Reforms

		Gorbachev's Motives in Holding Elections in Russia		All Soviet Leaders the Same?		Comparing Gorbachev's Interest in Making USSR a Freer Society with Past Soviet Leaders		
		Sincere	Insincere	Agree	Disagree	More Interest	Equal Interest	Less Interest
Maximum	1	36	27	25	55	62	16	3
		57.1%	41.9%	31.3%	68.8%	76.5%	19.8%	3.7%
	2	103	114	112	135	153	68	24
Attention to		47.5%	52.5%	45.3%	54.7%	62.4%	27.8%	9.8%
Reforms	3	57	123	111	80	78	97	13
		31.7%	68.3%	58.1%	41.9%	41.5%	51.6%	6.9%
Minimum	4	17	42	45	26	13	39	11
		28.8%	71.2%	63.4%	36.6%	20.6%	61.9%	17.5%
Total		213	306	293	296	306	220	51

Source: 1987 Foreign Policy Attitudes Survey, Lexington, Kentucky.

Note: Entries are cell frequencies (first line) and percentages (second line). Percentages are based on raw frequencies.

Although we display only three representative questions from the many in Table 2-6 to simplify our presentation, the same tendencies are found with virtually all other items. Specifically, while only about 27 percent of those who pay no attention to reports of Soviet reforms believe Gorbachev's electoral reforms to be sincere, more than twice as many (57 percent) of those paying a great deal of attention to news reports see his actions as well motivated. Conversely, the proportion of respondents perceiving the general secretary's actions cynically declines as individuals pay closer and closer attention to the media.

Along the same lines, individuals who pay a great deal of attention to news about the USSR are far less likely to believe that Soviet leaders are cut from the same cloth. Moreover, they are far more likely to believe that, relative to his predecessors, Gorbachev is concerned with making Soviet society freer. In short, those without much information about the Eastern bloc tend to resort to stereotypical (and quite negative) judgments about the Soviet system—its government, leadership, and policies—while the relatively better informed Americans have a greater capacity to appreciate differences and innovations in current Soviet politics.[3]

We close this section by quoting from two respondents who, during the course of the interview, displayed very little information about Soviet society and registered starkly negative attitudes toward the USSR. When asked why they disliked the government of the Soviet Union, both individuals mentioned isolated actions taken by Soviet officials rather than citing more general Soviet policies. Referring to a West German youth's daring landing of a small private aircraft in Red Square in the summer of 1987, an elderly woman expressed indignation at "putting that boy in prison over there for riding in that airplane." A young male indicated his displeasure with "the way they [Soviet officials] treated Sylvester Stallone when he was filming *Rocky IV* over there."[4] The point is not that all negative images of the USSR are lacking in sophistication and information but that individuals with less knowledge about the Soviet Union are more likely to base their judgments about that country on the most accessible information, which, in this case, is likely to be extremely negative.

Antecedents of Anticommunism in the United States

What makes Americans unique in their fear and loathing of the USSR? We noted above that, while other democracies probably have more to fear from the Soviet Union in objective terms, the level of distrust and hostility vented toward Eastern bloc countries is much higher in the United States than in Western Europe (a point also made later in this volume by Stephen White). Moreover, this typically American reaction toward communism and the Soviet Union has been a mainstay of our popular culture at least since the Cold War period of the 1950s (Stouffer, 1955). At the outset of this chapter we sought to describe the characteristics of Communist countries that Americans find so threatening. Here we ask: What is it about American society that helps to account for the anti-Communist beliefs of its citizenry? Certainly, the sources of such beliefs are diverse and complex and a full treatment is beyond the scope of this essay. However, our ongoing research on the subject suggests that the following three factors are particularly important antecedents of anticommunism: nationalistic values, religious values, and the persistent influence of political elites.

Nationalistic values run high in American society. The patriotic love and pride that most Americans express toward their country and its symbols, such as the American flag, are exceptional. Not only do we display high levels of affection for the country, but also a majority of Americans believes that our system of government is without equal in the world and should be emulated by other countries. Most Americans agree wholeheartedly with unabashedly ethnocentric statements like: "While the American form of government may not be perfect, it is the best form of government yet devised," and "Other countries should try to make their governments as much like ours as possible" (Hurwitz and Peffley, 1987a, 1987b). The fact that these patriotic feelings and ethnocentric beliefs are important antecedents of a fear and loathing of Communist countries is not surprising, for an ardent faith in the "American Way" is a natural counterpart to anti-Communist sentiment. Ingroup loyalty often translates into out-group hostility (Levinson, 1957; Rosenberg, 1965; Kegley and Wittkopf, 1987) and the long-standing "out-group" in foreign affairs has been Communist countries that, for the patriot, tend to represent an anti-ideal group whose values and interests are antithetical to ours.

Another characteristic of American society that appears to augment anti-Communist sentiment is the high level of religiosity in this country. Compared to the citizens of thirteen other Western democracies, a higher percentage of Americans belongs to church or religious organizations (57 percent) and believes in the existence of God (95 percent) and heaven (84 percent) (Neuhaus, 1986). Thus, a common reason cited for disliking the Soviet Union in our Lexington study was the lack of religious freedom in that country. Several of our respondents commented on the "godless" nature of the USSR when asked why they disliked the government of the Soviet Union. Recall, also, that almost three quarters of the Lexington sample thought that "one of the worst things about the Soviet government is that it prevents the Soviet people from worshipping God."

In a national study we were able to pinpoint one religious group that is especially hostile to communism and the Soviet Union: Christian fundamentalists who believe that the Bible should be interpreted literally rather than figuratively. The roots of anticommunism among fundamentalists may be found, first, in the strong anti-Communist rhetoric of many fundamentalist ministers, such as Jerry Falwell and Jimmy Swaggart; second, in this group's adherence to traditional (American) values; and, third, in the (partly accurate) perception that Communist regimes are often hostile to organized religion (Hurwitz and Peffley, 1987c). One fundamentalist in our Lexington study, for instance, remarked: "I think the humanistic, atheistic society that the [Soviet] government is forcing on the people is very bad."

A final source of this great fear and loathing in American politics emanates from Washington. As noted above, the belief that the spread of communism in the world must be contained by the United States has been a central tenet of American foreign policymaking in the executive branch for the last four decades. And, as Charles Ostrom and Brian Job (1986, p. 544) have argued:

> These beliefs have led U.S. Presidents to identify most unrest and turmoil in the world as the result of an international communist movement and to focus on the USSR as the primary challenger to U.S. interests. Furthermore, these beliefs have created the presumption that forceful actions are a necessary component of the containment strategy.

It goes without saying, then, that in order to boost public (and thereby congressional) support for greater defense appropriations at home or the use of military force abroad, presidents must often fan the flames of anticommunism to convince the public that Eastern bloc countries pose a serious threat to our national security. Thus, to varying degrees, all American presidents have helped to reinforce a hostile view of Communist countries.

Clearly falling in this tradition of modern presidents, Reagan has been able to take full advantage of the presidency as a "bully pulpit" to promote his view of the Soviet Union as an "evil empire." Reagan's persuasive skills and his long-standing credentials as a "Cold Warrior" have allowed him to capitalize on public anxieties in the aftermath of such events as the 1979 Soviet invasion of Afghanistan and the Soviet downing of a South Korean airliner in 1983. In our analyses we have discovered one clear sign of Reagan's success as the "Great Communicator": younger Americans, who tend to be more affected by short-term political forces than older Americans (Converse, 1976), have a much more negative image of the Soviet Union than their elders do. In an apparent reversal of trends in the 1970s, where youth appeared to champion détente and sought an end to U.S. military intervention against Communist revolutions, youth now are more supportive of containment policies than older cohorts (Hurwitz and Peffley, 1987c).

Some Consequences of Anticommunism

Thus far we have examined public attitudes at a fairly general level of abstraction. It is now appropriate to ask whether these general orientations affect the mass public's more concrete foreign policy views. In other words, to what extent can public support for more concrete foreign policy proposals, like the nuclear freeze or U.S. military involvement in Central America, be explained by more general attitudes toward Communist bloc countries? And in what ways does this sentiment make its way into the foreign policymaking process, if at all?

In answer to the first question, a fear and loathing of communism and the Soviet Union (that is, anticommunism) guides public preferences across a wide range of otherwise unfamiliar policy terrains in international politics. For the ordinary citizen not attuned to the esoteric details of public policy in foreign affairs, more global attitudes, like anticommunism, can be used to evaluate quickly and efficiently more concrete policy options.

Indeed, anti-Communist sentiment has been found to be an extremely powerful predictor of Americans' more specific positions on a wide range of international policies (Hurwitz and Peffley, 1987a, 1987b). Not only do anti-Communists tend to support dramatic increases in defense spending at home—in the form of further spending for Star Wars, augmenting the country's conventional forces, and expanding its nuclear arsenal—but also they tend to oppose negotiating an arms control treaty with the Soviets if that means reaching an agreement before the United States has a chance to build up its own nuclear arsenal. In short, on defense-related matters, anti-Communists are very much in sync with the foreign policy initiatives of the Reagan administration.

Anti-Communists also show strong support for Reagan's Central American policy to increase U.S. military involvement in that region. More specifically, they favor uping the ante of U.S. military aid to the contras fighting to overthrow the government of Nicaragua and would support sending U.S. troops to stop the spread of communism in Central America. In addition, should the Soviet Union invade West Germany or Poland, anti-Communists stand ready to send American troops to confront the Soviets directly on foreign soil. For many Americans a fear and loathing of communism translates into a militant policy of protecting ourselves at home and using our military might overseas.[5]

Although anti-Communist beliefs translate into specific policy preferences for the mass public, this is a far cry from saying that these attitudes have any real impact on public policy. Among policymaking elites the extent to which public opinion provides guidance is difficult to determine precisely. The conventional wisdom on the subject holds that the public is generally "permissive" in accepting the foreign policy initiatives advanced by its leaders (Almond, 1950). But a closer look at the conventional wisdom suggests that this permissiveness may stem less from apathy and ignorance than from the consensus on the major goals of foreign policy shared by the public and the presidents it elects. According to Charles Kegley and Eugene Wittkopf (1987, p. 36), for the last four decades two tenets have been uppermost in the minds of American foreign policymakers:

1) Communism comprises the principal danger in the world, and the United States must use its power to combat the spread of this menace.

2) Because the Soviet Union is the spearhead of the Communist challenge, American foreign policy must be dedicated to the containment of Soviet expansionism and influence.

From our examination of the survey evidence cited above we conclude that a large majority of the American public adamantly supports these goals of containment. Thus, if the public and its leaders are in agreement on the ends of foreign policy, the masses may grant some leeway to policymakers to select alternative policy instruments that lead to the goal of containment. Serious opposition may be mobilized only when other goals the public holds dear become threatened, such as the desire to avoid any long-term engagement of American troops.

Influence in foreign affairs is therefore a two-way street. As we have argued, elites (that is, presidents) do help to reinforce anti-Communist attitudes among the American public through the policy initiatives they adopt and their attempts to generate support for them. But, in embracing anti-Communist values, American presidents are only echoing the sentiments of the public that elected them in the first place.

Rather than conclude that presidents have a virtual "free hand" in foreign affairs because of public indifference (Lipset, 1966), we prefer the analogy that public opinion acts like a system of dikes to keep the policy flow within certain boundaries (Key, 1968). And in foreign policy, because of the public's strong tradition of anticommunism, the dikes that restrict the government's efforts to cope with the Eastern bloc are extremely wide, thus allowing the president considerable discretion.

Notes

[1] The average telephone interview, conducted by the professional staff at the University of Kentucky Survey Research Center, lasted from twenty-five to thirty minutes. The demographic characteristics of the sample come reasonably close to approximating those found in the Lexington population. According to the 1980 census, blacks make up 13 percent of the Lexington population: our sample includes 9 percent blacks. Women comprise 52 percent of the population: our sample is 49 percent. More educated and affluent individuals are slightly overrepresented in our sample. The median income in Lexington is $15,915, while the median income category in the sample is $20,000

to $30,000. Respective population and sample characteristics for education are "less than high school," 29 percent and 13 percent; "completed high school," 28 percent and 26 percent; "some college," 18 percent and 26 percent; and "graduated college," 25 percent and 34 percent.

[2]Respondents were asked: "How much attention would you say you have paid to news stories about reforms going on in the Soviet Union—a great deal, a fair amount, only a little, or almost none at all?"

[3]The same patterns are found when we cross-tabulate responses to these questions with other cognitive variables, such as education levels or the amount of general information about foreign affairs held by people.

[4]The latter incident was a purely imagined occurrence, since *Rocky IV* was not filmed in the Soviet Union.

[5]It should be pointed out that we have described only a general tendency for most, but not all, anti-Communists to support tough, militant policy measures. Many people who dislike communism and the Soviet Union also oppose more militant foreign policies, largely because they prefer accommodation to confrontation as a means of dealing with Eastern bloc countries. In fact, when this group of more accommodating anti-Communists is added to more liberal groups in foreign affairs that are not anticommunistic, we find a majority coalition among the mass public that is opposed to such policies as sending U.S. troops to Central America (65 percent opposed), increasing aid to the Contras (56 percent want this aid decreased), and building up the U.S. nuclear arsenal (75 percent are opposed to a buildup). Thus, the majority sentiment against communism and the Soviet Union in this country does not translate into a majority sentiment in favor of militant anti-Communist policies.

Bibliography

Almond, Gabriel. *The American People and Foreign Policy.* New York: Harcourt, Brace, 1950.

Converse, Philip E. *The Dynamics of Party Support: Cohort Analyzing Party Identification.* Beverly Hills, CA: Sage Publications, 1976.

Epstein, Leon D. *Political Parties in Western Democracies.* New Brunswick, NJ: Transaction Books, 1980.

Hurwitz, Jon, and Peffley, Mark. "How Are Foreign Policy Attitudes Structured? A Hierarchical Model." *American Political Science Review* 81, no. 4 (1987).

———. "Foreign Policy Attitudes and Political Behavior." Report prepared for the National Election Service 1987 Pilot Study. 1987.

———. "The Roots of Anti-communism in American Public Opinion." Unpublished manuscript. 1987.

Kegley, Charles W. Jr., and Wittkopf, Eugene. *American Foreign Policy: Patterns and Processes,* 3d. ed. New York: St. Martin's Press, 1987.

Key, V. O., Jr. *Public Opinion and American Democracy.* New York: Knopf, 1968.

Lane, David. *Soviet Politics.* New York: New York University Press, 1985.

Levinson, Daniel J. "Authoritarian Personality and Foreign Policy." *Journal of Conflict Resolution* 1 (1957): 37–47.

Lipset, Seymour M. "The President, the Polls and Vietnam." *Transaction* (September-October 1966): 19–24.

McAuley, A. "The Distribution of Earnings and Income in the Soviet Union." *Soviet Studies* 29, no. 2 (1977).

Neuhaus, Richard John. *Unsecular America.* Grand Rapids, MI: William B. Erman, 1986.

Ostrom, Charles W., Jr., and Job, Brian L. "The President and the Use of Political Force." *American Political Science Review* 80, no. 2 (1986).

Reilly, John E. *American Public Opinion and U.S. Foreign Policy 1983.* Chicago: Chicago Council on Foreign Relations, 1983.

Rosenberg, Milton J. "Images in Relation to the Policy Process: American Public Opinion on Cold War Issues." In Herbert C. Kelman, ed., *International Behavior.* New York: Holt, Rinehart and Winston, 1965.

Simon, Rita. *Public Opinion in America: 1936-1970.* Chicago: Rand-McNally, 1974.

Stouffer, Samuel. *Communism, Conformity, and Civil Liberties.* New York: Doubleday, 1955.

3

Who Are the Soviets?
The Importance of Accurate
Perception in the Age of Trident

Burns H. Weston

In his farewell address over one hundred ninety years ago, President George Washington counseled his fellow Americans "to steer clear of permanent alliances with any portion of the foreign world."[1] Today, in our increasingly interdependent and interpenetrating global community, this advice does not endure. At the present time, and from now into the future, there is no way, certainly no important way, that we can deny our essential connectedness with the rest of humanity. But another warning in Washington's farewell address does endure: his admonition that we Americans should beware of "inveterate antipathies against particular nations."[2] Said Washington: "The nation that indulges toward another an habitual hatred... is in some degrees a slave. It is a slave to its animosity... which is sufficient to leadeth it astray from its duties and its interests."[3]

The Soviets: The Allegations

Washington's advice has special relevance today because, since the coming to power of the Reagan administration especially, our government has exhibited toward our adversary the Soviet Union such a "habitual hatred" as to make us, to paraphrase Washington, in some degrees a slave to our animosity. Even after Reykjavik and the arrival of *glasnost* (openness), we have been told that the Soviet Union is "the focus of evil in the world," that it is principally to blame for the "hot spots" around the globe, and that it is unreliable, never to be trusted to keep its international agreements. As a consequence of these anti-Soviet perceptions and charges, relations between the United States

and the Soviet Union, until very recently at least, have been reminis-
cent of the Cold War of the 1960s. Well over a decade after President
Richard Nixon and Chairman Leonid Brezhnev negotiated the SALT I
Accords and toasted one another in Moscow in 1972, a policy of un-
paralleled military buildup—based on the view that the USSR can be
dealt with only as a hostile, dangerous force that knows and understands
only military power—has caused, at times, even the hopes of détente
to fade.

No sensible person would say that the USSR poses no threat or
that it is essentially a benign power somehow gone astray—let alone
that it is, in the late General Secretary Konstantin Chernenko's prepos-
terous phrase, "the hope for mankind." To overlook the subjugation of
Eastern Europe, to ignore the repeated repression of political dissidents,
or to somehow excuse its crude and barbarous behavior from the Berlin
blockade to Afghanistan would be folly in the extreme—naïveté writ
large. There is legitimate and ample reason to disapprove of Soviet
comings and goings, both at home and abroad.

In this Age of Trident it is likewise folly and naive to indulge our
penchant for oversimplification and thereby to perceive our adversaries
inaccurately. Very simply, the risks are too high. As seductively appealing
as it may be to view our relations with the Soviet Union as an eternal
struggle between the forces of good and the forces of evil—as if requiring an inevitable shootout at the OK Corral—it is well to recall that
today's protagonists are not using six-shooters. They are using nuclear
weapons, the average firepower of which is some eighty times greater
than the primitive bombs dropped on Hiroshima and Nagasaki.

It therefore behooves us to ask, if only in our own self-interest,
just how evil the Soviets really are, just how much they really are
responsible for the world's hot spots, and just how much they really
cannot be trusted to keep their international commitments. If nothing
else, the simple instinct of survival requires us to ask: Are we the
beneficiaries of skilled and patient thought, or are we the victims of
dangerous mythology?[4]

The USSR as the "Evil Empire"

Consider, first, the allegation that the Soviet Union is an "evil empire,"
driven by the forces of godless communism. The Soviet regime is without doubt repressive, but its practices have little in common with revolutionary terror as we ordinarily are led to believe. The Russia of Joseph
Stalin is not the Russia of Mikhail Gorbachev. Or, as recently put
by one of our leading students of Soviet affairs, Dimitri Simes: "The

modern Soviet state bears a closer resemblance to a superbly armed Austria-Hungary than to Nazi Germany."[5]

However much Communist ideology enjoins the Soviet people to reject theistic religion as "the opiate of the masses" and to substitute for it the religion of the state, Marxism-Leninism is firmly rooted in Judeo-Christian ethics and morality. The Marxist idea of socioeconomic equality is one of humankind's most noble aspirations. Despite the great material progress made in recent years, evident both in the statistics and in the general scene visible to the visitor, the Soviet Union has not yet won the struggle for socioeconomic equality (no more than has the United States or any other major power, for that matter). As Gorbachev points out, the Soviet economy stands exposed before the world as unjust and clumsily mismanaged in many critical respects. But let us not overlook the solid achievements: Every Soviet citizen is legally guaranteed free education through the university level, provided that the appropriate exams are passed. Every Soviet citizen is legally guaranteed a right to work—not necessarily at a job of one's choosing but at a wage appropriate to maintain a more or less adequate standard of living for self and family. Every Soviet citizen is legally guaranteed free medical care and health services that, although not always the best, nonetheless ensure longer life expectancies than ever before in Russian history. Every Soviet citizen is legally guaranteed at least minimal housing at stable and nonexploitative rentals. These, and other, achievements must not be ignored by observers of the Soviet condition because they form a measure of systemic performance that certainly contributes to an underlying legitimacy.

Also, let us not overlook what any visitor to the Soviet Union invariably encounters among the people he or she meets, whether they be of the elite or proletarian classes: a pervasive and vigorously expressed longing for world peace, born of firsthand suffering from repeated invasions throughout the last two to three centuries, but especially during World War II, which claimed Soviet citizens for over one half of its victims. Let us not forget, either, that it is the Soviet Union, not the United States, that has declared itself officially committed to a policy of no first use of nuclear weapons and, more recently, to a comprehensive test ban treaty.

Before concluding that the USSR is an unmitigated evil in the world, it is worth remembering that the Soviets, although guided by different ideologies and not without their faults, are, nonetheless, human beings with hopes and dreams not unlike those that animate each and every one of us. Just as we can see error in the Ayatollah Khomeini's characterization of the United States as "the Great Satan," we also should be able to see error in our one-sided characterizations of the Soviet Union.

The USSR as "Hot Spot" Culprit

Consider, next, the claim that if the Soviet Union did not exist the world would be more or less free of turbulent hot spots. This assertion is made at our peril. In addition to being just plain wrong, it foolishly denies the enormously complex and intricate nature of the contemporary global system, interdependent and interpenetrating as never before.

Former Undersecretary of State George Ball made the point very well when he noted that OPEC's precipitate 1973 oil price increases, which dislocated the world's economy and helped to bring about a global recession, were an initiative

> not of the Politburo but of a group of Third World nations exploiting their monopoly of a key source of the world's energy. Nor did the Soviets overthrow the Shah of Iran. He was pushed off his throne not by external forces, but because he had...managed to alienate almost every sector of Iranian society. Even the most paranoid ideologues cannot blame Moscow for the Iran-Iraq war. Nor is Moscow in any way the cause of the festering Arab-Israeli struggle, or the agonies of Lebanon, the communal bloodshed in India, the menacing racial tensions in South Africa, the religious feuding in Northern Ireland, the quarrel between the Moroccans and the Polisario in North Africa, Libya's threat to the Sudan, the comic opera conflict in the Falklands—or any of numerous other "hot spots" [that Washington has sought to blame on the Soviet Union in recent years].[6]

In other words, most troubles between nations are local or regional in character, a lesson that our current adventurism in Central America suggests we still have not learned despite the travesty of Vietnam. Close to fifty shooting wars are now in process around the globe, and all but a few stem from ethnic or religious conflicts, from racial animosities, from intolerance and repression in all its forms, from inequities and inequalities, from ancient boundary disputes, or from historic arguments that are no less bitter for having lost all discernible relevance to today's realities. To bend and twist these disputes to fit the doctrinaire concept of the polarized East-West conflict is not only foolish but also dangerous. It produces humiliating and tragic fiascos, such as we suffered in Lebanon where we sought to legitimate our thoughtless involvement in a long-standing factional conflict by portraying Syria as merely a Soviet puppet. We pay heavily for the damage and dislocations we mindlessly encourage by insisting that complex, parochial feuds are intricately related to the quarrel between the United States and the Soviet Union.

The USSR as a Breaker of Promises

Finally, what truth is there in the claim that the Soviet Union is a mendacious state, a breaker of treaties, a nation run by unprincipled thugs who believe that legal promises are like fences—made to be climbed? For over two generations, political points have been won by indulging in this sort of rhetoric, and obviously the Reagan administration is no exception. For example, it has charged the Soviets with violating the SALT agreements and also has accused them of supplying chemical weapons for use in Kampuchea and Afghanistan—the so-called yellow rain—in violation of international agreements and unilateral pledges.

With very minor exceptions, however, the Reagan administration has come up short with the proof. Regarding the SALT treaties the evidence is far from persuasive, and, in any event, the U.S. government has failed to resort to the procedures specified by those agreements for raising claims of violation. President Ronald Reagan defiantly ceased observing the shared expectations surrounding the SALT II Treaty, summarily rejected Soviet offers for a comprehensive test ban treaty, and has now threatened a unilateral reinterpretation of the ABM Treaty, our only real arms control treaty with the Soviet Union, so as to permit the testing of Star Wars antiballistic missile components, widely agreed to be prohibited by the treaty. As for the supply of chemical weapons, neither guilt nor innocence ever has been definitively established, although there appears now to be substantial credible evidence linking the yellow rain to the feces of bees—scarcely a Soviet plot.

As we assess the outcome of these thrusts and parries, it would be well to note that most far-reaching treaties and declarations of high principle—the UN Charter and the Helsinki Accords, for example—are couched in language that is easily susceptible of differing interpretation, and that narrower covenants and resolutions, precisely because of their specificity—the SALT treaties, for instance—are riddled with built-in ambiguities. Because nations sometimes have difficulty in reaching agreement on critical points, they "paper over" their disagreements by ambiguous language that contains something for all sides, permitting signature and entry into force of the agreement but leaving problems of interpretation to a future day.

Thus, it is easy to accuse the Soviets of not living up to their international commitments. However, in so doing we substantially rewrite the historical record. The United States already has concluded over one hundred treaties with the Soviet Union, and so far Moscow's performance under them has raised no serious doubts about Soviet dependability. As any American businessman will testify, the Soviets have been reliable partners in their commercial dealings: tough bargainers who keep the bargains they make. And, as any intellectually honest foreign policy expert is obliged to admit, we already do trust the Soviets to keep their word. As Richard Barnet of the Institute for Policy Studies has usefully pointed out,[7] every day we rely on their technology, as well as ours, to send and receive messages to prevent nuclear war. Every day we count on their septuagenarian leaders, as well as ours, not to make fatal miscalculations in their confrontations with us. Every day we trust that the persistent communication of an escalating threat will intimidate rather than provoke, that it will encourage cool rationality rather than acts of desperation, and that leaders that seem all too subject to human frailty will demonstrate superhuman prudence, cunning, and cool.

To borrow from Barnet again, the question that political leaders and the general public should be asking, as part of a wiser American foreign policy, is not "Can we trust the Russians?" but rather "In what way is it prudent for us to trust the Russians, for what, and how far?"[8] Unless we acknowledge that trust is, and must be, a central aspect of Soviet-American relations, and that it cannot be displaced by faith in the Soviets' perception of their own self-interest or by technological eavesdropping devices, we are unlikely to alter our catastrophic course, and we are unlikely to arrest the slide toward a war to which we now have been headed for some time.

The Soviets: The Reality

It behooves us to ask who the Soviets really are. That is, if they are not the focus of all evil in the world, if they are not the primary cause of the global hot spots, and if they are not an immoral people never to be trusted to keep the bargains they make, then who are they? We must face up to this question objectively; otherwise, we become the victims of our own distorted propaganda, the victims of policies that are entirely unsuited for our collective survival in the Age of Trident.

A comprehensive portrait of who the Soviets really are would be difficult to cover within this single chapter. Prime Minister Winston Churchill once said that "Russia is a riddle wrapped in a mystery inside an enigma."[9] But it is warranted to sketch in broad outline at least two propositions that should inform our relations with, as well as our study of, the Soviet Union. Were our government to accept these propositions, or to give them at least some credence, we would stand a greater chance of perceiving common interests, common concerns, and common problems instead of perceiving only irreconcilable conflict, mutual threat, and the necessity of attaining military and technological superiority.[10]

Historical Ambivalence toward the West

First is the proposition that the conflict and tension that mark Soviet-American relations today are in no way unique to the post-1917 period, nor simply the consequence of the differing theologies of the Communist East and the capitalist West. The Soviet Union's conflicted relationship with the West is rooted deep in Russian history. It must be recalled that Russia never participated fully in the Renaissance, the Enlightenment, or in the social, economic, and political transformations that shaped early modern Europe. Also, it did not share substantially in the evolution of Roman Christianity, being influenced, instead, by Byzantium. Lying half in Europe and half in Asia, Russia was fundamentally distanced for centuries from the mainstream of Western European cultural development and, to some extent, still is.

Thus, ever since the early eighteenth century, when Czar Peter the Great tried forcibly to westernize his country, Russia has been troubled by a kind of national schizophrenia. While some Russians enthusiastically embraced Western culture and agonized over their country's supposed inferiority, others—the so-called Slavophiles—resisted it, in particular its materialism and rationalism. They asserted, instead, an otherworldly orthodoxy, one that emphasized Russia's uniqueness and superiority, its spiritual purity and holy mission. Later, Marxist G. V. Plekhanov and others rejected the bourgeois individualism and social inequalities spawned by nineteenth-century capitalism and adopted utopian or Marxist visions of a just society. Underlying this ambivalence toward the West was an enormous tension that inheres in a process of cultural borrowing that, in turn, presupposes the backwardness, inferiority, and dependence of the recipient country.

The Soviet Union continues to struggle with this ambivalence and tension today,[11] its frequently obdurate posture often masking a genuine insecurity that its backwardness will forever place it in some precarious dependence on the West. Twice in this century—during the two world wars—the Soviet Union has paid a huge price for its economic underdevelopment, experiences that understandably reinforce an already deep distrust of the West. The memory of American troops joining other intervening forces in 1918 in an effort to crush the Russian Revolution, along with the strident anticommunism of successive

American administrations, also remains vivid in the Soviet psyche. And the secret development of the atomic bomb, precisely when the Soviets were bearing the brunt of the war against the Nazis, aroused suspicion, envy, and fear. This history, remembered so differently in the United States, continues to feed Soviet distrust of the West, in general, and the United States, in particular. The memory of explicit or clearly implied threats by the United States to use nuclear weapons first against the Soviet Union in a series of critical conflicts—Iran in 1946, Korea in 1953, Berlin in 1961, and the Persian Gulf in 1980—further exacerbates the Soviets' distrust.

In sum, the Soviet Union's love-hate relationship with the West, deeply rooted and not easily changed, is part of a national heritage that does not rest alone or even primarily on the experience of superpower conflict nor on the intense ideological combat of the twentieth century. It is a historical reality that is not likely to be altered substantially, much less "beaten" or "overcome" by Western military and technological prowess.

Czarist-Soviet Continuities

A second proposition also helps to put things into proper perspective, namely, that there exist important continuities or similarities between the czarist and Soviet political cultures. This is a fact that appears not to be properly fathomed in Washington. For example, both the czarist and the Soviet states have appeared to dominate—at times to consume—society. This behavior represents a pattern that is perhaps most obviously apparent in statist attempts to effect large-scale socio-economic transformations on an unwilling populace, as illustrated by Peter the Great in the eighteenth century and Stalin in the twentieth. There are also the repressive uses of state power, whether by the czars or by the commissars. Like Andrei Sakharov and other dissidents today, Feodor Dostoevsky was banished to internal penal exile for alleged crimes against the state in the mid-nineteenth century. Such an inflated role of the state has created a chasm between state and society, a chasm that is characteristic not only of the modern period but also of the Imperial era as well.

Perhaps even more important, because it is so hard for Americans to accept, is the inescapable continuity from Imperial to Soviet Russia of broadly shared political and social values as between the official elite and the masses as a whole—for example, the historical absence of democratic politics in the Western sense not only within the czarist and Soviet regimes, which is rather obvious, but also within broad segments of the population. Additionally, there are the patterns of top-down directiveness, authoritarianism, and hierarchal political organization. And, not least, reflecting the fears of social anarchy that lie in the twentieth-century experience of revolution and world war as well as in the great peasant rebellions of seventeenth- and eighteenth-century Russia, there are the deeply rooted patterns of subordination to constituted authority, the historic absence of institutionalized opposition, and the enduring patience with endless bureaucracy that confounds the contemporary observer of Soviet society as much as it encouraged Nikolai Gogol to write *The Inspector General* (1835), his great satire on bureaucratic corruption and lethargy. The motto "autocracy, orthodoxy, and nationality," expressing the principles that were applied to early nineteenth-century Russian education, was used by Czar Nicholas I to suppress liberal thought, control the universities, increase censorship, persecute religious and national minorities, and strengthen the secret police. The historical similarities are no mere coincidence.

Now at least two pregnant points may be drawn from this second proposition that important continuities define the political cultures of both czarist and Soviet Russia. First, one may legitimately question whether the ideology of Marxism-Leninism and the organizational strength of the Soviet Communist party are the overriding determinants of twentieth-century Soviet experience. Second, one might conclude that the current Soviet regime may well be in power not only, and perhaps not primarily, because of its exercise of coercive power but, rather, because it reflects and responds to important values shared by broad segments of Soviet society: a deep concern with order, stability, regularity, and directed change, as well as a generalized acceptance of a one-party system and an acceptance of the historically inflated role of the state vis-à-vis society.

Yet the West is regularly confronted with a formidable body of literature—to say nothing of the rhetoric emanating from Washington—that would have us believe that the twentieth-century Russian experience has been decisively determined by the organization and ideology of the Bolshevik party, hell-bent on the destruction of the Western capitalist system; that the Soviet population accords its government no legitimacy whatsoever; and that the Soviet regime is, in reality, on the point of imminent collapse. Rather than adopting a multicausal approach to the contemporary Soviet system and studying it as social scientists would study any other society, we shy from weighing the influence of a multiplicity of conditioning factors; we shy from understanding precisely what drives the Soviets and from identifying clearly their fundamental aspirations, concerns, and fears; and we shy from charting long-term patterns of continuity and change. The result is that we find it hard to accord the Soviet Union a basic legitimacy, or to see it as anything other than an ominous and ubiquitous threat.

The Consequences of Inaccurate Perception: Policy Choices

Thus, forgetting George Washington's wise counsel, our foreign policy becomes "a slave to its animosity...which is sufficient to leadeth [us] astray from its duties and its interests," as perhaps most characteristically demonstrated by our response to Nikita Khrushchev's famous challenge: "We will bury you." Reading Khrushchev's words automatically to mean the threat of physical destruction, U.S. policymakers responded over time with between $10 and $20 billion of extra military appropriations. It is regrettable that the White House and Foggy Bottom did not read Khrushchev's statement for what it really was: a boastful prediction that the Soviet system ultimately would bury capitalism in a shower of consumer goods. Knowledge may not be a panacea, but ignorance certainly can be a poison.

The problem, however, is really much worse, for when we let our habitual hatred of the Soviet Union becloud the accuracy of our perceptions we acquire the visage of our adversary, adopting its principles, aping its practices, and diminishing our country in the process. Consider, for example, that in the last six to seven years the United States, in its dealings with the United Nations and its allied agencies, has moved steadily from a long-established policy of multilateralism to one of unilateralism; that it has held up and refused to sign the new Law of the Sea Treaty, and later refused to pay the United Nations assessed dues for the treaty's implementation; that it has held that UN peacekeeping forces in Lebanon were part of the problem rather than, as traditionally understood, part of the solution; that it invaded a small Caribbean island on the flimsiest of pretexts and in violation of international law, and then vetoed the Security Council resolution critical of our actions; and that it indiscriminately laid mines in the harbors of Nicaragua and, upon learning that we would be sued in the World Court, in a transparent, undignified, and arguably unconstitutional manner, informed the World Court that we would not accept its jurisdiction in the matter. You may recognize a familiar historical ring. The Soviets are supposed to be the champions of strict limits on international institutions, the withholders of funds, the critics of peacekeeping, the invaders of defenseless countries, and the evaders of courts. On top of all this, in response to its fear and hatred of the Soviet Union the United States, since 1980, has committed itself to military expenditures exceeding $1.6 trillion over six to seven years, which is the equivalent of over $2.2

million for every day of every week of every year since the birth of Jesus Christ. None of this is healthy in this, the Age of Trident.

Conclusion

The issue is clearly drawn. On the one hand, there is the view of the Soviet Union, one of the world's two superpowers, pursuing an expansionist and aggressive foreign policy that is inimical to the historical preeminence and vitality of the Western democracies. On the other hand, there is the view that Soviet foreign policy represents less a purposeful threat to the West than a reflection of Soviet conservatism, bureaucratic inertia, and a deeply ingrained sense of vulnerability to external intervention, validated by centuries of depradation and plunder at the hands of hostile foreign powers. The differences between these two views are fundamental. Where the first tends to commit the West to a path of permanent military competition and confrontation the second holds forth the possibility of Soviet tractability, and therefore the potential for negotiation and compromise over the tension that divides the East and West.

Those who hold the first view do so with some justification. Because of the severe deprivations suffered during the two world wars and at other times, the power to defend the homeland aggressively and not just the ability to retaliate has long been a central objective of post-World War II Soviet military policy; and Soviet weapons and weapons systems have been developed and deployed in ways reflecting this fact. But, as suggested by Arthur Gladstone in a seminal essay published in 1959, there are other, including psychologically complex, reasons that help explain our perception of the Soviet Union as intractable and aggressive. Having the Soviet Union as an enemy, he observed, makes for several "advantages" and "satisfactions":

We have the very considerable stimulation to our economic system provided by the manufacture of armaments and preparations for war in general.... We are provided with a satisfying explanation for many conditions and events that displease us. Politicians are provided with a sure-fire campaign issue and vote-getter. The rest of us are provided with a crusade in which all can participate. Let us not underestimate the great psychological satisfaction provided by a crusade. There is the smug satisfaction arising from the recognition that we are morally superior to the Russians. There is the self-respecting satisfaction arising from the feeling of being needed by the cause, of being able to make a social contribution. And there is the red-blooded satisfaction of being able to hate and to prepare, to kill and destroy without feeling qualms of conscience.[12]

To this Gladstone has added: "Similarly, the Russians derive great advantages from having the United States as an enemy."[13]

Continuation of this pattern of habitual and mutual hatred makes nuclear war, in the author's judgment, ultimately a certainty. One day, because of mutual distrust and competition, a miscalculation or a megalomaniacal act somewhere in the world will unleash upon both societies—and others far beyond—the apocalypse that all of us hope to avoid. So long as distrust and hostile competition remain dominant in U.S.-Soviet relations the tendency to favor burgeoning military budgets and expansionist definitions of national security will continue to push both superpowers down a road neither wants to travel.

The core issue, then, is to consider whether at least we in the United States possess the imagination and will to escape the distrustful competition that now threatens us as never before, and to realize that the benefits of a less militarized and less expansive conception of national self-interest far outweigh the risks of a complex, interdependent world. The growing potential for nuclear war renders it imperative that the policy elites of the United States and the Soviet Union overcome—or at least radically reduce—their mutual distrust and competition at the earliest possible moment, and that this effort be accompanied simultaneously by a similar yet deeper reorientation among their respective populations generally, which for decades have been nurtured to believe the worst about the other.

We must take seriously the wise words of President Washington. We must search deeply among ourselves for ways in which the United States and the Soviet Union might construct a durable and stable relationship based on reciprocal forbearance and mutual tolerance, together with a joint commitment to the peaceful resolution of our disputes when our national interests collide. We must cap the volcano before it is too late.

Notes

[1]J. Richardson, ed., *Messages and Papers of the Presidents 1789-1817*, vol. 1 (Published by authority of Congress, 1901), pp. 213, 223.

[2]Ibid., p. 221.

[3]Ibid.

[4]For pertinent discussion see "Rethinking the Enemy," in Burns Weston, ed., *Toward Nuclear Disarmament and Global Security: A Search for Alternatives* (Boulder, CO: Westview Press, 1984), p. 267.

[5]Dimitri Simes, "The New Soviet Challenge," *Foreign Policy* 55 (Summer 1984): 113.

[6]George Ball, "Slaves to Animosity," *Bulletin of the Atomic Scientists* 40, no. 7 (August-September 1984): 5.

[7]Richard Barnet, "Why Trust the Soviets?" *World Policy Journal* 1, no. 3 (Spring 1984): 461–66.

[8]Ibid.

[9]BBC radio broadcast, October 1, 1939.

[10]The two propositions are derived in part from a public lecture, from which I borrow liberally hereinafter, presented by Professor Heather Hogan of the Oberlin College department of history on November 30, 1983, at Oberlin College. My indebtedness to Professor Hogan is confirmed in Hogan, "Reading, Writing and Reds: The Place of Russian Studies in a Liberal Education," *Oberlin Alumni Magazine* 80, no. 2 (Spring 1984): 15.

[11]"Somewhat ironically, it is the exiled Solzhenitsyn who captures much of this tension so well and whose criticisms of the West so confused Americans a few years ago. Americans wanted to believe that Solzhenitsyn was fleeing a merciless dictatorship for the freedom of the West—what they heard was a stinging condemnation of Western materialism and moral superiority of Orthodox, Mother Russia. To be sure, Solzhenitsyn was profoundly critical of the Soviet regime, but the intertwining of his perceptions and concerns illustrate how conflicted Russian attitudes toward the West and toward their own national experience can be." Ibid. 2:17.

[12]Arthur Gladstone, "The Conception of the Enemy," *Journal of Conflict Resolution* 3, no. 2 (1959): 132–33.

[13]Ibid.

4

Religious Faith in Soviet-American Relations

Bruce Rigdon

Contacts and Conflict

It was not until the middle of the 1950s that Protestant churches in the United States sought to have any relationship with the churches in the Soviet Union. The time was not auspicious for exploring possible new ties. In the United States, McCarthyism looked with deep suspicion on any contacts between Americans and Soviets and often struck out at church leaders when they appeared to be soft on communism. In this dangerous ethos of confrontation, a small delegation of American church leaders, headed by Eugene Carson Blake, then president of the National Council of Churches, set out on a mission to contact co-believers in the Soviet Union and to establish relations with sister churches.

The success of their visit is indicated by the fact that, within a relatively short time, the first official delegation of church leaders from the Soviet Union arrived on American shores to continue discussions begun in Moscow. The times were still not encouraging for such a venture. In the Soviet Union, Nikita Khrushchev had come to power and was beginning a new period of persecution and oppression of the churches that would last for about six years, involve considerable human suffering, and lead to the closing of approximately 15,000 parish churches before it ended.[1] Despite these and other difficulties that marked the times, a strong relationship between Soviet and American churches was established, which has continued to grow and deepen across more than three decades.

One of the results to which these visits contributed occurred in November 1961, when the Protestant and Orthodox churches in the Soviet Union (and elsewhere in Eastern Europe) became members of the World Council of Churches. Few people at the Third Assembly of the World Council of Churches meeting in New Delhi, India, were aware of the tremendous pressures under which the delegates from the Soviet churches were working as a result of the deteriorating conditions of church life at home. It soon became apparent, however, that the Soviet government recognized that the churches of the USSR might prove to be useful instruments in relation to its foreign policy objectives. Nevertheless, Soviet churches were eager to break out of their isolation and were willing to cope with the dilemmas created by this effort in their relations with the state authorities. Thus, in quite different ways, church leaders from both sides were under pressure from home to represent the ideological positions and the foreign policy objectives of their respective governments. It may have been precisely because of such pressure and constraints that church leaders in both the United States and the Soviet Union recognized from the beginning the enormous importance of giving visible evidence of Christian unity across geographical, political, ideological, and even theological boundaries. In any case, church unity has been a concern at the center of these relations from the outset.

The entrance of Soviet Christians and their churches into the international life of the ecumenical movement had a great impact on Christians everywhere. No longer could it be said of the World Council of Churches that it was largely Western in its outlook and Protestant in its composition. Amid the strains and stresses that this new fact sometimes created, American and Soviet church leaders learned to know one another and to trust each other; and they discovered that it was possible to disagree about many things, yet continue to work together. They discovered many things that they and their churches shared in common, and they learned to respect and value their diversities as well. Problems often became occasions for growing and learning together. This developing mutual trust has been nurtured through the years by frequent meetings of Soviet and American church leaders, not only in the context of ecumenical organizations, such as the World Council of Churches, but also through frequent bilateral meetings around issues of mutual concern, such as human rights, security, peace, and disarmament. Some meetings have had a rather dramatic character, as when church leaders from both sides gather during Soviet-American summit meetings to hold a vigil of prayer on behalf of positive agreements on nuclear disarmament. In other instances, long years of study and discussion have created significant agreement and new common ground among the churches in relation to their commitments for the future of our world. What is clear is that the churches will continue to work closely together whether Soviet-American relations improve or decline.

Environment of Soviet Religions

As the 1980s draw to a close, the question is: What are the churches and church life like in the Soviet Union? In 1988 the largest of the churches, the Russian Orthodox Church, commemorates the event that it recognizes as marking its 1,000th anniversary—the baptism of Prince Vladimir of Kiev and, with him, all people of Kievan Russia. Statistics on religious communities in the Soviet Union are not easily available, but even the most conservative estimates concerning the size of this church indicate a membership of at least 40 million people. More liberal estimates run as high as 85 million. The number most frequently cited is 60 to 65 million, a figure larger than the combined memberships of all of the Protestant and Orthodox churches within the National Council of the Churches of Christ in the United States.[2] For Americans who may be accustomed to thinking of the Soviet population as a faithless mass, such a figure is shocking indeed. But this is only the beginning of the statistical picture, sketchy though our information may be.

In the Baltic republics of Latvia, Lithuania, and Estonia, about one half of this region's population continues to identify itself with either the Roman Catholic or the Lutheran Church, while additional small minorities of Methodist and Reformed Christians exist in Lithuania. Roman Catholics trace their presence in this area to the fourteenth century, and Lutheran churches are mentioned in historical records as early as the end of the sixteenth century. Neither is, therefore, a newcomer to the history of these peoples.

There are two churches in the Soviet Union even older than the Russian Orthodox Church, churches already well along in their second millennium of life. The first and oldest of these is the Armenian Apostolic Church, with its ancient center just outside Yerevan at a place called Etchmiadzin. Even before the Roman emperor Constantine had become a Christian, the Armenian king had chosen to be baptized, and with him all of his people. The Armenians are proud to claim that theirs is the oldest national church in history. Armenian history is, in large measure, a history of oppression and suffering, including a holocaust in 1915 in which Turks massacred 1.5 million Armenians. During that long and tragic history it was the Armenian Apostolic Church that kept alive the language, art, music, folk wisdom, and literature of the whole nation. The result is that every Armenian feels a sense of gratitude and relationship with the institution that is so profoundly bound up with national identity. It is not unheard of in Armenia to find members of the Communist party in attendance at the great cele-bration of Easter each year. One of them commented, when asked about his attendance at this religious service, "But you don't understand that I am also an Armenian," suggesting that national identity and the church were in some respects inseparable.

Georgia, Soviet Armenia's northern neighbor, can also claim that the beginnings of its church are to be found in the fourth century, a few decades after the conversion of the Armenians. In Georgia, as well as in Armenia, the church has played such a central role in relation to the identity and survival of the whole nation and its culture that it continues to be valued by the population. Vigorous leadership in both these churches over the past few decades has increased the sense of energy and vitality that visitors receive when attending services and special events.

Evangelical Christian Baptists (together in the All-Union Council of Evangelical Christian Baptists) are found almost everywhere in the Soviet Union today, in rural areas as well as in large cities. In 1974, 550,000 baptized members of these denominations were estimated to exist in the USSR.[3] Many more unofficial, nonbaptized adherents are Pentecostalists or belong to the *Initsiativnaia gruppa* (action group), neither group a part of the registered All-Union Council. The number of congregations, and the number of baptized members within the All-Union Council, has grown significantly in recent years despite the split over the issue of registering congregations with the Soviet authorities that led to the breakaway of many believers from the Evangelical Christian Baptists. As a result of this division, a significant number of Baptist and Pentecostal churches carry on their life in a more or less clandestine fashion and are often referred to as "underground" churches. In recent years some of them have agreed to the conditions of registration and have either been reunited with the All-Union Council of Evangelical Christian Baptists or have chosen to remain outside, although living a quite public church life. Taken together, all practicing Baptists, Evangelical Christians, and Pentecostals now prob-ably number nearly 2 million, including all unofficial adherents and children in their communities who have not yet been baptized.

Other Protestant churches in the Soviet Union today include Hungarian-speaking Reformed churches along the Soviet-Hungarian border, Mennonites, and Seventh-Day Adventists. Jehovah's Witnesses are also found in the USSR but have not been granted legal status. Eastern Rite Catholics, sometimes called Ukrainian Catholics or

Uniates, whose members in the Ukraine may number in the millions, must be included as well. Since 1946 this church has not been legally recognized by the Soviet government, and it has been forced to lead a more or less underground existence.

In addition to Christians, other religious communities exist in the USSR. About 40 million Moslems form the fastest growing segment of the Soviet population.[4] Buddhists also are to be found in the Asian republics of the USSR, with active adherents numbering perhaps 500,000, and a much larger population is affected by Buddhist culture. The world's third largest Jewish community, consisting of 2.5 to 3 million people, lives in the USSR.[5] Although it is a highly secularized community, Soviet Jews wish to continue to find their identity in Jewish culture, history, and tradition. Among them are many who remain practicing Jews in terms of their religious faith. Whether practicing or nonpracticing, living a Jewish life in the Soviet Union involves many problems and difficulties.

Added together these figures indicate that today, seventy years after the Great October Revolution of 1917, there are still more than 100 million citizens who identify themselves with active religious communities. This total stands in stark contrast to the membership of the Communist party, which now includes about 18.75 million members. It would be ill-advised at this point to attempt to draw any political conclusions from these figures, but the discovery that people who profess religious faith in the USSR outnumber Party members certainly challenges many of the stereotypes about Soviet people that exist in the minds of Americans.

Religion and the State

Statistics such as those cited above take on special significance when viewed against the historical background of the struggles between church and state in the Soviet Union since the October Revolution. Each religious community has its own story to tell; but throughout this chapter primary attention is given to Christian churches, and principally to the Russian Orthodox Church.[6] One of V. I. Lenin's first acts in early 1918 was to declare the separation of the church—meaning the Russian Orthodox Church—from the state and school. Church property was confiscated, and all of its temporal functions (marriage, registration of civil status, education) were ended.[7] The Communist party, which he led, quite naturally included within its ideology a Marxist orientation toward all religious phenomena. This orientation was not developed on Russian soil but rather was the product of Karl Marx's own observation and analysis of the religious situation in Western Europe during his lifetime. As Marx observed the sprawling industrial slums and the de-humanizing working conditions of nineteenth-century Europe, he also saw that religious establishments tended to side with power and wealth. At the very least, churches tended to treat the poor as objects of charity and to refrain from any basic challenges to the structures of society that were exploitative.

Marx concluded that religion was a symptom of massive social illness—an opiate that encouraged people to project their deepest human needs into a future life, thus making masses of people passive and accepting of intolerable conditions of life. Religion, he concluded, was therefore an enemy of progress and a bulwark of the ancien régime in Europe against change. It seemed quite logical to Marx that when change did come to a society, when ordinary people experienced justice and economic progress, they would no longer need religion or turn to religion for comfort and hope. Who would pray for daily bread when it was already assured and abundant? From then on, Marx taught that religious institutions should not be singled out for attack, that they would deteriorate and wither away when they no longer had any role to play or need to fulfill in a new Socialist society.

As in many other instances, Lenin found that Marxist theory at this point needed revision in order to fit new Soviet realities. The October Revolution was followed on Soviet soil by the bitter years of civil war, and many prominent figures, as well as large numbers of ordinary people in the Russian Orthodox Church, identified themselves with the enemies of the new regime. Lenin, therefore, from the beginning took a much more aggressive position vis-à-vis the churches than classical Marxist theory would have advised.

During the decade of the 1920s the Communist party sought, through a variety of means, to bring religious life and institutions to an end. Basic to this task was the use of the educational system at every level to propagate scientific materialism and thus to persuade young and old that religion was the product of ignorance and superstition. Not only in schools and universities but also in a great variety of special organizations—such as atheist leagues (the League of the Militant God-less, for example) and youth and student movements—the Party sought to call the nation's citizens away from religious belief and practice. Mass media were also employed for this same purpose. Secular alternatives to popular religious rituals, such as baptisms, weddings, and funerals, were created and commended to the citizenry. Church properties were confiscated and many religious institutions were closed. There were confrontations with religious leaders and institutions in an effort to manipulate and control the life of religious communities so that they would conform to the interests of the state. The arrest and confinement of the recently elected patriarch, or head, of the Russian Orthodox Church is one such example from the early years of the decade. Its outcome, however, was that the patriarch, whose name was Tikhon, sought to establish a new basis for the existence of his church in Soviet society by accepting the Soviet state and pledging his political allegiance and that of his church to the Soviet government. This in turn contributed to great controversy and led to schisms within the Russian Orthodox Church, both at home and abroad. Thus, directly and indirectly the state sought through manipulation to weaken the strength and influence of religious institutions within the country.

However, all of this was to appear quite mild when compared to the Stalinist purges of the 1930s, which cost the lives of millions of people. Although the purges were directed against the Party itself, few institutions in Soviet society suffered more than the churches. Those remaining theological seminaries and academies were closed, as were countless local parish churches. Church leaders were harassed, arrested, and imprisoned. Most of the few monasteries still in existence were closed, and those that survived did so under daily threat of closure. By the end of the decade, only a handful of bishops in the Russian Orthodox Church remained in their sees; the others had been killed, imprisoned, sent to labor camps, or gone into exile. Some had taken to wandering from place to place offering their ministries as they passed from one village to the next. It did indeed appear that formal institutional church life in the Soviet Union at the end of the 1930s was on the brink of extinction.

The invasion of the Soviet Union by the forces of nazism in 1941 changed everything, including Joseph Stalin's religious policies. He might well have feared that as invading armies crossed the Ukraine and reopened churches that he had closed they would be greeted as liberators. In his efforts to solidify the nation, Stalin turned to the churches to seek their support. That support was forthcoming in many forms: churches raised funds to assist in the war effort, and the Russian Orthodox Church equipped an entire tank corps, for example, and gave to it the name of St. Alexander Nevsky.

Doubtless the churches' greatest contribution, however, came in their deep identification with the suffering of the Soviet people. In this respect the churches were not simply opportunistic or subservient to state authority. From the days of the Tartar Mongol invasion and occupation of the Russian lands, the church had identified itself deeply with human suffering and had played an active role in the national struggle for liberation. It is no accident that one of the central and compelling themes of Russian theology deals with the reality and meaning of all human suffering.

Nonetheless, the change in Stalin's religious policies can only be understood as pragmatic, utilitarian, and self-serving. In 1943 he released a number of bishops from prison and permitted a church council to be convened to elect a patriarch, thus filling the office that had been vacant since the death of Tikhon nearly twenty years earlier. Gradually, some churches, theological schools, and monasteries were permitted to reopen. In a nation that had experienced the death of more than 20 million of its citizens, a number larger than the combined total of all those around the globe who had died in World War II, it is perhaps not surprising that a massive religious revival occurred. The years that followed the end of the war were not easy ones for the churches; nonetheless, religious institutions rose from the ashes like the fabled phoenix, and the churches were crowded with worshippers.

Reference already has been made to the repression that set in during the Khrushchev era. Convinced that one of Stalin's many mistakes had been his postwar relative tolerance toward religion, Khrushchev set about reversing all such policies. Although willing to attempt to use the churches for his own purposes in international affairs, between 1959 and 1965, Khrushchev took a hard line against all religious communities. In the Russian Orthodox Church alone he is said to have closed more than 15,000 parish churches, while at the same time drastically reducing the number of functioning theological schools and monasteries.

It is against such a historical background that the survival of religious communities is so astonishing. Clearly the prevailing ethos in the Soviet Union has not been one in which there were any societal rewards or benefits for publicly professing faith or joining a church. Still, the churches not only survive, but they also presently appear to be growing in membership and in vitality. Within crowded sanctuaries, one can see increasing numbers of men, middle generation, young people, and especially the older women who have always been the backbone of all the churches. Occasional editorials in newspapers such as *Pravda* and *Izvestiia* admit that growing numbers of young people are finding their way to the churches, and these editorials often decry the failure of antireligious propaganda and call for new and more effective measures.

It is clear now to the Party and to all concerned that the churches are not going to disappear. Furthermore, a new generation of leadership is emerging in both church and state, a generation that has grown up in Soviet society and is somewhat removed from the bitterness that characterized church-state relations after the revolution. There is no doubt that the church leadership wishes to live as loyal citizens of the Soviet Union and that the churches wish to be able to make positive contributions to Soviet life. It is true that, because of the affirmation of atheism, which is necessary to be a Party member, the wall between church membership and Party membership is as solid as ever. Despite this, the emerging leadership in the Party has a somewhat different view of the churches than its forebears: one that recognizes the churches as an important part of Russia's past and thus of its culture; one that sees the potential usefulness of the churches in supporting state objectives; and one that may, as a result, take a more tolerant and open position in relation to the churches.

Some movements in this direction have been evident since the Brezhnev years. During the 1970s and 1980s the churches have been permitted to be much more active both internationally and domestically. Larger and larger numbers of men and women from the churches have been allowed to participate actively in the affairs of international ecumenical and denominational organizations. Meetings of these same organizations are frequently hosted by the Soviet churches inside the USSR, and exchanges of delegations with churches all over the world are now a daily occurrence. Russian Orthodox theological schools, although too few in number, have more than doubled in size during the past ten years. Discussions are under way with several other churches about the possibility of opening centers for theological education. Church leaders, for the first time, have been given prominent places in the national and local leadership of secular Soviet organizations such as friendship societies and peace committees. And the churches have hosted a series of large international, interreligious assemblies on issues related to peace and nuclear disarmament, which were given major attention in all of the Soviet media. Such activities go far beyond the narrow definition of the rights of religious persons and communities granted by the Soviet constitution, which limits such rights to one function and only one—that is, to religious "cult" or worship. It would be naive not to recognize that in all of the cases cited, and in many others that might be included in the list, the Soviet state has a decided self-interest, which it pursues in all of its decisions and policies regarding religious organizations. That this sometimes places church leaders in an ambiguous and difficult position is not surprising; yet, it is true at the same time that the churches are being given new opportunities to offer their witness and service.

One of Leonid Brezhnev's final orders before his death was that St. Daniel's Monastery, the oldest in Moscow, should be returned to the Russian Orthodox Church. Confiscated by the state nearly sixty years ago, the monastery lay in virtual ruin after decades of use as a prison and rehabilitation center. Today, after three years of intensive labor by hundreds of people, the monastery is nearly ready to play its role as the new center for the administration of the Patriarchate of the Russian Orthodox Church and the centerpiece for the millennial celebrations of 1988. Within its walls, older than those of the Moscow Kremlin, stand five newly restored churches, buildings old and new to house the monastery itself, a large restored building for the several hundred staff workers of the church's department of foreign relations, and a new structure designed to serve as the official residence of the patriarch and to house the Holy Synod, which administers the affairs of the church. Outside the wall the church is building its own hotel to house the guests that it will welcome for conferences and meetings in the future.

St. Daniel's Monastery is by any standards beautiful and impressive, but is it a tangible symbol of a better future at least for the Christian churches in the USSR? Does it symbolize a process of change in the policies toward all religious communities in the nation? It is still too early to know.

Mikhail Gorbachev has many battles that must be won to achieve his goals in Soviet society. His opposition is formidable and the risks are real. He has not made any public remarks that indicate anything about his plans, if there are any, for changing present policies with regard to religion. Nonetheless, religious people in the Soviet Union stand to gain, as will all other citizens, from the greater openness that he seeks to achieve in Soviet society. Some church leaders have even expressed concern privately that if the Gorbachev administration sought radically to change the policies with regard to religion it might prove to be the straw that would break the camel's back. That is, Gorbachev's own political position may not enable him to make a substantial break with past policies toward religion. Such persons are confident that, in the long-term future, the present directions being taken in Soviet society will lead to far greater openness for the church's work and witness. This is more than simply wishful thinking, for in two nations that have preceded the USSR in its developing reformist policies—Hungary and China—the situation of the churches has been significantly changed for the better.

In 1987 a few changes were evident in that direction. One was the release of religious prisoners, the first large group in the spring of 1987, and the promise that all of those remaining would be released by November of that year. At the same time the number of Soviet Jews being given permission to emigrate is significantly higher than it has been for many years.

At the end of the summer of 1987 a Soviet official responsible for administering government religious policy indicated that churches could be reopened or new churches built from that point on without the usual bureaucratic delays and resistance that have kept new churches to a minimum in the past. Is this in fact a new policy? Only time will tell, but in the past few months some new churches have been authorized.

In the area of publications, several new developments may be observed. Permission has been given to the Russian Orthodox and the Baptists to publish new editions of the Scriptures, and churches and Bible societies abroad have been allowed to assist in this process. The Hungarian Reformed Church has been permitted to send Scriptures and service books to their cobelievers in the Soviet Union. The publishing house of the Russian Orthodox Church is engaged in a number of significant projects with larger quotas of paper assigned to them to increase both the number and the volume of their publications. All of these developments bode well for the future.

However, we must ask what will happen if the Gorbachev era should prove to be short-lived? It does not require much imagination to see that to return the Soviet people to a previous status quo, after their hopes have been aroused and they have begun to experience a different sort of life from the one they have known, would require the use of rather massive repression. It is not unthinkable that, in the midst of such a scenario, the churches and other religious communities might pass through an even darker night of the soul than they have yet known in this century. For the present there is no reason to believe that such a pessimistic picture is necessary or inevitable. On the contrary, the future at this point appears to be quite promising.

One thing, however, can be predicted about the future. It is surely the conviction that hundreds of American Christians have carried away from the Soviet Union after spending time in recent years with their fellow believers in the churches there. It is the same conviction that Eugene Blake and his delegation brought back from their visit more than thirty years ago. It is grounded in the experience of the quality and intensity of the faith and devotion of Soviet Christians themselves. It is the conviction that whether the times are good or bad, whether the cost of religious commitment is relatively easy or full of hardship, the Christian communities in the USSR will still be there sharing the joys and sorrows of the Soviet people and offering to them their witness and service.

Notes

[1] "Russian Churchmen Face New Trials," *Times* (London), January 3, 1965.

[2]Variation in estimates of numbers of Russian Orthodox believers can be seen by comparing Paul A. Lucey, "Religion" in *The Soviet Union Today*, ed. James Cracraft (Chicago: Educational Foundation for Nuclear Science, 1983), pp. 295–303, with Radio Liberty Research no. 58, February 2, 1976, p. 1.

[3]David Lane, *Soviet Economy and Society* (New York: New York University Press, 1986), p. 251.

[4]Alexandre Bennigsen, "Soviet Muslims and the World of Islam," *Problems of Communism* 29 (March-April 1980): 40.

[5]Nora Levin, "Will 'Glasnost' Reach the Jews?: Gorbachev and Soviet Anti-Semitism," *Commonweal* (October 23, 1987): 597–98.

[6]For one of the most recent and comprehensive treatments of relationships between the Russian Orthodox Church and the Soviet state see Dimitry Pospielovsky, *The Russian Church under the Soviet Regime, 1917–1982*, vol. 2 (Crestwood, NY: St. Vladimir's Seminary Press, 1984).

[7]Robert J. Osborne, *The Evolution of Soviet Politics* (Homewood, IL: Dorsey Press, 1974), p. 468.

5

Soviet and American Health Care: The Uneasy Comparison

Mark G. Field

In almost any discussion of the Soviet social landscape, socialized medicine is likely to emerge as its single most redeeming feature. It thus assumes the redemptory quality of a clause that follows a critical statement, prefaced by that little word "but." Certainly, Benito Mussolini was a cruel dictator, *but* he made the trains run on time (which, incidentally, we are told, he did not). Or, we hear of a petty tyrant at work, or even of Nazi concentration camp guards, *but* at home they were good to their families and kind to their dogs. In a dialectical sense, Soviet socialized medicine represents the antithesis to the thesis that the Soviet Union is a totalitarian state epitomized by the image of the Gulag. A synthesis would describe Soviet society as a land of concentration camps *but* equipped with hospitals and clinics. It is true that today we are witnessing changes in policy under Mikhail Gorbachev regarding, for example, political dissidents, but these are much too recent to accept as a portent of liberalization and democratization. After all, a quarter of a century ago Nikita Khrushchev also inspired hopes for important reforms, many of which were dashed after he was removed from office.

The contradictory images evoked by the "Gulag/hospitals" synthesis are difficult, intellectually and emotionally, to accept. On the one hand, we see violations of human rights and dignity, the disregard of the interests of the individual at the expense of an all-powerful and ruthless state, and the denial of freedom and self-expression. On the other, we see care and concern for the health and well-being of the individual. We see medical institutions and doctors in white coats working with dedicated nurses and other personnel to save lives and alleviate suffering. These, then, are not only the two sides of a complex reality, but they also can be better reconciled through a utilitarian perspective. The system of socialized medicine—which, incidentally, saw its greatest expansion under the reign of Joseph Stalin—is not so much an expression of the concern of the regime for the well-being of the population per se. Rather, it is that the health of the population, its ability to work, an extended life expectancy, stamina, and energy are seen as important assets the regime needs to fulfill its twin programs of industrialization and militarization launched by Stalin after 1928, and to rebuild the economy devastated by the Second World War. It is this utilitarian element that provides a key to the conundrum enunciated earlier: one cannot build socialism and defend the motherland with a sickly, uncared-for work force, afflicted with high levels of morbidity and mortality. We shall see later how well this system performs its job.

Appeal of Socialized Medicine and the Health Crisis

For many outside the Soviet Union the concept of socialized medicine (separated from its Soviet ground) has a certain magic, if not ideological, appeal. It articulates an idea that all human beings are entitled to state-of-the-art medical care regardless of income, ability to pay, social position or origins, and on an equitable basis. It furthermore implies the end of the private practice of medicine by physicians more interested in their incomes than the provision of medical care, and who cater primarily to the rich or the affluent. It represents the decommercialization or decommodification of health care and its transformation into a public service. It thus removes the corrupting influence of the cash nexus between patient and doctor. The latter can then apply his art and science to help the suffering individual without having to worry about his next meal. The appeal of socialized medicine, in its abstract form, is that it is expected to provide health security from birth to death—or, as the English put it, from the cradle to the grave.

Toward the end of the twentieth century, this concern for health security has emerged in the West as a critical political, ideological, and economic issue. A recent newscast, for instance, on the fate of cancer patients in the United States concluded with these words: "Poverty is often a death sentence for cancer patients." People are dying of cancer because they cannot afford the expensive treatment available, and there are too few free clinics. Report after report states that medical care costs are running out of control. Such costs constitute almost 12 percent of the GNP, and by the end of the century, if allowed to rise at the present rate, would absorb about 20 percent of the national wealth, an unacceptable amount in view of the many other needs of our society. At the present time, we spend more on health than on any other sector, almost twice as much as on defense (which absorbs about 7 percent of the GNP). It is no wonder that the rapidly escalating costs of health care have become the major issue in the last quarter of this century. (In the 1960s the critical question was access to health care.) It is also no wonder that the present crisis situation has led to many schemes and attempts, largely unsuccessful, to contain these costs.

This crisis is relatively new and became particularly salient after World War II. In the nineteenth century, health care was small potatoes. There was little that physicians really could do to help the sick. The hospitals were places where indigents went to get a bed—and most often to die. It probably did not absorb more than 1 or 2 percent of the GNP. The situation changed radically in this century. It was only after 1910, as someone remarked, that a patient consulting a physician chosen at random had more than an even chance of benefiting from the encounter.

At the same time, the increased effectiveness of medical and surgical interventions and the continuing disparity, up to the present day, between the poor and the rest of the population have raised the ideological question of equity before suffering, disease, and death. This debate often resumed as to whether health was so fundamental a component of the individual's existence that care should be made available to all regardless of ability to pay. In the United States the jury is still out. It is also still out on the question of the proper role that the polity should assume in these matters. This is in contrast to education, which has been socialized almost from the time of Thomas Jefferson, and in which it is the state that has assumed the responsibility to see to it that all children be given elementary and, in some instances, secondary education, irrespective of their parents' income or social station.

Health care in the United States, particularly personal health care as against public health, has followed a quite different path. In the nineteenth century, public health was considered primarily a responsibility of the states (under the doctrine that what was not specifically a matter for the federal government belonged by right to the states).[1] But personal health care remained a private matter. It was considered an item of personal consumption that one bought if one could afford it, or received as a charity, or went without, but certainly not something to which one was "entitled" as a citizen. Until at least the Second World War the view persisted among many that medical care was like a Cadillac: If you could not afford one, that was too bad, but society did not owe you one. The federal government became more involved in health matters in the twentieth century, particularly as a result of the 1937 Supreme Court decision on Social Security, but the establishment of a national and universal program to guarantee all citizens health security has never been approved by Congress.

There is a "socialized" health care system operated by the federal government—that is, an arrangement whereby the government is in the business of directly providing personal health care at taxpayers' expense. It does this by hiring personnel (physicians and nurses) and by building, owning, managing, and financing health facilities (hospitals or clinics). But access to these facilities is not universal; it is categorical: it is reserved for members and former members of the armed forces and some of their dependents, merchant seamen, and Indians on reservations.

The landmark Medicare and Medicaid legislation, passed in 1965, mandates not so much a health care system or service as financial mechanisms that enable the aged and the indigent to purchase medical care. This purchasing ability, or effective demand, it is assumed, would stimulate the growth of services and facilities, primarily in the private (either voluntary or proprietary) sector. In addition, the federal government is involved in a myriad of activities related to health—for example, the splendid research facilities of the National Institutes of Health that have made the United States the world leader in medical research. However, these constitute, in the main, a congeries of activities rather than a national commitment to a comprehensive tax-supported scheme to provide for, or to deliver, equitable medical care and allied services to the entire population as a right of citizenship.

The Soviet Health System

Given the many unresolved issues we have in the United States regarding health care, it is only natural that we should use the comparative perspective to see how other large-scale industrial and urban nations have attempted to come to grips with the question of fair and affordable health care for their populations. The Soviet system of socialized medicine—the oldest in the world—suggests itself as a possible model. It was born in the turmoil of the 1917 Revolution, and the basic principles that initially guided it have remained, more or less, the same over the years of the Soviet regime.[2]

According to Article 42 of the present Constitution (1977):

Citizens of the USSR have the right to health protection. This right is ensured by free, qualified medical care provided by state health institutions; by extension of the network of therapeutic and health building institutions; by the development and improvement of safety and hygiene in industry; by carrying out broad prophylactic measures; by measures to improve the environment; by special care for the health of the youth, including prohibition of child labor...and by developing research to prevent and reduce the incidence of disease and ensure citizens a long and active life. [This right is implemented through socialized medicine described as a] socialist system of government and community of collective measures having as their main purpose the prevention and the treatment of illness, the provision of healthy working and living conditions, the achievement of a high level of work capacity and long life expectancy.

This basic mission is made operational in terms of the following principles:[3]

1) Public health and medical care (the distinction between the two is not as sharp as in the West) are a responsibility of the state and a function of the government. It is thus a public service that, in essence, rejects private initiative, private medical care, or charity. Physicians are employees of the state and salaried. Incidentally, the private practice of medicine has never been illegal in the Soviet Union, although it is surrounded by all kinds of restrictions, heavily taxed, and ideologically fated to disappear. There are no private medical facilities; however, there are their equivalent, as we shall see.

2) The development of all medical and public health measures takes place within the framework of a single plan. The health service is thus not considered a separate entity operating independently of the goals, needs, commitments, programs, and, particularly, resources of the regime. The system is financed almost entirely by the state; therefore, such integration is possible through the control of budgets and allocations. Since all health personnel are paid salaries by the state, and all facilities are state owned, it is possible (to a degree undreamed of in the United States) to determine, control, and predict what the aggregate bill will be for that sector.

3) The centralization and the standardization of the health system under the overall jurisdiction of the USSR Health Ministry (functionally equivalent to a federal department in our structure) and through the health ministries of the constituent union republics (roughly equivalent to our states), and eventually through health departments at the different administrative levels reaching down to the localities, provide a high level of consistency and integration.

4) Medical and allied services are made available to the population at no direct cost at the time of the services. The entire system is financed from general revenues and contributions of enterprises.

The Soviet citizen who receives medical or hospital care does not pay for this care any more than the American citizen who sends his children to a public school receives a personal tuition bill. The major exceptions are that drugs prescribed for outpatient care (but not those needed to treat specified chronic conditions) are to be paid by the individual; there are, in addition, certain so-called paying polyclinics where patients, for a modest fee, may see better qualified physicians with less waiting. These polyclinics are perfectly legal and supervised by health authorities.[4]

5) Prevention is said to be the linchpin of the Soviet health system, although, as is the case in the West, more than 90 percent of expenditures go for clinical rather than preventive services.

6) A system of priorities exists in the provision of medical services, thereby reflecting that Soviet society, contrary to popular belief, is a heavily stratified society,[5] and the provision of medical and allied services follows, as in most societies around the world, that stratification. Over time there has emerged within the Soviet Union a series of distinctive health subsystems reserved for different segments of the population—from the elites (who are taken care of by the fourth administration of the Health Ministry), to departmental or ministerial health systems reserved for their own members, and to facilities for other members of the population, including some industrial workers. These subsystems have sometimes been described as "closed" because they are not accessible to the general population, which obtains its care through the "territorial" or "open" network. That network consists of facilities available to the population on the basis of residence or catchment area. The population is divided into administrative units, called medical districts, of about 40,000 persons (three fourths of whom are adults, the rest children or adolescents), but the size may vary. That population is served by a district polyclinic, essentially an outpatient facility. The district population is further divided into microdistricts (uchastki) of about 4,000 persons or sometimes less, and each microdistrict is usually the responsibility of one or two general physicians (terapevti) and one pediatrician, as well as a nurse. These doctors provide primary care and access to the individual who is assigned to them on the basis of his home address. Physician and patient are thus matched automatically; there is no mutual selection. The microdistrict physician will see patients at the polyclinic (usually for one half of his or her working day) and will make house calls for the other half.

Specialists, also based at the polyclinic, are assigned the responsibility for more than one microdistrict depending on morbidity rates, population needs, and personnel availability. Polyclinics are affiliated with, or attached to, hospitals to which they refer patients, but the general physician does not follow the patient into the hospital.[6] The patient becomes the responsibility of hospital physicians until discharged, at which time he is returned to the microdistrict doctors. In cities where the population is quite dense the microdistricts are geographically very small. In the countryside where the population is scattered the microdistricts tend to be very large, and there are problems of communication and transportation.

We know very little about the facilities reserved for the top elites and the members of the Soviet establishment except, as might be expected, that they have available to them the best facilities and personnel.[7] Generally speaking, the elites and the rich everywhere know how to take care of themselves. Soviet elite hospitals, clinics, and rest homes are, in essence, the equivalent of private facilities in the United States, with the exception that in the Soviet Union they are available not on the basis of payment but as part of perquisites of rank, financed by the state.

Christopher Davis has tried to estimate the different percentages of the population served by these health systems.[8] On the basis of these figures (see Table 5-1), it can be estimated that .4 percent of the Soviet

Table 5-1. Distribution of the Soviet Population between the Six Subsystems of Medical Care, 1975

	People Served (000s)	Percentages
Elites	1,000	0.4
Departmental	12,700	5.0
Capital cities	49,900	19.4
Industrial	20,200	8.0
Medium cities	40,900	16.1
Rural districts	129,400	51.1
Total	254,100	100.0

Source: Christopher M. Davis, "The Organization and Performance of the Contemporary Soviet Health Service," in G. Lapidus and G. Swanson, eds., State and Welfare USA/USSR (in press).

population receive superlative care, provided through the fourth administration of the Health Ministry. Twenty-five percent have access to departmental and capital cities facilities that can range from relatively high to average or worse. Another 24 percent receive relatively decent to poor services in medium cities or industrial subsystems. About 50 percent of the population receive low, substandard, or sometimes abysmal quality care in rural districts. One of the problems is that physicians usually avoid, or attempt to avoid, serving in the countryside, and the bulk of care is in the hands of physician-assistants (feldshers) whose qualifications often leave much to be desired.[9]

Health Care Problems of Soviet Society

What the Soviets have developed over the last seventy years is the blueprint for a comprehensive and reasonably adequate, although differentiated, health care service, managed by the state, financed through taxation, and covering, in theory at least, every Soviet citizen. Yet, in the last few years, there have been increasing indications of major problems with the general Soviet health system.[10] These difficulties may be just as serious, and perhaps just as intractable, as those faced by the United States. Andrei Sakharov, the noted Soviet dissident, has written:

A free health service...is no more than an economic illusion in a society in which all surplus value is expropriated and distributed by the state. The hierarchical class structure of our society, with its system of privileges, is reflected in a particularly pernicious way in the health service and in education. The condition of the health service...is clearly revealed in the run-down state of public hospitals.[11]

Criticisms of the health system are not limited to dissident critics like Sakharov. An examination of official Soviet data, both quantitative and qualitative, and a careful reading of the literature, as well as public pronouncements by officials,[12] point to the problematic state of nonelite medical care in the Soviet Union today.[13] But to judge from the data, little has been, or perhaps could be, done. Among the major problems, at least five warrant elaboration.

First, and most dramatic, has been a worsening of the health situation in the Soviet Union, reflected through increases in mortality, particularly infant[14] and male adult mortality,[15] and, therefore, a retrogression in the life expectancy of the population. Simultaneously, we have seen an increasing (and almost unbelievable) gap in the life expectancy of males and females of about ten or more years.[16]

It is, however, most important to bear in mind that vital rates or health statistics do not exclusively nor necessarily reflect the quality and the quantity of medical services alone, and thus not all the blame should be laid at the feet of the health system. Mortality and morbidity are profoundly affected by social and economic conditions—poverty, for example.[17] There is evidence that in the Soviet Union there is a relatively large proportion of the population (35 to 40 percent) that lives at or below the officially defined poverty line.[18] Thus, we must be careful in examining or assessing the degree of variance that is attributable to the health system.

In the last decade it was noteworthy that the Soviet Union began suppressing the publication of a series of vital statistics (for example, infant mortality after 1974),[19] and it is only recently, with the policy of "openness," that a partial resumption of the publication of such data took place (for example, national infant mortality figures for 1980, 1983, 1984, and 1985 were published in October 1986).[20] These figures, incidentally, show that the Soviet infant mortality is more than 2.5 times higher than the American one. On the other hand, Americans do not have much to be proud about either.[21] Although the infant mortality rate has steadily decreased since the beginning of the century, the gap between black and white infant mortality remains two to one.[22] In Washington, DC, where the population is overwhelmingly black and poor, the infant mortality is almost 2.5 times higher than the national figure and thus is approaching the Soviet figure.[23] Again, comparative assessments are rendered difficult by the constriction in statistical data in the last few years. It may be hoped that the openness policy initiated by Gorbachev will remedy this lack of data. Indeed, the policy of the suppression of information was protested in no uncertain terms by a well-known sociologist writing in *Pravda*:

> We hold one of the last places among the developed countries in the level of social statistics....There has been a real downturn in this respect since the second half of the 1970s....Among data...not published...are statistics on the distribution of crime, on the frequency of suicide, on the level of consumption of alcohol and drugs, the condition of crime, on the frequency of consumption of alcohol and drugs, [and] the condition of the environment....And why does the secrecy extend to the categories of diseases among the Soviet population[?]...Even if all these areas were to exhibit negative trends, would it not be better to draw public attention to them and to join together in discussing ways to resolve any problems?[24]

At the same time, one can also note an increase in what are called voluntary health risks—that is, behaviors on the part of the population that increase the probability of morbidity. Alcoholism is the best known of such risks (and female alcoholism is also on the rise),[25] as well as increased smoking by both sexes, and drug addiction, which recently has been officially recognized as a national problem. Alexander Vlasov reported a figure of 46,000 registered addicts—probably a vast underestimate of the situation in a population of over 270 million.[26] Until recently, the Soviet Union denied that AIDS was even a problem (it has identified thirteen AIDS carriers, all but one foreigners). The Soviets also made the incredible announcement that AIDS was first developed by the U.S. Defense Department as part of its biological warfare program.[27] At the present time, there are indications that the Soviets are worried about the future, and that they believe that the epidemic is bound to move eastward as it has moved westward. Tied to the problem of AIDS transmission is that the Soviet Union has not had, until now, a supply of disposable syringes. (A perennial complaint is the shortage of medical equipment.) Homosexuality in the Soviet Union is not often discussed and is considered to be a criminal offense.

A second major health care problem is the maldistribution of physicians between the urban centers and the rural areas. There is on the books a series of administrative regulations that should assure a more equitable distribution of physicians, but these regulations tend to be flouted or circumvented through legalities and technicalities. The problem may gradually become less salient as an ever-increasing proportion of the population becomes urbanized. It illustrates, however, that even a regime as centralized as the Soviet one is incapable of imposing and enforcing a distribution of its professional manpower resources according to the needs of the population. It may be interesting, in the comparative context, that the United States has faced that same problem of maldistribution for many years, and most administrative measures failed to resolve the issue. It is only in the last decade or so that the increasing supply of doctors—and, indeed, its impending glut—has led to a more equitable distribution of American physicians over the territory; they must go where there are patients rather than settle where they would like to live and work, as used to be the case.[28]

Third, there also has been a decrease over the last two decades in the percentage of the total budgetary allocations earmarked for health, on the order of about 20 percent, as well (although this is difficult to calculate) as in the percentage of the GNP allocated to health.[29] This trend is contrary to what is taking place in the United States, where the proportion of the GNP devoted to health care has more than doubled over the same period of time and reached an alarming level of just below 12 percent. Although such calculations are fraught with difficulties, and show differences whether calculated in rubles or dollars, it can be estimated that the percentage of the Soviet GNP going into health (in terms roughly comparable to American calculations) is somewhere between 2 and 3 percent (thus 4 to 5.5 times smaller than in the United States). Estimates of per capita expenditures measured in 1978 dollars show that, while the United States spends 25 percent more on defense than the Soviet Union, it spends 3 times as much on education and 4 times as much on health. In calculations on an intra-country basis, the United States spends 50 percent more on defense than it does on health, but the Soviet Union spends 4.8 times as much on defense as it does on health.[30]

The overall background for such decreases in allocations, and the possible link with increased mortality and morbidity, may not be the result only of a stagnant industrial economy and a poorly functioning agriculture. Instead, the diminished allocations to health also may be traced back to the Cuban crisis of 1962, the removal of Khrushchev in 1964, and the decision by the Soviet leadership never to find itself in a position of military or nuclear inferiority to the United States. The willingness of the Soviet regime, in the name of national security, to match the United States in every weapon system, with a GNP that is about 55 percent that of the United States, has meant a defense burden at least twice as heavy as that shouldered by the United States—probably more (3 to 4 times) if we include the expensive cover of the Sino-Soviet border, the steady drain of combat in Afghanistan, and the maintenance of large forces in Eastern Europe. Given these commitments it is hardly surprising that the standard of living of the general population, and of its health, should suffer. The nonelite health system is not a high-priority element in the Soviet scheme.[31]

A fourth major problem in the Soviet health system thus arises as financial anemia and bureaucratic sclerosis afflict the nonelite segment.[32] But the problem does not stop there. As the GNP expands, and even with a budgetary percentage reduction, the amount of rubles per capita devoted to health is bound to increase. The rub, however, is that, in many instances, money itself will not be sufficient when it cannot be spent to acquire either buildings, materials or labor for repairs and expansion, or equipment, if such are unavailable, or reserved for high-priority items. Thus, year after year, health authorities have to return millions of unspent rubles to the Health Ministry.[33] As former Health Minister Boris Petrovskii once complained, many hospitals exist only on paper.[34]

Finally, the presence of what one might call a health crisis is not only evident from a steady stream of governmental and Party decrees aimed at improving the health system but also from the constant litany in the Soviet press about deficiencies in the health service. Among these the most prominent are those of corruption (for example, purchasing admissions to medical schools),[35] the need on the part of the population to give gifts[36] or money "under the table" to physicians, nurses, and other health and hospital personnel (thus making the claim of free medical care a sick joke),[37] and the fact that polyclinic physicians are overburdened with cases and paperwork resulting in an assembly-line rhythm whereby each patient is processed in no more than a few minutes. Dr. G. Ivanov from Leningrad wrote to *Izvestiia* that he was so pressed for time (one half of which was consumed by paperwork) that he had to make diagnoses and prescribe treatments as speedily as a jet pilot makes decisions in aerial combat.[38] A woman doctor complained: "I go through my appointments without looking up (at the patient)." She has thirty-six patients to examine in four hours. On the average she has seven minutes per patient, and more than one half of that time is consumed by paperwork.[39]

There are constant complaints on the part of the population about the bureaucratic attitudes of personnel in the polyclinics and hospitals,[40] especially about their indifference and rudeness. Patients going into hospitals come armed with sheafs of rubles to obtain the most elementary services, medications, and changes of linen, and it is customary for their relatives to bring them additional food. There is a perennial shortage of pharmaceuticals,[41] some of which are stolen by pharmaceutical and hospital employees and resold on the black market. In a case reported in the press, nurses at a pediatric hospital stole medicines and replaced the liquid with distilled water or dipheryl-hydramine hydrochloride for a period of over two years until they were caught and sentenced.[42] What amazed the reporter was not so much the stealing but that ostensibly experienced pediatricians failed to notice the ineffectuality of the supposedly powerful drugs they used on their patients. There is a lack of medical equipment of all sorts, including thermometers and absorbent cotton. Surveys have shown that many physicians are inadequately trained and poorly motivated, and food destined for hospital patients is diverted into illegal personal trade.

Thus, the quality of clinical care for the nonelite citizens is likely to be poor or, in some cases, abysmal. A few years ago, Dr. William Knaus reported on medical care as he had seen it in Soviet hospitals and clinics, and he was not impressed.[43] Indeed, he was horrified. The same general impressions were conveyed more recently by Dr. Kenneth Prager, who is on the faculty at the Columbia College of Physicians and Surgeons in New York, and who was in the Soviet Union in the spring of 1986. His view is that the Soviet medical care system is decades behind the West in technology.

In particular, Prager says that the level of sophistication necessary to attend properly to such chronic and complex ailments as cancer and cardiovascular diseases is what one would expect of a developing nation, not one of the world's Great Powers. There is a virtual absence of disposable items such as syringes, needles, catheters, and intravenous tubing. Reused items increase rates of infection, while intravenous needles and scalpels that have become dull increase pain and discomfort. Most of the staples of modern medical treatment like Tagamet for ulcer diseases, Sinemet for Parkinsonianism, beta blockers and calcium channel blockers for angina and hypertension, and antihistamine-decongestant preparations for the relief of common cold symptoms are extremely hard to come by, if at all. Here is the description of one of the first patients that Prager was asked to visit—an eighty-year-old man in severe pain because he was unable to urinate:

> His bladder was markedly distended and he obviously needed to be catheterized immediately. The urologist who had been summoned to his home complied with my request for a rubber glove to examine the patient's prostate gland....I was startled when the physician requested that I wash the glove so that it could be reused. She then relieved the patient...by passing her only, reusable catheter into his bladder after lubricating it with butter. She had sterilized the catheter by boiling it in a pot of water in the...kitchen.[44]

In one sense the problems of the Soviet medical system are but a reflection of the basic nature of the Soviet system and are not likely to be remedied either through declarations or high-minded resolutions passed by the Party and the state, or even through an infusion of large sums of money alone. As David Shipler has put it: "The system of medical care expresses the full range of strengths and weaknesses of Soviet society; it is a model of the country's hierarchy, reflecting instincts of authoritarianism, conservatism, and elitism that pervade all areas of life."[45]

Conclusion

The Soviet health care system is a good illustration of the proposition that such a system can never be understood apart from the parent society and culture in which it exists, thus the difficulty in making comparisons between Soviet and American medicine. A Soviet hospital, as anyone who has visited or been a patient in one will attest, is first and foremost a Soviet institution, and only second a medical one. Anyone who has confronted Soviet bureaucrats in Soviet hotels, restaurants, or other institutions will have an easier time grasping the nature of the Soviet health system. That system is the result of a dialectical combination of confrontation of two cultures: the *universalistic* aspects of medical knowledge and techniques and the *particularistic* aspects of Soviet society. The last ones are, perhaps, more significant. For instance, when available, Soviet statistics showing there are more physicians per capita than in any other country, or more hospital beds, reflect not only a belief that a quantitative attack on health problems may eventually turn to qualitative improvements (which appears doubtful at this moment) but also must be taken with a large grain of Siberian salt. Hospital mortality statistics (if available) also would reflect the policy that hospitals often will not admit a terminally ill patient because it would adversely affect their mortality rate. Thus, the manipulation of data by managers and directors in no way stops at the doorstep of the health care system.

Soviet medicine is a good illustration of that famous Gallicism: "*en principe.*" In principle the idea, or blueprint, is bold, audacious, attractive; it appeals to a universal human need and yearning. It reminds us that in the United States we still have millions of people who have no health insurance and for whom illness can be a devastating event, personally and financially. But the implementation of that blueprint in the reality of Soviet society is something else again. Perhaps under different circumstances, in another setting, in a society with more resources, it might have worked and blazed a trail for mankind to emulate. It reminds us of what George Bernard Shaw is supposed to have said about Christianity: it's a great idea; too bad no one has yet tried it.

Notes

[1] For a discussion of this issue see Mark G. Field, "The Health System and the Polity: A Contemporary American Dialectic," *Social Science and Medicine* 14A (1980): 397–413.

[2] Mark G. Field, *Soviet Socialized Medicine* (New York: Free Press, 1967), pp. 42–48.

[3] Yuri Lisitsyn, *Health Protection in the USSR* (Moscow: Progress Publishers, 1972); Christopher M. Davis, "The Soviet Health System: A National Health Service in a Socialist Society," in Mark G. Field, ed., *Success and Crisis in Health Care Systems: A Cross-National Approach* (London: Routledge, in press).

[4] "Paying Polyclinics: For and Against," *Izvestiia*, July 11, 1986.

[5] Mervyn Matthews, *Class and Society in Soviet Russia* (New York: George Allen and Unwin, 1972).

[6] For greater details see Michael Ryan, *The Organization of Soviet Medical Care* (London: Martin Robertson, 1978).

[7] On stratification and medical care see William A. Knaus, M.D., *Inside Russian Medicine* (New York: Everest House, 1981), pp. 299–312.

[8]Christopher M. Davis, "The Organization and Performance of the Contemporary Soviet Health Service," in G. Lapidus and G. Swanson, eds., *State and Welfare USA/USSR* (in press).

[9]Mark G. Field, "Changements dans la profession médicale aux EU et en URSS: Demande et commande," *Cahiers de sociologie et de démographie médicales* 24, no. 4 (October-December 1984): 291–317.

[10]David E. Powell, "The Emerging Health Crisis in the Soviet Union," *Current History* 84, no. 504 (October 1985): 325–28, 339–40.

[11]Andrei Sakharov, "Postscript to Memorandum Sent to Brezhnev," *Sakharov Speaks* (New York: Vintage Books, 1974), p. 155.

[12]See, for instance, Central Committee of the Communist Party of the Soviet Union and Council of Ministers USSR, "On Additional Measures to Improve the Health Protection of the Population," *Pravda*, August 26, 1982.

[13]Aaron Trehub, "Quality of Soviet Health Care under Attack," *Radio Liberty Research* RL 289/86, July 28, 1986.

[14]Mark G. Field, "Soviet Infant Mortality: A Mystery Story," in D. Jelliffe and E. F. Jelliffe, eds., *Advances in International Maternal and Child Health* (Oxford: Clarendon Press, 1986), pp. 25–65.

[15]Christopher M. Davis, "Reviewing Soviet Health Care Problems," *Wall Street Journal* (European ed., October 31, 1986).

[16]Vladimir G. Treml, "A Turning Point in the Availability of Soviet Economic Statistics?" *Soviet Economy* 2, no. 3 (July-September 1986): 277.

[17]See, for example, John Kosa, Aaron Antonovsky, Irving K. Zola, *Poverty and Health: A Sociological Analysis* (Cambridge: Harvard University Press, 1969).

[18]Alastair McAuley, *Economic Welfare in the Soviet Union: Poverty, Living Standards and Inequality* (Madison: University of Wisconsin Press, 1979); Mervyn Matthews, "Poverty in the Soviet Union," *Wilson Quarterly* 9, no. 4 (Autumn 1985): 75–84.

[19]Christopher M. Davis and Murray Feshbach, *Rising Infant Mortality in the USSR in the 1970s* (Washington, DC: Department of Commerce, June 1980); Bureau of the Census Report, Series P-95, no. 74.

[20]Treml, "A Turning Point," p. 277.

[21]A. Saunders, *The Widening Gap: The Incidence and Distribution of Infant Mortality and Low Birth Weight in the United States, 1978, 1982* (Washington, DC: Government Printing Office, 1984); *Infant Mortality* (Washington, DC: Government Printing Office, 1984).

[22]Anonymous, "Cheating Children," *New York Times*, February 20, 1983.

[23]Bernard Weintraub, "Don't Throw Out the Baby with the Medicaid-Medicare Bath Water," ibid., July 22, 1981; Richard A. Knox, "Fund Cuts Are Linked to Infant Death Rise," *Boston Globe*, May 24, 1984; Kathleen Newland, *Infant Mortality and the Health of Societies* (Washington, DC: Worldwatch, 1981); *Worldwatch Paper*, no. 47 (1981).

[24]T. Zaslavskaia, "Questions of Theory: Restructuring and Sociology," *Pravda*, February 6, 1987.

[25]See Field, "Soviet Infant Mortality," pp. 49–51.

[26]A. V. Vlasov, "Insidious Grams of Narcotics: The Minister of Internal Affairs Answers Questions of Readers," *Pravda*, January 6, 1987. See also Theodore Shabad, "Soviet Discloses 1977 Survey of Narcotic Use," *New York Times*, March 27, 1987 (based on a report published by Anzor Gabiana in *Zaria Vostoka* [Tbilisi], February 20, 1987).

[27]Philip Taubman, "AIDS Peril Worries Soviet Leaders," *New York Times*, February 6, 1987; Thomas W. Netter, "Countries Moving in Battle on AIDS," ibid., March 22, 1987.

[28]See Field, "Changements dans la profession médicale," pp. 312–13.

[29]Imogene Edwards, Margaret Hughes, and James Noreen, "US and USSR in the Comparisons of GNP," *Soviet Economy in a Time of Change* (Washington, DC: Government Printing Office, 1979), 1, pt. 2:369–401.

[30]"World Military and Social Expenditures-World Priorities," *New York Times*, September 20, 1981.

[31]Davis, "The Soviet Health System."

[32]O. Frantsen, "Diagnosing Oneself: Remarks from a Meeting of the Collegium of the Ministry of Health USSR," *Pravda*, February 15, 1987.

[33]"Repair in the Old Way Creates an Artificial Deficit of Hospital Beds," *Meditsinskaia gazeta*, no. 20 (March 10, 1982): 2.

[34]Boris Petrovskii, "High Duty of Doctors," *Izvestiia*, February 24, 1977.

[35]S. Bablumian, "Face to Face with the Law: Pseudo-Students," ibid., September 11, 1981.

[36]David K. Shipler, "Soviet Medicine Mixes Inconsistency and Diversity," *New York Times*, June 26, 1977.

[37]See, for example, "The Debatable and the Indisputable," *Literaturnaia gazeta* (January 5, 1977): 13. See also, *Current Digest of the Soviet Press* 29 (February 9, 1977): 16.

[38]G. Ivanov, "Frankly," *Izvestiia*, February 7, 1986.

[39]A. Paikin and G. Silina, "The Sector Physician," *Literaturnaia gazeta* (September 27, 1978): 11. English translation in *Current Digest of the Soviet Press* 30, no. 40 (November 1, 1978): 4–5.

[40]Zh. Mindubaev, "The Line to the Physician," *Izvestiia*, November 14, 1984.

[41]Mark Popovskii, "Medicines for the Toilers," *Russkaia mysl'* (Paris), no. 3542, November 8, 1984 (in Russian); "The Individual Came to the Pharmacy," *Meditsinskaia gazeta*, no. 100 (December 14, 1984): 1.

[42]O. Parfenova, "On Duty and Honor: Sisters without Mercy," *Trud*, August 11, 1985, in *Current Digest of the Soviet Press* 37, no. 52 (January 22, 1986): 22.

[43]Knaus, *Inside Russian Medicine*, pp. 105–47, 217–25, 252–61.

[44]Kenneth M. Prager, "Soviet Health Care's Critical Condition," *Wall Street Journal*, January 29, 1987.

[45]David K. Shipler, *Russia: Broken Idols, Solemn Dreams* (New York: Times Books, 1983), p. 216.

6
Aging in the USSR and the United States: Demographic Trends and Policy Responses

David E. Powell*

Both the United States and the Soviet Union are classified by the World Health Organization as "old" countries, that is, nations with a substantial part of their population over the age of 60. There is a certain irony in this since leaders in Washington and Moscow alike regularly link today's stable political order with their states' tumultuous revolutionary beginnings. In fact, America in 1987 celebrated the 200th anniversary of the adoption of the Constitution, while the other superpower congratulated itself on the 70th anniversary of the Bolshevik Revolution.

Because the political elites in both countries define their national security policies in a global context, they allocate immense sums of money to the defense sector. If, somehow, funding levels could be reduced, additional resources might be made available to improve the health, education, and welfare of the people of both nations. Some of the savings, one suspects, would be diverted to mass consumption, conspicuous or otherwise. But with appropriate cues from responsible leaders, some sort of rational link between needs and resources could be devised and additional monies could be made available to the truly needy. Even now, despite the fact that they spend far more dollars and rubles on "social security" (in the broadest sense) than on national defense, both superpowers find themselves faced with seemingly intractable problems on the domestic front. Examined here will be one aspect of social security in the two nations: the numbers of, problems experienced by, and official responses to, men and women who have reached retirement age.

*The author would like to express his appreciation to the National Institute on Aging for its research support.

The Soviet Union

The Communist (formerly Bolshevik) party has been responsible for a number of extraordinary achievements in the period since 1917. In addition to transforming a relatively backward country into a modern nation-state, the authorities have made great strides in expanding educational facilities and opportunities, raising public health standards, developing irrigation schemes, feeding and housing a population of some 283 million, creating a large-scale industrial base, guaranteeing full employment, and making many public services available free of charge. Regarding the elderly, the government generally has been successful, although not in all ways or at all times.

Before World War I, female life expectancy in the Russian Empire was 33 years; for males the figure was 31.[1] After gaining power, V. I. Lenin and his followers invested considerable effort in constructing water-purification facilities, dams, and irrigation canals. They also built thousands of hospitals and trained millions of doctors, nurses, and paramedics. Far more slowly they introduced various pension arrangements, which they extended gradually to cover more and more workers.

Despite the ghastly toll exacted by the civil war, the famine, Joseph Stalin's industrialization and five-year plans, the collectivization of agriculture, the purges, and World War II, life expectancy among Soviet citizens has increased. From the mid-1960s until the early 1980s, however, male life expectancy fell by at least four years, and female life expectancy by one year. Indeed, the USSR Central Statistical Administration published no new data on life expectancy for the fifteen years from 1971/72 to 1985/86. Today, average life expectancy for the Soviet population is 69 years, less than the figure of 70 that prevailed from 1963/64 to 1971/72. Life expectancy for men, which peaked at 66 in the mid-1960s, fell to 62 in 1978/79 but is now back up to 64. Female life expectancy, which rose to 74 in 1964/65 and remained at that level for almost a decade, is now 73.[2] We will now look at these numbers from several vantage points. At the same time, we will examine the Party's response to these developments and try to determine its purposes and assess its efforts.

Regional Disparities

There are major differences in life expectancy among people living under different climatic conditions, between urban and rural populations, and, related to these two variables, among groups differing with respect to socioeconomic status, access to medical care, and "overall cultural level and health standards."[3] For example, life expectancy in the northern and eastern reaches of the Soviet Union is lower than in the European part of the country. The explanation for this phenomenon involves many factors, the most important of which undoubtedly is the harsh climatic conditions prevailing in the North and East. Other factors include poor housing and transportation, nutritional deficiencies, and an inadequate public health infrastructure in these regions—that is, too few hospitals and doctors, a lack of medical specialists, shortages of diagnostic equipment and medicines, and remoteness even from provincial centers.

For many of the same reasons, life expectancy among the urban population is higher than in rural areas. The differences are less palpable than one might expect, since city dwellers, who have more and better medical services available to them, are also more likely to experience the harmful consequences of "modernization," such as environmental pollution, hypertension, depression, obesity, and an increased incidence of various chronic diseases. Still, there is a real and, it would appear, growing gap between the city and the countryside. In the late 1930s, on the eve of the Second World War, life expectancy among the urban population was less than that in rural areas. (The figures were 45 and 48 years, respectively.) This is a remarkable fact and, if true, suggests that the horrors of collectivization, the policy of underfunding the agricultural sector, and the apparent seriousness with which Stalin viewed Karl Marx and Friedrich Engels's observation about "the idiocy of rural life" were not necessarily worse than forced industrialization, the Stakhanovite movement with its constant increases in production quotas, a massive housing shortage in the cities, and extremely rigorous labor discipline at factories and construction projects.

By 1958/59 life expectancy in urban areas was almost equal to that in the villages: 68 years among the former, 69 among the latter. At the beginning of the 1970s the relative positions of the city and the countryside finally were reversed, and ever since then the life expectancy figure for urban areas has exceeded that in the villages. According to the most recent data available (released in early 1987 after having been kept secret for almost two decades), life expectancy among the urban population in 1984/85 was 69 years, whereas in rural districts it was only 66.[4]

Ethnic Differences

While life expectancy figures for the country as a whole remain low, there are significant differences among ethnic groups, thereby making the demographic picture more complicated. Indeed, in some parts of the Soviet Union, one can find astonishing numbers of people who are over the age of 80, 90, or even 100. According to scholars at the Institute of Gerontology, 20,000 Soviet men and women are 100 or more years of age—more than twice the U.S. figure, and higher than that in any other industrialized country. These people are known colloquially as *dolgozhiteli* (individuals who have lived a long life), rather than as "old men" or "old women." An "old" person is simply someone who has grown old, whereas *dolgozhiteli*, it is said, have lived long without growing old.[5]

Claims of extraordinary longevity among certain ethnic groups have been challenged by a number of non-Soviet gerontologists who point out that historical documents indicating when these people were born are almost never available. There are also questions involving the use of a lunar calendar, which provides a much shorter year than our 365.24 days. Moreover, the existence of sentimental, chauvinistic, anti-Russian, or antiscientific attitudes contributes further to inaccurate reporting. Still, it appears that large numbers of people *do* live for a very long time in certain areas. The best known are the Abkhazians (who live in their own autonomous republic in Soviet Georgia) and certain central Asian nationalities, especially some of the smaller groups that inhabit relatively remote mountain villages. In the Abkhazian ASSR, whose population is roughly 500,000, there are said to be 3,500 persons 90 years of age or older—"a world gerontological record."[6] Most of these individuals reside in small villages far from centers of industry, commerce, and transportation, and their longevity is attributed to their diet (which includes substantial quantities of yogurt and fresh fruit, alleged to possess remarkable medicinal properties), and to "an active life-style."[7]

While discussions of Abkhazia are shrouded, to an undetermined degree, in a romanticized view of the people who live there, we can speak far more authoritatively about other regions of the country. Thus, the 1970 census (the last to publish comprehensive age-related data) reported that 11.8% of the Soviet Union's population were 60 years of age or older; however, in the Baltic States and a few other areas, there were far higher percentages of people in this age bracket. These are not *dolgozhiteli*, who continue to thrive in their native villages; instead, they consist largely of men and women who have retired within the past decade, whose health has begun to fail, and who represent a considerable drain on the state treasury. The figures for Latvia (17.3%), Estonia (16.8%), and Lithuania (15.0%) were higher than those reported for any other republic. In contrast, a relatively small proportion of the population of Central Asia was 60 years of age or older: the lowest figures reported—7.2% and 7.5%—came from Turkmenia and Tadzhikistan, respectively.[8]

These disparities are not an expression of differences in life expectancy per se. Instead, they can be explained by three other factors: 1) historical and cultural patterns, especially the extremely low birth rates prevailing in Estonia and Latvia, along with the extraordinarily high birth rates in the "Muslim" parts of the country; 2) vast differences in urbanization, industrialization, and educational levels in these two areas, as well as equally sharp differences in the quantity and quality of medical care and sanitary-hygienic practices; and 3) the overall character of the infrastructure that has been erected during the past century in the sphere of public health.

Estonia, for example, has had one of the lowest birth rates in the world since the turn of the century. In some years the figure has been so low that the number of deaths exceeded the number of births, a circumstance that helps to explain why there still are 4% fewer Estonians today than there were before the outbreak of World War II. Years and years of low birth rates, which have made the "graying" of the Estonian population all but inevitable, will continue to promote this process in the future. As of 1970 only 23.6% of the republic's population was 15 years of age or younger, the lowest percentage to be found in any of the Soviet Union's fifteen republics. Since ethnic Estonians, on average, are older than the other nationalities in the republic (especially the Russians who comprise about 18% of Estonia's population), the age structure of the indigenous group will shift even further toward the elderly.[9]

Today, ethnic Estonians are highly overrepresented among the older age groups in "their" republic. Almost one fourth (23%) is past retirement age, as compared with only 12% of the republic's non-Estonian population. Prospects for the future are bleak, for "replacement rates" are even more disadvantageous from the Estonian point of view. Some 60% of the nonindigenous peoples of the republic are between the ages of 16 and 29. In contrast, only 20% of the native population are in this age bracket. Further exacerbating the problem is the unusually low marriage rate and high marriage age among Estonians. These practices almost definitely will contribute to a further drop in birth rates as well as an even more rapid aging of the Estonian nation. In addition, mortality rates among young Estonian males are extremely high. Combined with the general reluctance of this ethnic group to marry "outsiders," the end result is a substantial number of unmarried Estonian women—yet another factor contributing to the low birth rate and the increase in the proportion of the population that is elderly.[10]

The Gender Gap

There are also sizable differences in the life expectancy of men and women throughout the country. This pattern, which existed long before the Great October Socialist Revolution in 1917, has grown more vivid during the first seven decades of Soviet power. As increments in life expectancy among men began to level off in the late 1950s (rising almost imperceptibly from 64.42 years in 1958/59 to 64.56 years in 1968/71), the figure for women continued to increase at a more satis-factory pace (from 71.68 to 75.53 years during this same period).[11] In fact, the gap between female and male life expectancy grew for several decades: in 1926/27 it was five years (47 for women, 42 for men), in 1958/59 it reached eight years (72 for women and 64 for men), and by 1981 the difference was a full ten years (74 for women versus 64 for men).[12] As recently as 1984/85 the Soviet statistical authorities put the gap at a decade (73 for women, 63 for men), but more recent reports indicate that it has narrowed to nine years (73 for women, as against 64 for men).[13]

Living Conditions

Virtually all men and women who reach retirement age, whether or not they are gainfully employed, continue to live in the same apart-ments or homes where they had been residing. A very small number of older people, primarily the frail elderly and the "old-old" (in contrast with the "young-old," who are closer to retirement age), live in nursing homes. The few Soviet surveys that have looked into the question of housing preferences among the elderly have determined that almost all of them want to live with their children or, a distant second choice, alone. They will choose, or at least be willing to move to, a "home for labor veterans" only in extremis—that is, if they cannot take care of themselves, and no family member is able or willing to assume respon-sibility for them.

A typical study, carried out in the city of Sverdlovsk, found that only 1.4% of people between the ages of 60 and 75 expressed a desire to live in such an institution.[14] Their attitude appears to be the product of three factors. First, the tradition of the three-generation family unit, common in rural areas, continues to seem natural to large numbers of urbanites, most of whom are recent migrants—or the offspring of recent migrants—from the countryside. Second, there continues to be a shortage of old-age homes, and those that are in use tend to be designed poorly and are not well suited to the needs of older persons, are maintained inadequately, and are overcrowded. And third, while elderly widows and widowers experience intense feelings of loneliness, not many of them wish to live with strangers, even if the latter are in the same position.

Although few in number, elderly bachelors or widowers are more likely than women their age to wind up in a home for labor veterans. Soviet scholars have found that the various social roles performed by women (as mothers, grandmothers, and housewives) make it relatively easy for them to adapt to their new lives, even though they are cut off from their jobs and the network of friends and colleagues with whom they worked. Men generally find the phenomenon of isolation more troublesome; the small number who manage to outlive their wives face the added difficulty of shopping, preparing meals, and taking care of themselves in other ways—responsibilities for which few males in the USSR, especially those who are now advanced in years, are prepared.[15]

Medical Care

Having chosen to allocate an increased proportion of its GNP to the military and investment programs, the Politburo has had to reduce the rate of growth of public health expenditures. In 1960, 6.6% of all budgetary allocations went to health care. By 1970 the figure had dropped to 6.0%; in 1975 it was 5.3%, and by 1980 it had fallen to 5.0%.[16] Even now, the number continues to plummet: in 1985 it represented 4.6% of the country's GNP, while in 1987 it will be only 4.4%.[17]

The decline in the public health sector's share of the nation's wealth has accelerated the deterioration in the quality of medical care. Despite, or perhaps because of, the government's traditional quantitative approach to health care—training more physicians and nurses, building more hospitals and polyclinics, and adding more beds—there is little evidence that "care" for patients is valued by doctors. Physicians, like other workers and employees in the USSR, are assigned certain quotas; if they are to fulfill (or, if possible, overfulfill) their plan, they simply do not have the time to be solicitous of their patients. According to William A. Knaus, an American physician who worked for the U.S. government in the USSR and who interviewed numerous public health experts in that country, Soviet doctors are required to see eight patients each hour (nine for surgeons). This rigid schedule allows them a mere seven minutes per consultation. Furthermore, surveys have shown that the average polyclinic physician "needs at least five minutes to fill out the forms for the patient's medical record, his trade union, and to excuse the patient from work." Thus, the health care provider actually has only two minutes to discuss symptoms, perform a physical examination, discuss the prognosis, offer advice, and discuss medications or the possible need for further tests.[18]

This arrangement, which emphasizes quantity rather than quality, has come in for considerable criticism since the policy of *glasnost* (openness) was introduced. Leading medical authorities have condemned the phenomenon of "paper fever,"[19] complained that they have "to make diagnoses and prescribe treatments as quickly as a jet pilot has to make decisions in aerial combat,"[20] and criticized the practice of training ever greater numbers of doctors, just to "put them to work scribbling."[21] One physician from the city of Tula asserted that the emphasis on quantitative indicators was actually self-defeating rather than helpful. Writing in *Izvestiia*, he said that "it is practically impossible to extract information about the effectiveness of treatment from all the numbers. Has the patient's health improved? Stayed the same? Deteriorated? There is no way of knowing."[22]

Problems that afflict the Soviet medical system in general weigh especially heavily on older men and women, since they are far more likely than their children and grandchildren to require medical assistance. For example, those who are over 50 years of age, roughly 20% of the country's population,[23] make about 25% of all visits to physicians and are the object of more than 50% of all home visits by doctors. Even more striking is the fact that persons who are age 60 or older are three times as likely to be hospitalized during any given year as the average citizen. Between one fourth and one third of the former group is hospitalized for some period of time each year.[24]

These men and women appear to be the least satisfied of all Soviet health care consumers. However, it should be noted that the data are too skimpy to permit a firm declarative statement on this matter. One reason for this dissatisfaction is the typical doctor's tendency to attribute their complaints to "old age," and thus to ignore them rather than to take such patients seriously and make a genuine effort to ameliorate their condition.[25] A second, related factor is the priority given by physicians, nurses, and ambulance personnel of the Emergency First Aid Service to younger people, even if a call involving an elderly person had come in earlier. Informed citizens, when telephoning for emergency medical assistance, sometimes conceal the fact that the person in need is an older man or woman. As one doctor acknowledged candidly, Emergency First Aid Service personnel "are held strictly accountable if they fail to respond quickly to a call concerning a young patient."[26]

Similarly, a Soviet journalist described the experience of an elderly aunt who was crying when he came to visit. In response to his expression of concern, she explained why she was weeping: "I just barely succeeded in dragging myself to the [local] polyclinic and waited in line. Eventually, the doctor said, 'Why are you here? I don't even have time to examine the younger patients.'" The reporter who related this sad tale placed the blame on the various ministries and departments responsible for helping pensioners. They simply do not "measure up to our understanding of humanism, philanthropy, and charity." As a result, older people's lives "do not meet the standards of current conceptions of social justice." Perhaps the most telling remark was the reporter's conclusion: "Unfortunately, the notion of respect for old age has not yet found a place in our re-structuring efforts" (*perestroika*).[27]

Pensions

The number of persons receiving old-age pensions has increased dramatically, especially since Stalin's death in 1953. Much of the growth can be explained by legislative changes adopted in 1956 and 1965, but the rapid rise in the number of people of pension age also has been a major factor. In 1941 a mere 200,000 people received pensions,[28] but by 1961 the number had risen to 5.4 million; in 1976 it reached 29.4 million, increasing to 34 million in 1981 and to nearly 40 million in 1986.[29] How these people live, and how they feel about it, are matters that are only beginning to be explored by Soviet physicians, sociologists, anthropologists, and social psychologists.

Virtually all of the research published to date concerns the older generation's health and economic circumstances, as well as its ability and inclination to continue working after having reached retirement age.[30] Nonetheless, Soviet specialists are profoundly aware of the psychological trauma that reaching age 60 represents for men, and reaching age 55 means for women. One commentator, referring to "the drama of retirement," has emphasized that "it is difficult for someone to change the habits he has developed during his [working] life, to reconcile himself to the fact that he no longer is a factory director, a foreman, or a colonel, but just a pensioner, a modest urban dweller."[31]

Old-age pensions are far too low to meet the needs of the average pensioner, and "poverty" (at least as this term is understood by academics and public officials in the USSR) continues to be widespread among the older generation.[32] Both of these circumstances have prevailed for many years, although only in the recent past have Western social scientists recognized their existence, much less their significance. Thus, in 1940 the average pension consisted of a mere 6.9 rubles, roughly 20% of the average wage in the state sector. Over the next decade the average value of a pension rose by 46%, but this was only slightly more than one half of the 86% increase in the retail price index. The real value of pensions fell by about 20% during the ten-year interval. After collective farmers became eligible for state pensions in 1965 a majority of citizens of pension age was receiving retirement benefits—the first time in Soviet history that coverage exceeded 50% of those in the appropriate age bracket. By 1980 the proportion increased to 75%, and it continues to increase with each passing year.

In 1956/57, Soviet scholars specializing in the field of social security established—unofficially, for purposes of research and, perhaps, policy recommendations—a definition and a measure of "poverty" in the USSR. The term they used was "*maloobespechennye*" (underprovided for), rather than "poor"; families whose per capita monthly earnings were less than 25 to 30 rubles were included in this category. For our purposes, what is most relevant is the overlap between the elderly population and citizens whose income defined them as *maloobespechennye*. The average pension did not reach 25 to 30 rubles per month until 1960, which means that at least 50% of all old-age pensioners received monthly payments putting them below the poverty line. According to estimates prepared by the British economist Alastair McAuley, the average collective farm pension in 1965 was approximately 13 rubles per month, and the vast majority of elderly *kolkhozniki* and *kolkhoznitsy* actually received the minimum pension: 12 rubles per month.

Some progress has been achieved since then, but not much. The standard of living of people who have reached pensionable age remains "far short of the accepted poverty level."[33] In the mid-1960s a new definition of poverty was adopted, largely because inflation had altered the structure of incomes and prices. The threshold below which individuals were considered underprovided for was set at 50 to 56 rubles, but only at the end of the 1970s did the average pension actually reach this level. Thus, more than one half of all retirees had to live on incomes that were held below the poverty line, and, until recently, average pension levels were barely above the statutory minimum.[34] It is probably for this reason that the Soviet Constitution of 1977, unlike any of its predecessors, stipulates in Article 66 that just as parents are responsible for bringing up their children the latter "are obliged to care for their parents and provide them with assistance."[35] Often, elderly men and women would remain below the poverty level except for the willingness of their children to help out financially.

Since January 1, 1980, men and women of pension age have had the option of having their pension raised by 10 rubles per month for every additional year they work after becoming eligible to retire. (The new law, however, places a ceiling of 150 rubles on pension benefits for individuals who choose this scheme.)[36] Persons who have maintained an unbroken record of employment at any enterprise for fifteen years are eligible for a 10% increase in their pensions, while anyone with twenty-five or more years of uninterrupted service may receive an additional 20% on top of the 10% granted for fifteen years of uninterrupted work. (Women with children are eligible for the extra 20% if they put in twenty or more years without interruption at the same plant.)[37]

This elaborate array of financial incentives has had a definite effect on labor-force participation rates among older workers. Even though the available evidence is sketchy, it appears that the principal factor inducing men and, to a lesser degree, women to continue earning money is the promise of more income. The desire, or need, to continue earning money is cited by slightly more than one half the males questioned in several surveys; the figure for women ranges from about one fourth to two fifths. In contrast, the decision not to work seems to hinge on nonfinancial considerations. The most important of these is the desire to avoid heavy physical labor, but the lack of opportunities to work part-time or to work at home also pushes people toward retirement as soon as they become eligible. Not surprisingly, women approach the work-retirement decision with a very different mind-set from that of their male counterparts. In particular, women tend to retire in order to deal with family responsibilities—for example, to take care of grandchildren, or to liberate children or grandchildren to study, work, or enjoy additional leisure.[38]

At the present time, more than one of every three pensioners is employed. Most of these men and women have full-time jobs, while a few work part-time; some continue in the same position they occupied before reaching retirement age, while others have moved on (either voluntarily or involuntarily) to another job. Almost all of these individuals decided to continue working without interruption, even though they could have retired. Only a handful left the labor force, reconsidered their decision, and returned to work.

Virtually all pensioners who want to continue working after retirement have had to take full-time jobs, either staying on at their

regular place of employment or seeking a position elsewhere. Very few
have the opportunity to work part-time, whether a few hours a day or
a few days a week. Various surveys of pensioners with jobs have put the
number working at home at less than 1% of the overall sample; even
fewer—estimated between 0.3% and 1%—enjoy a reduced workday or
workweek.[39] According to one estimate, only 9,000 out of a total 2
million working pensioners in the Russian Federation—that is, less than
.5%—are employed part-time.[40] A more comprehensive and detailed
survey of Muscovites, carried out between 1973 and 1975, drew a picture that was only slightly more encouraging. According to the investigators, 86% of all working pensioners in that city had to put in a full
day, even though 58% of the sample expressed a desire to work part-
time.[41] Whether the absence of part-time, including at-home, employment results in a net gain in the labor force (because workers who
would prefer to work part-time must work full-time) or in a net loss
(because individuals who would like to work part-time cannot do so) is
unclear. What is certain is that existing programs and policies do not
meet the needs of older men and women.[42]

Throughout the country, more and more men reaching 60 years
and women reaching 55 are deciding to continue working. According
to the 1970 census, 12.4% of all pension-age people had jobs.[43] Five
years later the figure had almost doubled,[44] and it now exceeds one
third of all age-eligibles. In the larger industrial cities, where populations
tend to be a good deal older than the national average, the rate of
increase has been especially high. Perhaps most strikingly, in recent
years more than 60% of all new pensioners have chosen to work rather
than to retire.[45] Therefore, the total number of working pensioners can
be expected to rise still further.

Unless the authorities decide to increase pension benefits, financial
considerations will probably come to play an increasingly dominant role
in the work-retirement decision. Pension levels are inadequate today,
and, in view of other demands on the state's resources, they will become
more and more inadequate. As two Soviet economists observed at the
end of the 1970s: "In recent years, the income level of non-able-bodied
citizens in our country has begun to lag perceptibly behind the standard
of living of the population as a whole." In 1956, they pointed out, "the
highest old-age pension was more than one and a half times the average
wage. Now, the average wage is more than twice as high as the average
pension and is higher than the maximum old-age pension."[46]

In 1980 the average monthly pension for urban blue- and white-
collar workers was 70 rubles—that is, 41% of the average monthly
wage. Official plans call for a doubling of the average pension by the

year 1990 and a threefold increase by 2000. Even if this optimistic goal is reached, however, the average old-age pension at the end of the century will still be only 54% of the average monthly wage that will prevail then. The situation of collective farmers is even worse and will remain so throughout the 1980s and 1990s.[47]

The United States

A child born in the United States in 1986 could expect to live for 75.0 years, an increase of 0.3 years since 1985. (The previous year had evidenced no change in life expectancy in comparison with 1984; in fact, between 1982 and 1985, the figure rose by only 0.1 years.) As is true in the USSR, there are numerous differences among various subgroups of the American population. The male-female differential is especially noteworthy: life expectancy for boys born in 1986 was 71.5 years, while that for girls was 78.5. (The gender gap, a full 7 years, is substantial but still is 2 years less than the gap in the USSR.) In five of the last six years, male life expectancy at birth has increased. According to the National Center for Health Statistics, from 1979 to 1981 the figure was 70.1 years, in comparison with the 1986 level of 71.5. Among girls there was an increase in 1986—after a period of little or no growth since 1982. From 1979 to 1981 the life expectancy of newborn girls was 77.6 years; by 1986 the figure had grown by less than 1 year, reaching its current level of 78.5. Thus, the 7.5-year difference between the sexes from 1979 to 1981 has shrunk since then, but only slightly, to 7.0 years in 1986.[48]

Comparing life expectancy projections for whites and blacks, one can see equally sharp contrasts. Boys and girls of both races born in 1986 could expect to live far longer than infants born at the beginning of the century. Moreover, the gap between blacks and whites has narrowed considerably, especially among females. Nevertheless, it remains true that the "average" white outlives the "average" black, and the pace at which the two numbers are converging has continued to slow down over time.

During the first half of this century, between 1900 and 1902 and between 1949 and 1951, white male life expectancy at birth rose by 18.1 years, while white female life expectancy rose by 20.9 years. Over this period of five decades, then, the average annual increase was about 0.4 years. Among nonwhite babies the first half of the twentieth century witnessed a somewhat higher rate of increase: life expectancy among males and females rose annually by approximately 0.5 years.

During the 1950s, 1960s, and 1970s nonwhites once again saw their life expectancy increase more rapidly than was the case among white persons. For newborns in both categories, however, upward movement was far slower than it had been earlier—roughly 0.2 additional years annually among whites (a total of 6.2 years among white girls and 4.5 years among white boys), compared to 0.3 additional years annually among nonwhites (a total of 11.3 years among nonwhite girls and 6.7 years among nonwhite boys).[49]

Table 6-1. Life Expectancy in the United States at Birth, by Race and Sex, 1979-81 to 1986 (in Years)

Year	White				Nonwhite (including black)				Black			
	1979-81	1984	1985	1986	1979-81	1984	1985	1986	1979-81	1984	1985	1986
Male	70.8	71.8	71.8	72.0	65.6	67.4	67.2	N.A.	64.1	65.6	65.3	65.5
Female	78.2	78.7	78.7	78.9	74.0	75.0	75.2	N.A.	72.9	73.7	73.7	73.6

Sources: Various reports issued by the National Center for Health Statistics, in "New High for Expectation of Life," Metropolitan Life Foundation, Statistical Bulletin 68, no. 3 (July–September 1987): 11; New York Times, September 8, 1987.

The same pattern of continuing increases in life expectancy, espe-cially among nonwhites, has persisted throughout the 1980s. Between 1979-1981 and 1985 the figure rose by 1.0 years for white boys and by 0.5 years for white girls; among nonwhites the corresponding increases were 1.6 and 1.2 years, respectively. Despite these impressive changes, however, two troublesome facts must be noted. First, the category "nonwhite" is not coterminous with the category "black," and gains in life expectancy among blacks have not been as great as those noted for nonwhites. Second, there still are significant differences in life expec-tancy among whites, nonwhites, and blacks, as well as among males and females in each of the three categories. As Table 6-1 indicates, for those born in 1986 the highest figure (78.9 years) applies to white females, while the lowest (65.5 years) refers to black males born in 1985.[50]

The gap between life expectancy among blacks and whites, as well as that between whites and nonwhites, stems from a number of factors. Among the most important are wealth and income; education; infant mortality levels, which are closely related to prenatal and postnatal care, as well as the nutritional habits of expectant mothers; alcohol and drug abuse; teenage (and, to a lesser degree, adult) homicide and other forms of violence, including suicide; and motor vehicle accidents.

All of these matters, while interesting and important, need not be analyzed thoroughly to appreciate their relevance for life expectancy levels among different subgroups of the population. What is crucial for our purposes is that, even though the average white or nonwhite American today will live far longer than his or her parents or grand-parents did, racial differences continue to be unacceptably high. As one authoritative source has put it:

> Based on mortality conditions [existing] in 1984, 855 out of every 1,000 white women could expect to celebrate their 65th birthday, while only 744 out of every 1,000 white men were likely to do so. Among nonwhites, the chances of surviving until age 65 were 774 out of 1,000 for women and 622 in 1,000 for men. The likelihood of a person celebrating an 85th birthday was about 400 in 1,000 among white women and a little more than 310 in 1,000 for nonwhite women. Among men, the chances of reaching age 85 were just half those of women.[51]

A smaller proportion of blacks has reached the age of 65 than is the case among whites, although recent data indicate that the gap may be growing smaller. In 1980 some 7.8% of the black population were 65

years of age or older, while the figure for whites was 11.9%. The difference can be attributed primarily to two factors: higher birth rates within
the black community, and higher mortality rates among almost all age
cohorts of blacks. In the past decade or two, however, the proportion
of blacks who are elderly has been increasing more rapidly than the
figure among whites, a trend that is expected to continue for the fore-
seeable future.[52] Unfortunately, we do not know if this recent development reflects improvements in the medical care of blacks and a rise
in their socioeconomic status. Instead, it may be a result of continuing
high infant mortality rates affecting the greater number of black babies
being born, as well as very high rates of premature deaths among young
urban males through drug abuse or various forms of violence. It is
unclear whether the "graying" of the black population should be eval-
uated positively or negatively.

Expansion of the "Old-Old" Age Group

While race and gender clearly have implications for a given individual's
life expectancy, the proportion of the population classified as "elderly"—
that is, those who are 65 years of age or older—has been growing
steadily since the turn of the century. In 1900 the elderly numbered
3.1 million and constituted approximately 4% of the U.S. population.
By 1960 the total had grown to 16.6 million (9.2% of the population),
and by 1986 it reached 29.6 million (12.4% of the population). One
out of every eight persons living in the United States today is at least
65 years old.[53] Their number is expected to increase still further, as is
their contribution to the nation's total population. According to U.S.
Census Bureau projections, the number of elderly men and women in
America will reach 39.2 million by the year 2010, and two decades
later there will be 64.6 million persons in this category. If the Census
Bureau's predictions are accurate, the elderly will constitute 13% of the
total population in 2010, and 21% in 2030.[54]

   In 1985 approximately one third (32.2%) of all elderly persons was
65 to 69 years of age, while one fourth (26.6%) was 70 to 74 years old
and another one fifth (19.6%) between 75 and 79. Almost one tenth
(9.4%) of the elderly—that is, some 3 million people—was 85 years of
age or older. The same Census Bureau report stating that the number
of elderly men and women will rise by 9.6 million in the year 2010 also
suggests that more than one half of the increase (5.9 million persons)
will occur among individuals who will be 80 years or older.[55]

   The fastest growing segment of the U.S. population is, and over
the next seventy years will probably continue to be, men and women

aged 65 and over.[56] More precisely, it is the group aged 85 and over that is expanding most rapidly—four times as fast as the number of those who are 65 and older. In mid-1982 about 2.5 million persons were 85 or more years old; by the year 2000 their numbers are expected to more than double, reaching a total of over 5 million. By the year 2050 there should be more than three times this number—more than 16 million people, or roughly 5% of the country's entire population. (One fourth of the nation at that time will consist of men and women who are 65 years of age or older.)[57]

Of the approximately 2.5 million people who were 85 or older in mid-1982 more than 70% (1,722,000) were women. Population projections suggest that this gender-based disparity will grow even wider "as a result of women's more favorable survival record." By the end of the century the difference is expected to increase to 2.4 million, as against "only" 1 million in 1982. By the year 2050 the male-female differential among the "old-old" will be about 6.8 million. If these predictions materialize in 2050, men aged 85 and over will comprise 17.1% of all men in the 65-and-over age group; the comparable figure for women will be 28.6%.[58]

Where do these people live? In the USSR there is considerable regional variation in the proportions of the population that are elderly (65 and over) or "old-old" (85 and over). As of the 1980 census the states with the highest percentages of elderly persons were Florida (17.3%), Arkansas (13.7%), Rhode Island (13.4%), Iowa (13.3%), Missouri and South Dakota (13.2% each), Nebraska (13.1%), and Kansas (13.0%). Most of these states are in the Midwest, but a very different picture emerges if we look at the states with the largest number of residents 65 years of age or older. This list includes California (2.4 million), New York (2.2 million), Florida (1.7 million), and Ohio (slightly less than 1.2 million). This rather heterogeneous grouping consists of the Sunbelt states, as well as some of the major industrial states of the Middle Atlantic and Midwest areas. Some of these states offer the promise of a mild climate and "easy living"; others are populous, and therefore it is not surprising to discover large numbers of elderly people living there.[59]

The main contrast with the situation in the USSR involves a combination of two factors: the presence of, or restrictions on, freedom of movement; and the nature and intensity of cultural difference between the northern and southern regions of each country. Americans are far more mobile than Soviet citizens are, and, even under conditions of *glasnost* and *perestroika*, it is unlikely that large numbers of Slavs or Baltic peoples will be allowed to migrate to the sunbelt areas of central Asia, the Transcaucasus, or the Crimea. In fact, Moscow has been trying to persuade inhabitants of labor-surplus areas such as central Asia to resettle in labor-deficit regions such as Siberia.

A further impediment to any such population movement is the fact that the indigenous peoples of the southern parts of the USSR have not made Slavs living there feel welcome. History, language, culture, and strong feelings of ethnic self-identification among the southern nationalities act as deterrents to many Slavs who might otherwise choose to move south. A related deterrent is the deep attachment that Russians, Ukrainians, and other ethnic groups feel toward their native lands.

The same American states in which most of the elderly live also are home to the nation's very old (those who are 85 or more years of age). Ten states—California (218,000), New York (193,000), Pennsylvania (130,000), Florida (117,000), Illinois (115,000), Texas (112,000), Ohio (108,000), Michigan (82,000), Massachusetts (74,000), and New Jersey (72,000)—contain one half of the "old-old" population. At the other extreme, a mere 619 of the "old-old" age group live in Alaska, while Wyoming (3,473) and Nevada (3,640) rank forty-eighth and forty-ninth, respectively. All three states are sparsely populated and are subject to unusually severe climatic conditions; one would not expect to find very old men or women living there.[60]

For reasons that are far from clear, there is very little correlation between living in a state with a high proportion of elderly or very old people and the likelihood of living to 100. To be sure, the prospect of becoming a centenarian is very small, but it is far from nonexistent. Information obtained from census questionnaires is notoriously unreliable, but U.S. demographers and statisticians in the government and elsewhere have developed alternative ways of estimating how many people really are centenarians.

The figure most widely used today is 15,000, but these people are not distributed randomly throughout the United States. In certain states the chances of reaching 100 are far better than they are in other parts of the country. For every 100,000 persons currently residing in Hawaii, 1,713 will become centenarians. Other states where one's chances are relatively good are Minnesota (1,444), South Dakota (1,392), Iowa (1,379), and Nebraska (1,364). The odds against living to 100 are most formidable in Alaska (941), the District of Columbia (948), Louisiana (994), Nevada (1,004), and Pennsylvania (1,009).[61]

How can we account for these contrasts? One analyst, after reviewing the literature on centenarians, has concluded that "there is no fountain of youth, no elixir, no natural nutrient, no hidden valley and no isolated geographic area that promotes [an] extended lifetime."[62] Eugene Carlson, a reporter for the *Wall Street Journal*, has suggested that family income, climate, health care standards, and genetic background all play a part, as does interstate migration. He contends that Hawaii, Florida, and Arizona, states that attract substantial numbers of retirees, "have a relatively high proportion of residents over 100 because older people who move to a new state tend to be healthy."[63] In contrast, Pennsylvania has a large number of elderly inhabitants but a low percentage of centenarians. To explain this apparently contradictory phenomenon, Carlson cites unnamed demographers who argue that "Pennsylvania exports a lot of its healthy oldsters, while retaining those who lack the vigor to migrate to a retirement haven." His hypotheses are intriguing; unfortunately, they are not accompanied by any evidence. All we can say with certainty is that no one has yet explained why certain locales seem to be conducive to living a long life, or why certain people manage to do so.

A Sociological Profile of the Elderly

As we have seen, 90% of all Americans 65 years of age or older are white. Among all age cohorts in this population, the proportion of females is slightly higher among whites, as well as blacks. An even more noteworthy contrast exists between elderly men and women: their marital status. As of 1982 more than one half of all women in this age bracket was widowed; among women 75 years of age or older the figure rose to two thirds. In contrast, only 12.4% of elderly males were widowers, as were 21.8% of men aged 75 or more. Thus, for every widower there are approximately six widows, and, since the former are far more likely than the latter to remarry, the proportion of elderly women who spend their final years without a spouse is immense.[64]

The overwhelming majority of elderly males lives in "family households," most living with their wives but a small number with their children. Only one sixth of all elderly men lives alone. In contrast, slightly more than one half of all elderly women lives in family households, either with their husbands or their children; almost as many live alone, and a handful live with nonrelatives.[65] Over the past two decades the percentage of elderly men living in a family has remained fairly steady at just over 80%. During this same twenty-year period the proportion of elderly women living in a family has declined steadily, while the proportion of those living alone has continued to rise. Today approximately one third of the elderly population lives alone, and the figure has been rising with each passing year, especially among women. Indeed, 80% of those who are 65 or older, and who live alone, are women.[66]

There are significant differences in this respect between those who are relatively young (65 to 74 years of age) and those who are aged 75 or older. Approximately 38% of the former group live alone, whereas a far larger proportion of the "old-old" has chosen to live alone: 54% in 1985, a figure that is expected to increase to 58% by 1995.[67] Among those who are at least 85 years old, fully 30% continue to live independently. In contrast, only 16% live with their children, although the percentage is considerably higher in some states—for example, Hawaii (where the extended family tradition remains strong) and in the midwestern farm states (where a large proportion of these individuals is still working).[68]

Whatever their living arrangements may be, these men and women are among the first to live long enough to watch their grandchildren grow to maturity. As Tamara K. Hareven has pointed out, "The opportunity for a meaningful period of overlap in the lives of grandparents and grandchildren is a twentieth-century phenomenon." Equally important, she notes, this fact "runs counter to the popular myth of family solidarity in the past that was based on three-generational ties."[69] Elaine M. Brody also has tried to refute the idea that "there is widespread abandonment of the current generations of older people by their families." This notion, she observes, "has been disproved by research and clinical evidence, but it stubbornly refuses to be dispelled in popular belief."[70]

Numerous surveys have shown that elderly persons prefer to live apart from their children. According to Brody, "Most prefer to live near, but not with, their children."[71] Unless income or health poses a barrier, they want to live separately. Such an arrangement affords them privacy and, if and when they so choose, allows them to see their children or grandchildren. (This situation has been described by a leading gerontologist as "intimacy at a distance.")[72] The arrangement seems to work for most elderly people. Recent studies reveal that almost two thirds of parents aged 65 or older see their children at least once per week, while almost one fourth (23%) says they see their children daily, and another 40% do so once per week. Sixteen percent meet their children once per month, 18% once per year, and only 3% say they never see their offspring.[73]

More generally, the available evidence suggests that the elderly are content and even happy with their lives. A group of scholars at the University of Michigan's Institute for Social Research determined that "overall subjective well-being does tend to be higher among today's elderly population than among younger age groups." In attempting to explain their findings, the researchers suggested that older persons "seem to find life less burdensome and less trying than do younger people." In addition, the Michigan team hypothesized that "the narrowing of their global life roles is compensated for by a parallel reduction in the number of stressful disruptions of their daily lives." Finally, they observed that the higher incidence of religious belief found among older people also is related to "higher satisfaction levels."[74]

Health and Medical Care

Federal budgetary expenditures for the elderly have been increasing at a rapid rate, both in absolute and relative terms. In 1960 less than 15% of the budget was spent on programs for older Americans. By the 1985 fiscal year the proportion had nearly doubled, rising to 28% of federal outlays. A similar pattern can be seen if we examine expenditures on the elderly as a percentage of the GNP. Thus, pension and health care financing programs constituted 6.1% of the GNP in 1970; by 1986 the figure had increased to 9.6%.[75]

In 1985 funds for programs aimed at older citizens came to nearly one half of all federal spending on domestic health care—roughly $263 billion. Social Security represented 55% of these expenditures, and Medicare another 23%. The remaining money was allocated to special retirement programs (including several for those who have served in the armed forces), Medicaid, housing, Supplemental Security Income, and a number of smaller scale activities.[76]

As the elderly population, in general, and the number of very old, in particular, continue to grow, demand for federal spending on health care for those over 65 also will grow. The additional sum is likely to be substantial, partly because medical costs are expected to continue rising more rapidly than inflation and partly because of the expected increase in the number of very old, who are especially likely to require medical assistance.[77]

Medical costs are not confined to programs administered by the U.S. government, nor are all expenses in the sphere of health care absorbed by it. According to estimates proposed by various scholars and economic forecasting companies, total health care spending in 1987 was more than $500 billion, about 6.8% higher than the figure for 1986. This sum represents approximately 11.3% of the GNP, compared with 10.9% one year ago and 9.1% in 1980.[78]

Doctors' fees, which account for one fifth of all medical costs, rose 7.8% in 1986, despite the fact that the rate of inflation was only 1.1%. In addition, physicians are employing more expensive procedures and tests, a development that adds significantly to the nation's health care bill. As a *Wall Street Journal* reporter observed, there is something ironic about new technologies leading to cost increases. In most industries, he wrote, technological advances help bring about lower costs, but "in medicine, advances traditionally have been directed more at improving care than reducing expenses." Consequently, "new methods for treating patients often significantly add to the expense."[79]

These remarks are both perceptive and important, but they are even weightier in view of the "graying" of the U.S. population and the special needs of older people. As we have seen, about 12% of Americans are classified as "elderly"; but this portion of the population accounts for 38% of all hospital bed-days, 23% of all hospital discharges (a category that does not include men and women who die while being hospitalized), and 29% of all health care expenses.[80]

Some sort of crisis seems to be looming in the economics of health care. What one analyst has termed "the inexorable growth of the elderly population" already has begun to threaten the budgets of the federal, state, and local governments; charitable institutions; and individuals with elderly parents.[81] In 1985 sociologist Alice T. Day pointed out that changes in family and social structure were threatening the security of the nation's elderly. Increasing life expectancy and decreasing birth rates, she noted, were leading toward a situation in which there might be too few workers to support those 65 or older. In addition, more and more women were joining the work force. This circumstance, in turn, meant that fewer wives and daughters—the traditional source of help within the family—would be available to care for senior citizens who were ill. As Day put it, "The daughters of the very old are more likely than their counterparts in previous generations to be in the workforce, to have had their fewer children later in life, [and] to be divorced and remarried." Furthermore, "they are themselves growing older," thereby increasing the likelihood that they ultimately would "face a decade of widowhood, with no children available to care for them."[82]

The emerging crisis in Social Security, Medicare, and other governmental programs for the elderly will be extremely difficult to manage. The demographic picture is clear: while the number of retirees and the number of persons in the labor force are increasing, the rate of growth of the former population is much greater than that of the latter. Unless something changes dramatically, tax revenues and contributions to the Social Security fund will be insufficient to continue providing older persons with services and a steady stream of income. A prominent American journalist has noted that "the nation could face wrenching choices about the level of Social Security benefits, the payroll tax burden on workers, and the affordable level of spending on health care for the aged."[83] We are still in the early stages of this crisis, but it is certain to mature over the coming decades: whereas there are 3.3 workers today for every retired person, thirty years from now the ratio will be halved.

There are other reasons for concern about the nation's ability to remain solvent and also provide for the needs of the elderly. One involves a large increase in the number of veterans who are, or will be by the year 2000, 65 years of age or older. According to the Veterans Administration, the number of veterans classified as "elderly" will more than double in the next fifteen years—from 4 million to 9 million. During this same time period the number of veterans in the very old category will come close to doubling, increasing from 260,000 to about 515,000. But VA hospitals and nursing homes currently have an occupancy rate of 85%, and many of the system's nursing homes are 100% filled, with waiting lists for individuals willing to wait for an opening. How, if at all, they will handle the vast increases in their clientele remains to be seen.[84]

Another reason for being skeptical about the prospects for reconciling future supply and demand in the sphere of medical services is the failure of various cost-cutting arrangements to fulfill their promise. For example, the Reagan administration's Medicare "prospective payment system"—whereby the government pays hospitals according to a patient's diagnosis rather than his or her length of stay—seems to have saved money, but at the expense of proper health care. Under the new program, hospitals have an incentive to release patients as quickly as possible; predictably, this is precisely what they have done. While some of these individuals are able to recuperate fully at home, others apparently require more intensive care than their families can provide.[85]

The Role of Nursing Homes

The circumstances described above already have begun to exert pressure on the nation's limited network of nursing homes. Until a few years ago roughly 5% of America's elderly population lived in nursing homes and similar institutions. Even without an influx of older persons released early from hospitals, governmental studies were predicting a 57% growth in the nursing home population between 1980 and 1995. The supply-demand relationship is being strained still further by other cost-cutting devices—for example, limits on fees paid to nursing homes by state and federal agencies, and limits on the addition of new beds, as well as the construction of new facilities. Although these measures have helped to reduce the government's share of all nursing home costs—from 56% in 1979 to 48% in 1985—they also have "increased competition for existing facilities and may have heightened discrimination against [M]edicaid patients." Since the latter group pays less and requires more paperwork than private patients, nursing home administrators have little incentive to accept them.[86]

Few individuals have insurance that covers the cost of nursing home care. As a result, almost one half (49.4% as of 1984) of the total cost is paid by patients or their families. Most of the remainder (43.4%) is provided by Medicaid, but one of the prerequisites for Medicaid eligibility is that individuals must first exhaust their own resources.[87] In view of the high costs associated with medical care, increasing numbers of the elderly cannot afford the continuing financial burden of office visits and outpatient care. Others who enter nursing homes as "private-pay" patients quickly deplete their savings and wind up on Medicaid. According to estimates prepared by the Health Care Financing Administration (HCFA), a unit of the U.S. Department of Health and Human Services, approximately one half of all nursing home residents on Medicaid is comprised of "the newly impoverished—people who ran through most of their assets and income paying for nursing home care."[88] To a significant degree the function of Medicaid is no longer what its creators intended. "Nominally a medical safety net for the poor, the program has now become a payer of last resort for many middle-class nursing home patients whose medical expenses have made them poor."[89]

Total expenditures for nursing home care, which came to $4.7 billion in 1970, have increased at an extraordinary pace. By 1980 the figure had risen to $20.4 billion, and by 1984 it reached $32.0 billion. Projections developed by two HCFA economists suggest the total costs will be some $52 billion by 1990.[90] These developments are largely a consequence of two factors: the increase in the population of elderly persons, and the introduction and expansion of Medicaid and Medicare. The role of Medicare is relatively small in this regard, since the program covers only short-term stays in nursing homes and is available only to those recuperating from an illness or released from a hospital. Medicaid funding, however, has risen rapidly, as more and more demands are placed on this program. Thus, while nursing home patients comprise approximately 5% of Medicaid recipients, this group consumes more than 43% of the program's funds.[91]

The number of elderly persons residing in nursing homes has almost doubled since Medicare and Medicaid were established, and the number of very old has increased even more rapidly. Today, 20% of the latter group reside in these institutions; most are women, largely because females predominate among those who live beyond 85. Equally important, this segment of the population is most likely to need long-term care. At the beginning of the century, medical problems among the elderly were acute; today, they tend to be chronic, and the likelihood of developing a chronic illness, or some sort of major disability, increases with age. But the diseases that affect elderly males generally are fatal, while those affecting women usually lead to chronic conditions that require constant attention. Finally, because elderly women (especially those who are very old) are more likely than men of the same age to outlive their spouses, they are more likely to live alone and to require institutional care.[92]

Economic Status

America's elderly have improved their economic condition over the past fifteen years to such a degree that it is no longer appropriate to think of them as poor or "near-poor"—that is, those with incomes that are less than 150% of the poverty level. In 1972 approximately 38% of all elderly persons were poor or near-poor, in contrast with "only" 22% of the entire U.S. population.[93] Since then there has been a sharp decline in the incidence of poverty among older age groups, even during the 1981/82 recession. The major factors explaining this improvement are the significant increases in Social Security benefits introduced in the early 1970s, and the decision to "index" Social Security outlays, beginning in 1975, by linking them to the prevailing rate of inflation.[94]

Between 1970 and 1985 the poverty rate among older persons declined from 24% to 12.6%, and one year later the figure was 12.4%.[95] Despite the stereotyped view of some people that the elderly live in or near penury, the fact is that those 65 years of age or older are doing rather well. Indeed, recent research has found that elderly Americans are four times as likely to give regular financial assistance to their children as they are to receive it.[96] The point here is not that elderly citizens of the United States live in splendor but rather that they, as a group, no longer are impoverished. As Robert M. Ball, a former commissioner of Social Security, has observed: "The recent progress enjoyed by the elderly has not conferred upon them a favored economic position, but has merely brought them from a position of considerable disadvantage closer to parity with the rest of the population."[97]

From 1970 to 1983, Social Security benefits rose by 273%, almost twice the rate at which the average wage of working Americans increased (138%). To be sure, cumulative inflation of 156% eroded a large part of the elderly's gain, but it resulted in a loss, in real terms, for ordinary wage-earners. These developments lend support to one of the conclusions contained in the annual report issued in 1985 by the President's Council of Economic Advisers: "Elderly Americans have achieved basic economic parity with the rest of the population and they are no longer a relatively disadvantaged group."[98] While 24.6% of the nation's elderly lived below the poverty line in 1970 (twice the proportion of the rest of the population), by 1985 the number of elderly below the poverty line had shrunk to 12.6%, compared with 14% among other citizens.[99] In 1986 the figures were 12.4% and 13.6%, respectively.[100]

Even though in general the elderly are doing better and better, certain segments of the 65-and-older population continue to experience severe financial privation. For example, the very old are twice as likely to live below the poverty line as people aged 65 to 74. Gender differences are equally striking: in 1985, 15.6% of all elderly women were poor, in comparison with 8.5% of all elderly men. Among elderly women living alone the figure was 26.8%; among elderly black women it was 34.8%, and for elderly black women living alone the rate was 54%.[101]

As governmental programs for the elderly have expanded and an ever greater proportion of these people receives pensions from their previous employers, their incentive to continue working has diminished. "Early retirement" programs also have proved to be attractive, especially to males; as a result, labor-force participation rates among men have declined precipitously. This phenomenon is most visible among males in the 60 to 64 age bracket: between 1960 and 1984 the rate fell from 80% to 57%. A similar, although less pronounced, trend can be seen among men aged 55 to 59: between 1960 and 1983 labor-force participation within this group dropped from 92% to 81%.[102]

The pattern among women is more difficult to discern. As the authors of a General Accounting Office study observed, "Women with long-term jobs may be leaving the labor force earlier, but any such trend has been largely offset by increasing labor market entry."[103] Still, they reported a slight decline in labor-force participation among women who were 60 to 64 years old: in 1970 the rate was 36%, whereas in 1983 it was 34%. A parallel and reinforcing development also has been occurring: among women 55 to 59 years of age the rate of increase of job-holding has fallen in the past fifteen years.[104]

The proportion of people 65 years of age or older that continues to work has fallen sharply. In 1950 almost one half of all men in this age bracket was in the labor force, but by 1980 only 20% were. Among women in the same age bracket, labor-force participation rates barely changed during this period: at the beginning, about one in ten was employed, and the same figure was obtained in 1980. In 1985 approximately 7% of all elderly women were in the labor force; the proportion of elderly men who continued working was over twice as great, approximately 17%.[105]

The existence and growth of private pension plans have introduced a new element into the work-retirement decision. These arrangements, which were uncommon before the Second World War, have proliferated in the decades since then. In 1950 some 24% of private-sector employees were part of a pension program, but by 1979 the proportion had more than doubled, rising to 49%. The 1960s and 1970s witnessed a variation on this theme, as plans were introduced that allowed people to retire before the age of 65. By 1984 a majority of those enrolled in private-sector programs was eligible to receive benefits when they reached 62 years of age, without having to sacrifice any portion of their pension. Today, most private plans allow employees to retire as early as age 55, although those who choose this option, as a rule, will receive reduced benefits.[106]

Largely as a result of these changes, greater numbers of private-sector workers and administrators have decided to take early retirement. The median retirement age in this area of the economy is 62. According to a recent survey, 62% of the women and 48% of the men collecting Social Security benefits for the first time were 62 years old, the minimum age at which one is eligible to receive Social Security retirement benefits.[107]

The question of when to retire—affecting those employed in the private sector, those employed at one or another level of government, and those who are in business for themselves—generally hinges on two considerations. One involves the individual's health, including his or her concern about medical conditions that, in the not-too-distant future, may prove disabling or life-threatening. The other concerns his or her sense of financial well-being—that is, the availability and level of expected retirement income in comparison with anticipated needs and obligations. Because of improvements in both of these spheres, labor participation rates for older persons have declined substantially. Among elderly men the rate in 1983 stood at 17%, down from 46% in 1950, while among elderly women the drop has been less striking but still perceptible—from 10% in 1950 to 7% in 1983.[108]

Aging individuals and their families do not make work versus retirement decisions in a vacuum. Experts, lobbyists, and policymakers almost always play an important role. For example, the American Association of Retired Persons, with its membership of 26 million people—who are more likely than their children or grandchildren to be interested in political and economic developments, to contribute to candidates for office and to advocacy groups, and to vote in primaries and general elections—helps to frame public debate about issues of concern to the elderly. It also exerts considerable influence on politicians and bureaucrats alike.[109]

Federal, state, and local officials are even more powerful, for they determine the boundaries and also fashion and interpret the rules governing the range of choices available to older persons. A 1984 report by the Congressional Clearinghouse on the Future described the dilemma confronting political leaders:

> Concerns over the future costs of Social Security, federal retirement [arrangements] and other income programs for the elderly, lead policymakers to consider ways to prolong labor force participation.... On the other hand, provisions such as those in the 1983 Social Security Amendments to raise [the] retirement age from 65 to 67 after the turn of the century may penalize those who, because of health, discrimination, or unemployment, are forced to retire early with reduced benefits.[110]

Clearly, there is no "correct" choice. Virtually any policy that is adopted will delight some people and trouble others; or, put more positively, all interested parties are likely to experience both satisfaction and dissatisfaction. In a very real sense, that is what democracy and equity are all about.

Conclusion

The experience of the elderly in the United States is both similar to, and different from, that of older men and women in the Soviet Union. The main differences, it would seem, stem from six interrelated factors. First, America is a far richer country than the Soviet Union. Second, doctors in the United States are exceedingly well trained, well organized, and lobby effectively at all levels of government to keep their incomes high and limit other people's access to the profession. Third, a much greater percentage of the GNP is allocated to health care in the United States than is the case in the Soviet Union. Fourth, sophisticated technology and various kinds of pharmaceutical products that are abundant in the United States are all but unavailable in the Soviet Union. Fifth, the medical community in the United States is committed to keeping patients alive at all costs, a luxury that the Soviets simply cannot afford and that leads them to put a relatively low priority on caring for older citizens. Finally, older men and women in America, like other groups with shared values or interests, are able to publicize their views, organize their membership, mobilize public support for their ideas, and exert pressure on the government to adopt certain kinds of policies.

It is especially important to note that public opinion in the United States, among old and young alike, endorses the policy preferences of the elderly. Surveys carried out in recent years by Louis Harris and Associates, a major polling organization, have found that a majority of elderly persons (61%) and of young people—that is, those under 30 years of age (54%)—opposed increasing monthly premiums for Medicare, opposed increasing the deductible for Medicare coverage (65% of the elderly and 64% of the young), and objected to freezing Social Security cost-of-living increases (60% and 53%, respectively).[111]

Our national wealth, which at first glance might seem to offer nothing but advantages, is actually a mixed blessing. It has helped countless numbers of elderly persons to live longer, to avoid (or at least minimize) some of the problems that accompany the aging process, and has permitted them to enjoy their leisure or contribute to their own, their family's, or society's well-being. At the same time, however, the fact that our country and its people are so prosperous has contributed to the feeling of isolation that large numbers of senior citizens experience. It also has eased the conscience of many middle-aged individuals who "warehouse" their parents in nursing homes, thereby thrusting responsibility for the latter onto strangers or, at times, abandoning them altogether.

In addition, the system of private medical care that prevails in America, along with certain governmental programs such as Medicare, Medicaid, and Social Security, has reinforced the effects of great disparities in personal wealth and income. Whether or not an adequate "safety net" exists to support those who are needy, there certainly are great disparities in the quality of medical care available to rich and poor, blacks and whites, and those who live in major cities (especially those located on the East or West coast) versus those living in more sparsely settled areas.

The mere fact of living a long life is not, in and of itself, a source of pleasure for a given individual, even though it may say a good deal about medical services and pension arrangements in that person's society. Life expectancy in the United States is higher than in the Soviet Union, and the overall quantity of goods and services is greater here than there. But how the elderly in the two countries assess the quality of their lives may be the most important question of all. Perhaps in the future the policy of *glasnost* will permit Soviet and American scholars to carry out such an investigation and share its results with all their citizens.

Notes

[1]*Narodnoe khoziaistvo SSSR v 1973 g.* (Moscow: Statistika, 1974), p. 43.

[2]*Narodnoe khoziaistvo SSSR v 1985 g.* (Moscow: Finansy i statistika, 1986), p. 547.

[3]This paragraph and the one following rely heavily on *Vestnik Moskovskogo Universiteta, Seriia* 6, no. 1 (1981): 59.

[4]*Argumenty i fakty*, no. 18 (1987): 7.

[5]William A. Knaus, *Inside Russian Medicine* (New York: Everest, 1981), p. 262. The claim that 20,000 Soviet centenarians represent twice the number found in the United States is false. American specialists put the U.S. figure at approximately 15,000.

[6]*Sotsial'noe obespechenie*, no. 8 (1983): 49. For a more thorough discussion, which mixes scientific analysis with propaganda messages, see Georgi Z. Pitskhelauri, *The Longliving of Soviet Georgia* (New York: Human Sciences Press, 1982). For a scathing criticism of Soviet claims about *dolgozhiteli* see Neil G. Bennett and Lea K. Garson, "The Centenarian Question and Old-Age Mortality in the Soviet Union, 1959–1970," *Demography* 20, no. 4 (1983): 587–606.

[7]A museum in the Abkhazian district with the greatest concentration of the "very old" was opened recently. Its purpose is not only to celebrate longevity, or what the Party has done to make it possible, but also to promote healthy nutritional habits, vigorous exercise, and "clean living" in general. *Sotsial'noe obespechenie*, pp. 49–50.

[8]V. I. Kozlov, *Natsional'nostii SSSR: Etnodemograficheskii obzor*, 2d rev. (Moscow: Finansy i statistika, 1982), pp. 197–98. More recent data, published sporadically in medical or other scientific journals, suggest that the 1970 census data may be so outdated as to be misleading. For example, a Kirgiz medical journal has pointed out that the "geriatric coefficient" in the republic—that is, the proportion of the population that is 60 or more years of age—more than doubled between 1970 and 1979, increasing from 3.5% to 7.9%. See *Zdravookhranenie Kirgizii*, no. 6 (1982): 9.

[9]Kozlov, *Natsional'nostii SSSR*, pp. 197–98; Radio Liberty Research (hereafter cited as RL), Baltic Area SR/8 (December 9, 1986), p. 7.

[10]RL, pp. 8–12.

[11]*Itogi Vsesoiuznoi perepisi naseleniia 1959 goda: SSSR, Svodnyi tom* (Moscow, 1962), p. 85; *Vestnik statistiki*, no. 2 (1974): 95.

[12]*Vestnik Moskovskogo Universiteta*, p. 59.

[13]*Argumenty i fakty*, p. 7.

[14]A. V. Dmitriev, *Sotsial'nye problemy liudei pozhilogo vozrasta* (Leningrad: "Nauka," Leningradskoe otdelenie, 1980), p. 59, n. 14. See also Dmitri F. Chebotarev and Nina N. Sachuk, "Union of Soviet Socialist Republics," in Erdman Palmore, ed., *International Handbook on Aging* (Westport, CT: Greenwood

Press, 1980), pp. 409–10. The latter source cites a figure of 330,000 places in Soviet old-age homes in 1975.

[15]Dmitriev, *Sotsial'nye problemy*, pp. 56–57, 64–65, 68–70. See also *Sovetskoe zdravookhranenie*, no. 6 (1983): 12–16.

[16]Mark G. Field, "Medical Care in the Soviet Union: Promises and Realities," in Horst Herlemann, ed., *Quality of Life in the Soviet Union* (Boulder, CO: Westview Press, 1987), p. 68.

[17]*Narodnoe khoziaistvo SSSR v 1985 g.*, p. 560; *Pravda*, November 18, 1986.

[18]Knaus, *Inside Russian Medicine*, pp. 219–20.

[19]*Izvestiia*, January 7, 1986. This reference, as well as others in this paragraph, is taken from Aaron Trehub, "Social and Economic Rights in the Soviet Union," *Survey* 29, no. 4 (August 1987): 18–20.

[20]*Izvestiia*, February 7, 1986.

[21]Ibid.

[22]Ibid., June 13, 1986.

[23]*Itogi Vsesoiuznoi perepisi naseleniia 1970 goda* (Moscow: Statistika, 1972), 2:12–13. Presumably, the figure is higher now, but the relevant data have not been published.

[24]Chebotarev and Sachuk, *Union of Soviet Socialist Republics*, p. 408.

[25]See Trehub, *Social and Economic Rights*, p. 20.

[26]*Sobesednik*, no. 48 (1986): 5.

[27]Ibid.

[28]Alastair McAuley gives a figure of 225,000, adding that the total population of pensionable age at that time was 16.5 million. Thus, only 1.4% of those who were of pension age actually received financial support from the state. See McAuley's "Social Policy," in Archie Brown and Michael Kaser, eds., *Soviet Policy for the 1980s* (Bloomington: Indiana University Press, 1982), p. 157.

[29]*Sobesednik*, p. 4.

[30]For a discussion of trends in gerontological research and a listing of some of the most original studies in the field see Dmitriev, *Sotsial'nye problemy*, pp. 3–8.

[31]See the remarks of N. Gol'tsev, in *Literaturnaia gazeta*, November 21, 1984. See also T. V. Riabushkin, ed., *Demograficheskaia politika sotsialisticheskogo obshchestva* (Moscow: "Nauka," 1986), pp. 104–5. For a poignant example of this phenomenon as depicted in Soviet fiction see Natalya Baranskaya, "The Send-Off," *Mademoiselle* (November 1972): 184–85, 197–98, 213.

[32]This section is derived from McAuley, "Social Policy," pp. 150–62.

[33]Ibid.

[34]See Mervyn Matthews, "Aspects of Poverty in the Soviet Union," in Herlemann, *Quality of Life*, pp. 51–52.

[35]*Konstitutsiia (Osnovnoi Zakon) Soiuza Sovetskikh Sotsialisticheskikh Respublik* (Moscow: Izvatel'stvo "Pravda," 1977), p. 21.

[36]*Pravda*, October 2, 1979.

[37]*Sotsialisticheskaia zakonnost'*, no. 11 (1983): 54–55.

38William Moskoff, "Part-Time Employment in the Soviet Union," *Soviet Studies* 34, no. 2 (April 1982): 279–80. See also A. G. Novitskii and G. V. Mil', *Zaniatost' pensionerov: sotsial'no-demograficheskii aspekt* (Moscow: Finansy i statistika, 1981), p. 94.

39Novitskii and Mil', *Zaniatost'*; A. G. Novitskii, "Istochnik formirovaniia zaniatosti s rezhimom nepolnogo rabochego vremeni i v poriadke nadomnichestva," in A. Z. Maikov and A. G. Novitskii, eds., *Problemy nepolnogo rabochego vremeni i zaniatost' naseleniia* (Moscow: "Sovetskaia Rossiia," 1975), p. 60; *Kommunist*, no. 2 (1980): 54.

40A. Novitskii, "Dopolnitel'nyi istochnik rabochei sily sfery obsluzhivaniia," in *Narodonaselenia: naselenie i trudovye resursy*, p. 59.

41*Sotsiologicheskie issledovannia*, no. 1 (1976): 110.

42See *Gorodskoe khoziaistvo Mosvky*, no. 2 (1983): 26–27; *Sovetskaia kul'tura*, October 26, 1982; *Agitator*, no. 9 (1983): 24.

43V. P. Belov, ed., *Trudosposobnost' pensionerov po starosti, voprosy stimulirovaniia i organizatsii ikh truda* (Moscow: Tsentral'nyi nauchno-issledovatel'skii institut ekspertizy trudosposobnosti i organizatsii truda invalidov, 1975), p. 141.

44Ibid., p. 6.

45*Izvestiia*, January 6, 1976; *Nedelia*, no. 15 (April 9–15, 1979): 11.

46*Ekonomika i organizatsiia promyshlennogo proizvodstva*, no. 5 (1978): 29.

47Stephen Sternheimer, "The Graying of the Soviet Union," *Problems of Communism* 31, no. 5 (September-October 1982): 85, 86. In mid-1987 the authorities announced that a new system of "supplemental retirement annuities" would be introduced, on a voluntary basis, for workers, white-collar personnel, and collective farmers: anyone who wishes to may pay a regular premium from his or her wages. In the future, such individuals will be eligible for an annuity of 10 to 15 rubles per month. For details, see *Izvestiia*, August 24, 1987.

48This section relies on data gathered by the National Center for Health Statistics, published in Metropolitan Life Foundation, *Statistical Bulletin* 68, no. 3 (July-September 1987): 8–12.

49Ibid.

50Ibid., pp. 11–12; *New York Times*, September 8, 1987.

51*Statistical Bulletin*, p. 14.

52U.S. Bureau of the Census, *Demographic and Socioeconomic Aspects of Aging in the United States*, Series P-23, no. 138 (August 1984): 21–22, 26–27.

53Cynthia M. Taeuber, *America in Transition: An Aging Society*, U.S. Bureau of the Census, Current Population Reports, Special Studies, Series P-23, no. 128 (1983): 3; U.S. Bureau of the Census, *Projections of the Population of the United States, by Age, Sex, and Race: 1983 to 2080*, Publication P-25, no. 952 (1984): 43–44.

54U.S. General Accounting Office, *An Aging Society: Meeting the Needs of the Elderly while Responding to Rising Federal Costs*, GAO/HRD-86-135 (September 1986), pp. 8–9.

55*Projections of the Population*, pp. 43–44.

[56]See, for example, "United States Population Outlook," *Statistical Bulletin* 65, no. 1 (January-March 1984): 16–19.

[57]"Projections of Population Growth at the Older Ages," ibid. 65, no. 2 (April-June 1984): 8.

[58]Ibid., pp. 9–11.

[59]"Continued Increase in Elderly Population," ibid. 63, no. 3 (July-September 1982): 6–10.

[60]Charles F. Longino, Jr., "A State by State Look at the Oldest Americans," *American Demographics* (November 1986): 40–41. See also "Trends in Longevity after Age 65," *Statistical Bulletin* 68, no. 1 (January-March 1987): 10–17.

[61]"Profile of Centenarians," ibid., pp. 2–7.

[62]Ibid., p. 2.

[63]*Wall Street Journal*, May 19, 1987.

[64]"Projections of Population Growth at the Older Ages," p. 12.

[65]Ibid., pp. 10, 12.

[66]*Tomorrow's Elderly*, Report Prepared for the Congressional Clearinghouse on the Future, for the chairman of the Select Committee on Aging, U.S. House of Representatives, 98th Cong., 2d sess., October 1984, p. 4.

[67]"Housing for the Elderly," *American Demographics* 9 (April 1987): 62.

[68]"A State by State Look at the Oldest Americans," p. 42.

[69]Tamara K. Hareven, "Family Time and Historical Time," *Daedalus* 106, no. 2 (Spring 1977): 63.

[70]Elaine M. Brody, "The Aging of the Family," *Annals* of the American Association of Political and Social Science, July 1978, p. 14. See also Donald P. Kent, "Aging—Fact or Fancy," *The Gerontologist* 5, no. 2 (June 1965): 51–56.

[71]Brody, "The Aging of the Family," pp. 17–18.

[72]Leopold Rosenmayer, "Family Relations of the Elderly," *Journal of Marriage and the Family* 30, no. 4 (November 1968): 672–79.

[73]*Wall Street Journal*, April 28, 1987.

[74]*ISR Newsletter* 10, no. 4 (Winter 1982): 3, discusses A. Regula Herzog et al., *Subjective Well-Being among Different Age Groups*, ISR Research Report, 1982.

[75]*An Aging Society*, p. 14.

[76]Ibid.

[77]Ibid., pp. 14–15. In 1984 people 80 years of age or older received, on average, $8,321 in federal benefits. This figure was 17% higher than the $7,151 that the "average" 59- to 65-year-old person received. Ibid., p. 15.

[78]See *Wall Street Journal*, September 29, 1987.

[79]Ibid.

[80]Ibid., September 25, 1987.

[81]Julie Kosterlitz, "The Graying of America Spells Trouble for Long-term Health Care for Elderly," *National Journal* 17, no. 15 (April 13, 1985): 798.

[82]Alice T. Day, *Who Cares? Demographic Trends Challenge Family Care for the Elderly* (Washington, DC: Population Reference Bureau, 1985).

[83]*Wall Street Journal,* September 28, 1987.

[84]*Tomorrow's Elderly,* p. 33.

[85]Two studies, one by the General Accounting Office, the other prepared by the House of Representatives, Select Committee on Aging, reported that "local health providers and officials [are concerned] that the prospective payment system is causing hospitals to release patients both sooner and sicker." See Kosterlitz, "The Graying of America," p. 799.

[86]Ibid., pp. 798–99. Quotation on p. 798.

[87]"Nursing Home Care: The Need and the Costs," *Congressional Quarterly* 44, no. 22 (May 31, 1986): 1229.

[88]See Kosterlitz, "The Graying of America," p. 799. According to an authoritative health care newsletter, 50% of elderly Americans who enter a nursing home with their own resources will completely deplete, within one and one half years, their own funds and will then have to turn to Medicaid for coverage. *The Keckley Report,* December 22, 1986, p. 3.

[89]Kosterlitz, "The Graying of America," p. 799.

[90]Ibid.; "Nursing Home Care," p. 1229.

[91]"Nursing Home Care," p. 1230.

[92]*Tomorrow's Elderly,* p. 42.

[93]Ibid., p. 5.

[94]Michael J. Boskin and John B. Shoven, "Poverty among the Elderly: Where Are the Holes in the Safety Net?" National Bureau of Economic Research (Cambridge, MA), Working Paper no. 1923 (May 1986), p. 2.

[95]*New York Times,* July 31, 1987.

[96]Irene Hoskins, "Intergenerational Equity: An Overview of a Public Policy Debate in the United States," *Ageing International* 14, no. 1 (Spring 1987): 5.

[97]Quoted in *New York Times,* January 25, 1987.

[98]Cited in ibid., April 23, 1987.

[99]Ibid.

[100]Ibid., July 31, 1987.

[101]Hoskins, "Intergenerational Equity," p. 5. As appalling as these statistics are, they nevertheless represent a perceptible improvement over the situation that prevailed as recently as 1982. For details see *Tomorrow's Elderly,* p. 5.

[102]General Accounting Office, *An Aging Society,* p. 20.

[103]Ibid.

[104]Ibid. For a splendid discussion of the issues and the data concerning early retirement see Charlotte Nusberg, "Early Retirement Ubiquitous in Western Nations," *Ageing International* 13, no. 4 (Winter 1986): 26–32.

[105]General Accounting Office, *An Aging Society,* pp. 19–20.

[106]General Accounting Office, *Features of Nonfederal Retirement Programs,* GAO/OCG-84-2 (June 26, 1984); General Accounting Office, *Retirement before Age 65 Is a Growing Trend in the Private Sector,* GAO/HRD-85-81 (July 15, 1985), p. 2.

[107]Sally R. Sherman, "Reported Reasons Retired Workers Left Their Last Job: Findings from the New Beneficiaries Survey," *Social Security Bulletin* 48, no. 3 (March 1985): 22–30.

[108]*Tomorrow's Elderly*, pp. 12–13.

[109]For a fascinating interview with the association's chairman see *New York Times*, September 11, 1987.

[110]*Tomorrow's Elderly*, p. 11.

[111]Cited in Hoskins, "Intergenerational Equity," p. 8.

Part 2

AVOIDING CONFLICTS

7

Gorbachev and the West

Stephen White

Gorbachev's General Secretaryship: Some Major Themes

Mikhail Gorbachev was elected Communist party general secretary in March 1985, just a few days after his fifty-fourth birthday. In his acceptance speech he promised to continue the strategy of his predecessors, which he defined as "accelerated socioeconomic development and the perfection of all aspects of Soviet life."[1] An emphasis on continuity—particularly with Yuri Andropov, his mentor within the leadership—is appropriate in many fields, among them the Soviet Union's official ideology.

Soviet Marxism-Leninism is often regarded as the Communist Ten Commandments, yielding a clear and unchanging set of policy prescriptions for all areas of Soviet life. It, perhaps, may be regarded more profitably as a flexible body of doctrine that gives broad directives to officials and to the Soviet population at large and that changes considerably over time.[2] The most authoritative single statement of this official ideology is the Party program, of which there have been three so far. The third program, adopted under Nikita Khrushchev in 1961, was the one inherited by Gorbachev.

The 1961 program was an optimistic document, at least from the official viewpoint.[3] By 1970, it promised, the United States would be overtaken in gross and per capita production, and by 1980 communism "in the main" would be established in the USSR itself. Functions such as policing and sport would be taken over from the state by groups of citizens, and hard manual labor and town/country differences would gradually be eliminated. Everyone would have a separate apartment and a guaranteed one-month paid holiday.

Not only was this program not fulfilled, but it also soon became unmentionable, at least in print, and no more was heard of the dates by which its ambitious targets were to be achieved. Leonid Brezhnev (general secretary, 1964–82) introduced the notion of "developed socialism," which was a stage of development that would last for many years before a transition to communism could be contemplated.[4] His successors—Andropov and Konstantin Chernenko (general secretaries: 1982–84 and 1984–85, respectively)—made it clear that the Soviet Union was "only at the beginning" of developed socialism, and called for more attention to immediate and practical tasks than to what V. I. Lenin had called the "distant, beautiful and rosy future."[5] The program became increasingly out of line with these new emphases, and in 1981 it was decided to redraft it. The drafting commission, chaired latterly by Gorbachev, published a preliminary version of the new program in October 1985; a final slightly amended version was adopted by the 27th Party Congress in March 1986. Gorbachev told the Congress that some had argued that this should be a new fourth Party program, not a new version of the third, because the changes it contained were so considerable.[6]

The old program, for instance, was presented as a "program for the building of communist society"; the new program talks only about the "planned and all round perfection of socialism." In 1961 it was argued that socialism alone could abolish exploitation, economic crisis, and poverty; in 1986 it is claimed only that socialism offers "advantages" and is superior to capitalism. No dates or stages are presented through which the transition to communism is to proceed (forecasts of this kind are described as "harmful"); and there are no references to the increasing provision of free public services, to the one-month paid holiday, or to the withering away of the state, a classic Marxist goal. (Some had always maintained that the only thing that would wither away was the *idea* that the state would wither away. They turned out to be right.) Indeed, there are few references to "communism" of any kind in the new program; far more emphasis is placed upon eliminating defects such as profiteering, parasitism, and careerism. All this is in line with the tendency of recent years to retreat from utopianism and to place much more emphasis upon practical, short-term, and even disciplinarian objectives.

There has been some continuity, but perhaps a greater degree of change, in government and politics since Gorbachev's accession.[7] The process of leadership renewal, for instance, that was begun under Andropov, has been pushed far and rapidly; indeed, we have recently seen perhaps the greatest turnover in the Soviet leadership since the 1930s. Gorbachev showed his political strength just one month after his accession by bringing two associates (Yegor Ligachev and Nikolai Ryzhkov) straight from outside the Politburo to full membership, bypassing the candidate stage. In July 1985 his presumed rival for the succession, Grigorii Romanov, was compelled to resign on "health" grounds from both the Politburo and the Secretariat. More changes followed at the 27th Party Congress in March 1986, including the appointment of the first woman member of the leadership (Alexandra Biryukova, who joined the Secretariat) in the last twenty years. More changes have followed at the Central Committee plenary meetings in 1986 and 1987. The outcome is that well over one half of the membership of both Politburo and Secretariat is entirely new to the leadership since Gorbachev's own accession. These changes are particularly striking in the Secretariat, which has become the powerhouse of the new administration. There have been parallel and no less extensive changes in the Council of Ministers, the Komsomol, the diplomatic service, and elsewhere.

There also have been changes in what might be called political style, above all in terms of *glasnost* (openness). This has meant more open criticism of shortcomings in Soviet life and of those responsible, more attention to the "dark sides" of Soviet life—such as prostitution, drug addiction, and violent crime—and better statistics on all aspects of Soviet life including life expectancy and infant mortality. There has even been some openness to non-Soviet and non-Socialist points of view in the Soviet media—for instance, in the form of interviews with Western politicians such as Paul Warnke and Zbigniew Brzezinski, or in the form of articles in the Soviet press. *Pravda*, for example, began a new regular column early in 1987 entitled "From Different Positions," which allowed representative Western figures (the first was Senator Robert Dole) to set out their views in full and without editing before a Soviet audience. Western politicians like former West German Chancellor Helmut Schmidt have taken part in live Soviet television debates, and visiting Westerners, such as British Prime Minister Margaret Thatcher and U.S. Secretary of State George Shultz, have been interviewed on Soviet television and their remarks translated in full without significant distortion.[8]

Soviet leaders have become more accessible to ordinary members of the public through such means as walking tours of factories and neighborhoods and phone-in programs. Further changes in the direction of greater "democratization" of Soviet life have taken place in 1987, including the first multicandidate elections to local councils (Soviets) and the adoption of a law on referenda (the Soviet Constitution has always provided for such exercises, but none has so far been conducted). Changes in the criminal law (especially in the articles that concern "anti-Soviet agitation and propaganda") have been promised, and changes in the artistic and cultural sphere—with the publication of Boris Pasternak's novel *Doctor Zhivago*, and many previously unmentionable authors—have been perhaps the most striking of all.

There have been significant, if still rather modest, changes in the most important sphere of policy for all Soviet leaders: the economy. The main objective has been to reverse the stagnation and inertia of the later Brezhnev years, when, as Gorbachev put it to the 27th Party Congress, a "curious psychology—how to improve things without changing anything"—had been dominant.[9] It is easy enough in any political system to blame one's predecessors; more positively, the Congress adopted a new strategy with "acceleration" and "reconstruction" as its guiding principles. The rate of economic growth was to be raised (this was the "key to all our problems," in Gorbachev's view), and national income was to be doubled by the year 2000.[10]

Toward that end, science and technology were to be more closely associated with production; key sectors such as machine-tool building were to receive priority; more emphasis was to be placed upon reequipment and economy in the use of resources; Gosplan, the state planning committee, was to become more strategic and enterprises more independent of its control; and prices were to become more "flexible," although in ways that have not so far been made clear. The "human factor" was also to play a part, with greater rights for workers in their workplace, including—under a new law on the state enterprise adopted in 1987—the right periodically to elect the factory management. The private and cooperative sectors were to receive more prominence, especially through a law on "individual economic activity," which took effect in May 1987.[11] All this is not, despite what the *Washington Post* has suggested, the reintroduction of capitalism. The law on individual economic activity, for instance, explicitly excludes the employment of others or anything other than part-time work. However, it does show, as does the antialcoholism campaign, that this is a leadership prepared to address these issues more seriously and thoroughly than any we have seen since the Second World War.

Finally, we have seen what the Russians have described as "new thinking" in foreign policy and strategy.[12] Gorbachev attaches quite exceptional importance to this sphere, as his extensive travels abroad, for instance, have demonstrated. As evidenced by meetings in 1986–87 with Senators Gary Hart and Edward Kennedy and with former Secretary of State Henry Kissinger, he also has been willing to give time to visiting Westerners, even to those not currently in government. He has taken personal charge of the making of foreign policy through the appointment of Georgian Party First Secretary Edward Shevardnadze as foreign minister and through the recall of Anatoly Dobrynin from his post as ambassador to the United States to head the foreign policy apparatus of the Central Committee.

Gorbachev has clearly staked a great deal upon improvements in East-West relations and in arms control in particular. For Gorbachev the INF treaty is a vital demonstration of successful foreign policy. A good deal of his foreign dealings are oriented toward Western public opinion, and thus might be characterized as imagemaking. However, we have seen some evidence of genuine "new thinking" as well as a fair amount of public relations. Gorbachev's new thinking was particularly apparent in his speech to the March 1986 Party Congress, especially in his open admission that global problems could not be resolved by either East or West alone; rather, they required "cooperation on a global scale" in a world that had become increasingly interdependent. The general secretary gave several examples of problems that required such a global and cooperative approach. These included ecology—environmental pollution and the depletion of natural resources—as well as terrorism, the problems of the Third World, cultural values, and, above all, the threat of nuclear war. He called on both peoples and governments—social democrats, religious organizations, and others, as well as Marxists—to work together to resolve such issues.[13] There have been some signs in other areas of cautious rethinking: for instance, a guarded criticism of the Brezhnev Doctrine in late 1985, and a warning to Third World revolutionary movements not to let their use of violence provoke a larger conflict.[14]

So far as policy is concerned, the Gorbachev leadership has brought forward a whole series of initiatives, including, most notably, a moratorium on nuclear tests from August 1985 (the anniversary of the Hiroshima explosion) to early 1987, when the failure of the United States to reciprocate led to a limited resumption. In January 1986, Gorbachev proposed gradual and complete disarmament, a proposal that was incorporated into the new version of the Party program adopted by the 27th Party Congress. There has been, in addition, much greater flexibility than ever before on such matters as verification, chemical weapons, and the place of British and French weapons in more general East-West disarmament negotiations. In some areas that have made a particular contribution to East-West tension—such as the presence of Soviet troops in Afghanistan—Gorbachev has shown a willingness to seek a solution and to take more than trivial measures toward that end on a unilateral basis (in this case through major troop withdrawals). He also has shown flexibility in his dealings with individual Western states. In relations with Britain, for instance, agreement has been reached on joint measures to combat terrorism, and the issue of czarist debts, outstanding since 1917, was amicably settled in mid-1986.[15]

The Gorbachev Leadership and Western Responses

There will be a wide variety of views on the manner in which the Western states should properly respond to Gorbachev, even if it is accepted that this is a leadership attempting a more far-reaching process of change in all areas of Soviet life than any we have seen since

Khrushchev, if not the early 1920s. In what follows I will set out three guiding principles that reflect not only my own views but also, I believe, those of a much wider European constituency. Indeed, these principles may encompass the views of some previous U.S. administrations and many figures prominent in American public life today (George Kennan, George McGovern, and Robert McNamara are obvious examples).

The first of the principles I would like to suggest is: let us at least seek to cooperate with this new Soviet administration, wherever we can, which may not be everywhere, and without sacrificing our own vital and quite legitimate interests. This must apply, above all, to arms control, where the survival of the species itself is at stake. The urgency of seeking such an accommodation may be felt more acutely in Europe than in the United States. Europe, more particularly Western Europe, is small and very densely populated, and richly endowed with cultural artifacts—buildings, monuments, and galleries—of the historic past. The European nations, moreover, have had some experience in dealing with Russia, and more recently the Soviet Union, as a partner in the European balance of power since the eighteenth century, and, for Britain and France, as a partner in the two world wars. Seen from this perspective, Europe is indeed a "common home" in which the Western and Eastern nations have been obliged to coexist for many centuries, and one that offers some lessons for the conduct of the rather broader relationship between the two superpowers.

I claim no specialist knowledge of contemporary strategy, but seen at least from Europe there can be little doubt that the Soviet leadership is seriously interested in reaching an agreement on arms control of a kind that would involve concessions, if not the sacrifice, of vital security interests. The series of Soviet proposals for the reduction of arms, up to and beyond the Reykjavik summit, certainly conveys this impression. The same impression is amplified by an awareness of the nature of the burden that military spending represents for an economy little more than one half the size of that of the United States, by an understanding of the Soviet Union's historical past, and, above all, by the Soviet experience of the Second World War. The United States last had foreign troops on its own soil in 1812. The only direct casualties on American soil during the Second World War (so I have been told) were four men who died while chasing a military balloon. And, of course, the United States is separated by an ocean on each side from every serious military adversary. The Soviet Union, by contrast, has been repeatedly invaded (by the United States, among other powers), and during the Second World War lost an estimated 20 million lives, more than forty times the losses that were sustained by Britain, proportional to population, and more than seventy times those of the United States. Indeed, Soviet losses during this period were greater than have been suffered by any major nation in any war.[16] There can be very few visitors to the Soviet Union who have not been impressed by the strength of popular feeling on the question of the maintenance of peace that stems, in part, from this experience.

Seen again from Europe, there is some objective basis for an agreement of a kind that would not threaten the vital interests of the major parties, although no such agreement is likely to result unless there is some political will to achieve it. According to respected international bodies, such as the Stockholm Peace Research Institute and the International Institute of Strategic Studies, there is a rough strategic parity between East and West, although not necessarily in every theater or in each separate category of weapons. The stockpiles of weapons that presently exist are also far greater than could possibly be needed for the purposes of deterrence. The American arsenal alone can destroy all Soviet cities of over 100,000 population at least forty-one times.[17]

There has been no shortage of proposals of a kind that could translate this rough strategic parity into an agreement that would permit, first, the containment, and then the reduction of present levels of armaments. The Palme Commission, which had both Eastern and Western participation, proposed a number of initiatives in its report on "common security"; there was the formula agreed on in the famous "walk in the woods"; or there were the proposals advanced at Reykjavik, perhaps in some modified form. A very precise formula has been proposed by McGovern: the ending of nuclear tests in the United States as well as in the Soviet Union; the liquidation of old weapon systems, so as to remain within the limits prescribed by SALT II; and an agreement to limit research on SDI for the next ten years in return for the Soviet Union's agreement to a 50 percent reduction of strategic weapons and the total elimination of intermediate weapons. *Pravda*'s editor commented that this would be a "big step forward," if not as significant an agreement as could have followed the Reykjavik summit.[18]

An agreement along lines such as this, or at least some evidence of determined moves toward such an agreement, is important for U.S.-European relations and not just for relations between the superpowers. Right or wrong, the approach to East-West relations of the Reagan administration—terms like the "evil empire," the apparent influence of religious and émigré advisers, violations of international law as in the Libya bombings, and the declared intention of exceeding the limits of SALT II—has made a bad impression in Western Europe. In fact, if opinion polls on such matters can be believed, Gorbachev has become a more popular and trusted figure in many European countries than President Ronald Reagan has in the last several years. Gorbachev, according to West German polls, is seen as more genuinely committed to arms control, while Reagan is blamed for the failure of the Reykjavik summit. In Britain, again according to the polls, Reagan is trusted less than Gorbachev, and the Soviet leadership is seen as more genuinely committed to ending the arms race, although in neither country is there any sympathy for the Soviet system as such.[19] A constructive approach to East-West relations is vital if this widening gulf is to be contained, and I believe there is a greater willingness in Western Europe than before to help make this possible by, for instance, increased spending on conventional arms.

The main obstacle to moves in this direction is probably the "Russian threat"—the perception, widely held and not without foundation, of the USSR as a hostile, expansionist, and formidably armed power that represents a serious and immediate threat to Western interests. There can certainly be no doubt that the USSR, to take just one of these points, is formidably armed. Yet, we must try to keep a sense of proportion about such matters and remember to relate military potential to the relevant defense circumstances. The Soviet Union, for instance, defends an enormous area (about one sixth of the world's land surface), with the world's longest land frontier, and with important adversaries on its eastern as well as its western front. The Soviet Union may spend more on defense than the United States, although comparisons of this kind are fraught with difficulty; the USSR also maintains more men under arms and spends a greater proportion of its GNP on defense than is the case in the United States. But the NATO countries as a whole, even if France is somewhat artificially excluded, spend more on defense than the Warsaw Pact powers taken as a whole. NATO's military manpower is slightly superior, and its forces are almost certainly better trained, better equipped, and more reliable in combat situations.[20]

We also need to keep Soviet "expansion" in perspective. The USSR, in fact, has not been a particularly successful imperial power. As Michael Klare has detailed in Chapter 9, some advances have been achieved from the Soviet point of view in countries like Afghanistan and in parts of Africa, but this must be viewed in light of Soviet deemphasis on force projection in the Third World and must be set against the loss of China, Somalia, Indonesia, Ghana, and many other countries. The USSR's allies in Eastern Europe are mostly unreliable, and the world Communist movement has more or less collapsed. As Jane Curry discusses in Chapter 10, even in Eastern Europe "Europeanization" has loosened Soviet control. In fact, Soviet global influence is definitely in decline, according to an investigation recently made public by the Center for Defense Information in the United States. Over the entire postwar period (1945–80), the center found there had been a net increase in the number of countries under Soviet influence. However, the number of countries had greatly increased; thus, the proportion of countries worldwide under Soviet influence was actually down, from a peak of 14 percent in the late 1950s to about 12 percent in 1980. The same was true if the countries concerned were ranked in GNP or population terms. "If these data demonstrate anything," the report concluded, "it is the decline of Soviet world influence since the 1980s." [21]

Nor should we get carried away by alarmist reports—reports that our own military establishments have a vested interest in purveying—about the quality of Soviet armed forces. Other sources, particularly those that are based on the firsthand impressions of recent émigrés, convey a rather different picture, one of racial tension, indiscipline, and equipment that is often a more obvious danger to those who operate it than to the enemy. For instance, according to Alexander Cockburn's *The Soviet Threat* (1983), the T-64 tank, hailed in the West as a major advance in Soviet armaments, had to be taken out of production because of its poor reliability and the tendency for its mechanical loading arm to select the arm or leg of its gunner and load that instead of a shell. As one American army officer told Cockburn, "Perhaps that's how the Red Army gets its soprano section." And the T-72 tank, although conveniently small, was cramped inside, unreliable in service, and a sledgehammer had to be used to change gears.

Soviet troops, Cockburn also found, suffered from poor dietary and living conditions and had a drinking problem of epic proportions (certainly much greater than the comparable problems that exist in NATO armies). Soldiers officially were permitted no alcohol at all, but it was often mailed to them in a variety of containers, or equipment was sold to pay for it, or all kinds of substitutes were used including antifreeze and even shoe polish. The MiG-25 fighter-bomber, which needed about 1,000 pounds of alcohol for its braking and electronic systems, was known for this reason in the Soviet air force as the "flying restaurant." [22]

Some indication of the importance of these factors emerges from a report that appeared in the Western press concerning a Soviet tank that got lost on maneuvers in Czechoslovakia as night was falling. The tank was driven into a village where the only pub was still open and then sold to the pub owner for two cases of vodka with some pickles and herring thrown in "as a gesture of solidarity." The crew was found sleeping it off some days later; the tank itself, however, could not be found. It later emerged that the owner had sold it to a metal recycling firm that acknowledged that it had indeed received a large quantity of high-grade scrap.[23] An incident of this kind is hardly likely to be typical; and no one should doubt that the USSR remains a substantial and formidable military power, particularly when its own territory has been invaded. But neither should we exaggerate the threat it represents to Western interests, much as it would suit some sections of our own societies to do so.

If a more satisfactory relationship between East and West is possible, my final guiding principle would be that the negotiation of such a relationship is too important to be left to politicians or diplomats alone. My own view is that the best hope for an attainable and stable East-West accommodation must rest not on changing administrations or passing strategic fashions such as SDI but on direct popular links of various kinds based upon the fullest possible information, reciprocal access, and interaction. A process of this kind has been called "citizen diplomacy" or "détente from below"; it means the expansion of links between East and West of all kinds—for example, tourism, journalism, sports, foreign trade, academic and scientific exchanges, cultural and religious contacts, and medical cooperation.[24]

The essential element in such exchanges is people to people, rather than government to government. The development of closer links of this kind within Europe probably has helped to ease postwar tension, such as between France and Germany, which have fought three major wars since 1870. Direct popular links cannot dispose of basic differences of interest but at least can help to spread understanding and to avoid the unfortunate tendency to demonize one's opponents. It is a kind of "confidence building" between people. And the United States, as it happens, is particularly rich precisely in its tradition of citizen self-organization of this sort.

Contacts of this kind might typically embrace closer business and trading links between East and West. American trade with the USSR, for instance, apart from grain, has remained relatively small and subject to all kinds of political pressures. The United States presently sells less to the Soviet Union than to Belgium or Austria, and imports from the Soviet Union are at about the same level as those from the Ivory Coast—hardly a major trading nation.[25] Soviet trade with the United States (unlike Polish trade) does not enjoy most-favored-nation status, and embargoes of various kinds apply not simply to technology or to firms based on U.S. territory. Trading links of this kind can hardly hope to provide a stable basis for relations between the two superpowers, still less to accommodate the long-term, large-scale projects that are characteristic of Soviet economic management.

More important, however, are direct links between the two people (and between East and West more generally), which join people not just through what they produce but through the whole range of capacities that are characteristic of being human. One may legitimately hope for improvements, for instance, in the teaching of foreign languages and in media coverage of the USSR and its affairs. The appearance of a daily English-language edition of *Pravda* is another step in the right direction. Electronic means of communication also are of growing importance in this connection—for example, Soviet television broadcasts that are enriching many college programs (and not just Russian-language ones) and the "citizen summits," such as the television satellite link of early 1986 between Seattle and Leningrad. In 1987 a comparable "space bridge" linked U.S. and Soviet parliamentarians.[26] Links of this kind have been encouraged by the Esalen Institute of San Francisco, monitored by the Institute for Soviet-American Relations in Washington, DC, and furthered by bodies such as the Committee on East-West Accord.

To conclude, no one would wish to suggest that better knowledge and understanding can or even should resolve all the differences between the superpowers and their allies, but it can dispel some harmful myths and help to avoid extreme and sometimes dangerous courses of action. The same knowledge and understanding may guard against the tendency, particularly in America, to what has been called the "paranoid style" of politics.[27] There is certainly a lot of room for the improvement of our understanding of each other's societies, especially in the United States. A 1985 *New York Times* poll found that 76 percent of those asked were unable to identify Gorbachev as the Soviet Union's new leader, and 44 percent did not know that the United States and the USSR had been allies in the Second World War (28 percent thought they had been enemies). In another poll, 36 percent of those asked expressed the view that China, India, and Monaco were all parts of the Soviet Union.[28] It is surely incumbent on all of us, as scholars, students, parents, and citizens, to do what we can to change a situation of this kind, which is as dangerous as it is unfortunate.

Notes

[1] *Materialy vneocherednogo Plenuma Tsentral'nogo Komiteta KPSS, 11 marta 1985 goda* (Moscow: Politizdat, 1985), p. 9.

[2] For a fuller discussion see Stephen White and Alex Pravda, eds., *Ideology and Soviet Politics* (New York: St. Martin's, 1988).

³The program is reprinted with extensive commentaries in Leonard Schapiro, ed., *The USSR and the Future* (New York: Praeger, 1963), and in other sources.

⁴See Alfred B. Evans, Jr., "Developed Socialism in Soviet Ideology," *Soviet Studies* 29 (July 1977): 409–28; and Evans, "The Decline of Developed Socialism: Some Trends in Recent Soviet Ideology," *Soviet Studies* 38 (January 1986): 1–23.

⁵Chernenko's citation from Lenin is in his *Narod i partiya ediny: izbrannye stat'i i rechi* (Moscow: Politizdat, 1984), p. 456.

⁶*XXVII s'ezd Kommunisticheskoi partii Sovetskogo Soyuza 25 fevralya – 6 marta 1986 marta 1986 goda. Stenograficheskii otchet*, 3 vols. (Moscow: Politizdat, 1986), 1:116. The program, as adopted, is in ibid., pp. 554–623. An extensive documentary record of the Congress's proceedings is available in *Current Soviet Policies IX* (Columbus, OH: Current Digest of the Soviet Press, 1986).

⁷More detailed accounts of leadership changes under Gorbachev are available in the reports issued by Radio Liberty Research or the regular surveys of Soviet affairs in the *Yearbook on International Communist Affairs*, ed. Richard F. Staar (Stanford: Hoover Institution Press, annual).

⁸See, for instance, David Wedgwood Benn, "'Glasnost' in the Soviet Press: Liberalization or Public Relations," *Journal of Communist Studies* 3 (September 1987):267–76; and on Soviet television see Ellen Mickiewicz, *New York Times*, February 22, 1987.

⁹*XXVII s'ezd* 1: 24.

¹⁰The Broad Directives of the Economic and Social Development of the USSR for the period 1986–90 and up to the year 2000, as adopted by the Congress, are in ibid. 2:221–92. The recent performance of the Soviet economy is considered in Trevor Buck and John Cole, *Modern Soviet Economic Performance* (Oxford: Blackwell, 1987); and in the U.S. Congress Joint Economic Committee's symposium, *Gorbachev's Economic Plans* (Washington, DC: Government Publications Office, 1987).

¹¹See ibid. for an account of these changes. On current debates see Alec Nove, "Radical Reform, Problems and Prospects," *Soviet Studies* 39 (July 1987): 452–67.

¹²See, for instance, Margot Light, "New Thinking in Soviet Foreign Policy," *Coexistence* 24 (December 1987); and Stephen Shenfield, *The Nuclear Predicament: Explorations in Soviet Ideology* (London: Routledge, 1987).

¹³*XXVII s'ezd* 1:37–42.

¹⁴See respectively Yu. S. Novopashin, "Politicheskie otnosheniya stran sotsializma," *Rabochii klass i sovremennyi mir*, no. 5 (1985): 55–65, esp. p. 60; and *Pravda*, November 14, 1986. Yevgeny Primakov, director of the Institute of the World Economy and International Relations, has argued that the export of revolution is now "outdated" as a foreign policy concept. See *Pravda*, July 10, 1987.

¹⁵See, respectively, *The Guardian*, November 5, 1986; and *Financial Times*, January 29, 1987.

[16]Geoffrey Hosking, *A History of the Soviet Union* (London: Fontana, 1985), p. 296.

[17]Jim Garrison and Pyare Shivpuri, *The Russian Threat: Its Myths and Realities* (New York: Gateway Books, 1985), p. 18.

[18]*Pravda*, January 12, 1987.

[19]See *The Independent*, November 13, 1986; and *The Guardian*, November 4, 1986. Subsequent polls have indicated that up to eight times as many citizens of West Germany, Britain, and France give credit to the Soviet Union for recent arms control progress as give it to the United States. See *The Guardian*, June 8, 1987.

[20]Comparisons of this kind are available in *Military Balance* and *Strategic Survey* (London: International Institute of Strategic Studies, annual); and *World Armaments and Disarmament* (Oxford: Stockholm International Peace Research Institute, annual). On the Warsaw Treaty Organization more specifically see David Holloway and Jane M. O. Sharp, eds., *The Warsaw Pact: Alliance in Transition* (Ithaca, NY: Cornell University Press, 1984); and Daniel N. Nelson, *Alliance Behavior in the Warsaw Pact* (Boulder, CO: Westview, 1986).

[21]Center for Defense Information, "Soviet Geopolitical Momentum: Myth or Menace?" in Robbin F. Laird and Erik P. Hoffman, eds., *Soviet Foreign Policy in a Changing World* (New York: Aldine, 1986), pp. 704–6.

[22]See Andrew Cockburn, *The Soviet Threat* (New York: Vintage, 1983), chaps. 3, 8.

[23]*The Guardian*, August 5, 1985.

[24]Exchanges of this kind are considered, often with practical recommendations, in Clare Ryle and Jim Garrison, eds., *Citizens' Diplomacy* (London: Merlin, 1986); Don Carlson and Craig Comstock, eds., *Citizen Summitry: Keeping the Peace When It Matters too Much to be Left to Politicians* (Los Angeles: Tarcher, 1986); Ann Pettit, ed., *DIY Détente* (London: Quartet, 1987); and Craig Comstock et al., *Global Partners: Citizen Exchange with the Soviet Union* (Lafayette, CA: Ark Communications Institute, forthcoming). I am grateful to Paul Schicke for allowing me to see a copy of this last item prior to publication.

[25]*M. S. Gorbachev: Speeches and Writings*, intro. Robert Maxwell (Oxford: Pergamon, 1986), pp. 312, 314.

[26]*Soviet Weekly*, December 20, 1986.

[27]See Richard Hofstadter, *The Paranoid Style in American Politics* (New York: Knopf, 1965).

[28]Cited in Robert Karl Manoff, "The Media's Moscow," *American Association for the Advancement of Slavic Studies Newsletter* 26, no. 5 (November 1986): 3. For what it may be worth, what appears to be the first survey of its kind in the USSR has suggested that better Soviet-American relations would be welcomed by most Soviet citizens. In a poll carried out in several towns in the RSFSR following the Geneva summit, respondents were asked to define their attitude toward the American people, and were given a range of possible answers ranging from "with great sympathy" to "with hostility." Some 80 percent chose a "positive" response, 10 percent took a "watchful" attitude, 4.4 percent claimed to take an attitude of "great sympathy" toward the American

people, and only 0.4 percent had a "hostile" attitude. These and related findings are reported in V. N. Ivanov, "Bez'yadernyi mir i obshchestvennoe soznanie," *Kommunist*, no. 5 (1987): 117–19.

8

The Soviet-American Arms Control Dialogue before and after Reykjavik

Jack Mendelsohn

The U.S. Record

A review of the arms control dialogue during the Reagan administration reveals not only a remarkable series of retrograde U.S. decisions on the issue but also a marked determination to attempt to change the fundamental "rules of the game" that have regulated the Soviet-American strategic relationship for two decades. A brief recapitulation of U.S. actions during this period makes it difficult to draw any other conclusion.

In 1983 the Reagan administration announced its SDI program, described by the president as intended to render ballistic missiles—the mainstay of the Soviet Union's strategic deterrent—"impotent and obsolete." To many, Ronald Reagan's program was destined to undermine the relatively stable balance established between offensive and defensive weapons in the late 1960s. Then, one year later, the first in a series of "noncompliance" reports was released. These reports have been highly critical of Soviet treaty behavior, claiming that there exists a "pattern of Soviet violations" of arms control agreements to which they were a party.

In 1985 the Reagan administration unilaterally reinterpreted the ABM Treaty, the only existing strategic weapons agreement and the keystone of nuclear arms control. The reinterpretation, which totally reversed thirteen years of practice and the overall intent of the agreement, would permit rather than prohibit the testing and development of space-based and other mobile antiballistic missile systems based on exotic technologies. Furthermore, in 1986 the administration's political commitment not to undercut the essential provisions of the unratified SALT II Treaty was repudiated by Reagan. This repudiation was based on claims of alleged Soviet noncompliance with the treaty, accusations that the chairman of the U.S. House of Representatives Permanent Select Committee on Intelligence maintains are "highly ambiguous and have not been represented fully and accurately by the administration."[1]

More recently the United States has attempted to move closer to a decision to adopt as American policy the 1985 reinterpretation of the ABM Treaty, and to move (under the expanded development program permitted by this reinterpretation) to the testing and early deployment of elements of a space-based kinetic-kill ABM system.[2]

The Soviet Record

The Soviet Union, on the other hand, has been acting during the first two years of the Gorbachev period as though it might be seriously interested in some form of nuclear arms control. In August 1985 the Soviet Union initiated a unilateral nuclear testing moratorium, which was extended several times and eventually lasted for nineteen months. During this same period the United States tested at least twenty-six nuclear devices. In January 1986, a few months after the test moratorium was begun, the Soviet Union announced a comprehensive plan for disarmament by the year 2000. The plan combined a millennial vision of a future without nuclear weapons with practical suggestions for near-term agreements (for example, INF) and a sharp critique of the negative impact of the SDI program on strategic arms control.

In July 1986 the Soviets agreed to allow the National Resources Defense Council, a nongovernmental organization, to establish seismic monitoring stations in the Soviet Union to verify Soviet compliance with its own unilateral nuclear testing moratorium. The USSR showed further signs of overcoming its decades-old penchant for secrecy when it concluded a Conference on Disarmament in Europe agreement with first-time provisions for the on-site inspection by third parties of Soviet military activities. (The Soviet Union had previously agreed to on-site inspection of peaceful nuclear explosions [the 1974 Peaceful Nuclear Explosion Treaty] and of nuclear power facilities [a 1985 accord with the International Atomic Energy Agency], and had agreed in principle to on-site monitoring of a comprehensive test ban in 1978.)

The Soviet Union demonstrated amazing flexibility and diplomatic skill when, in October 1986, it agreed at the Reykjavik summit to accept steep reductions (about 50 percent) in strategic weapons and to eliminate intermediate-range nuclear weapons in Europe provided appropriate constraints were placed on the testing and development of SDI. The USSR followed up this far-reaching set of proposals in February 1987 when it offered to delink INF from an overall strategic/SDI settlement, to conclude a separate agreement on the elimination of intermediate-range weapons in Europe and, when shorter range INF became an obstacle to agreement, to withdraw or eliminate them as well. The signing of an INF accord at the third Reagan-Gorbachev summit in December 1987 reflects the consequence of such new Soviet flexibility.

Finally, in April 1987 the Soviet Union offered to carry out reciprocal nuclear tests at national test sites to help establish a better basis for estimating teleseismically the yield of explosions permitted under the unratified Threshold Test Ban Treaty. This apparent Soviet receptivity to arms control can be attributed to several factors. First, after a number of years of suffering under a "senilocracy," the Soviet Union, at last, is under the direction of a dynamic, "live" leader who is able to make decisions, to respond more flexibly to the challenges of East-West public diplomacy, and to appreciate the impact of Soviet behavior on other nations.

Second, this new leadership has been able to reassess its own policies and seeks to establish a new and more favorable image, particularly in view of the highly negative reaction to Soviet behavior generated between 1975 and 1985. In the late 1970s and early 1980s the Soviet Union provoked strongly adverse responses to its SS-20 deployments, its invasion of Afghanistan, its strategic modernization programs, and its walkout from the Geneva negotiations.

Third, the Soviet Union is embarked on an economic, social, and political modernization program for which relief from the pressure of an expanding military competition with the United States is clearly desired and actively sought. To aid in this modernization, the Soviet Union seeks improved relations with the technologically and economically developed world—that is, the United States and its allies.

Finally, the Soviet Union is in the midst of an extended internal debate over whether nuclear weapons can usefully further Soviet goals in theater warfare. This debate has raised serious doubts as to the utility of additional investment in nuclear weapons and focused increased attention on high-technology conventional weapons and to the refurbishment of the nation's industrial infrastructure to support the demands of modern, high-technology conventional warfare.

Control of the Agenda

Since arms control persists as the centerpiece of Soviet-American relations, and since the United States has been reluctant or unable to pursue a coherent policy in this area, the control, scope, and pace of the superpower agenda during the 1985 to 1987 period have been basically in the hands of the Soviet Union. This is strikingly evident when comparing key events in the arms control dialogue of the past few years. Contrast, for example, Soviet behavior during the 1985 Geneva and 1986 Reykjavik summits. At the November 1985 summit most observers believed that President Reagan succeeded in dominating the publicity, in projecting the image of a strong leader, in controlling the exchange with Mikhail Gorbachev, and in appearing capable of at least managing the Soviet-American dialogue, if not improving it.

At the 1986 summit, which was proposed by the Soviets, Reagan's performance was clearly outclassed by that of the general secretary. The president appeared confused and frustrated; returned home to speculation (which only reinforced the impression) that the United States had been "lured into a trap"; traded recriminations with Congress, the Joint Chiefs of Staff, and the Soviet leadership over who said what to whom; was criticized by even his staunchest conservative supporters; and ultimately lost the public relations battle to "smiling Mike."

Consider also the differences in the Soviets' handling of the 1961 and 1987 nuclear testing moratoriums. In 1961 the Soviet Union, after announcing on August 30 that it intended to resume nuclear testing (the United States had abandoned its commitment to the moratorium at the end of 1959 but had not resumed testing), launched an unprecedentedly intensive test series the following day. Within sixty days of the end of its moratorium the Soviet Union had conducted thirty atmospheric tests and exploded more megatonnage than the total of all previous tests. The series included a gigantic 57-megaton explosion, believed to be a scaled-down version of the Soviets' ultimate terror weapon, a 100-megaton warhead.[3]

The Soviet Union announced the end of its recent unilateral nuclear testing moratorium in December 1986 and linked its first test to the initial U.S. test in the new year. Only after two U.S. tests in 1987 did the Soviet Union explode one sub-20-kiloton weapon on February 26, on a day that found the event submerged in U.S. domestic news (the release of the Tower Report), and just two days before publicly proposing to delink the INF negotiations from the overall arms control package discussed at Reykjavik.

Finally, there are obvious differences between the Soviets' handling of the 1977 and 1986 U.S. strategic arms reduction proposals. In 1977, when the newly installed Carter administration attempted to propose reductions in the levels of strategic weapons agreed to at the 1974 Vladivostok summit, the Soviet Union angrily rejected the proposals, accused the United States of attempting to undo a previous accord, and sent Secretary of State Cyrus Vance home from Moscow empty-handed and frustrated. And, in 1981, when the West first put forward its "zero-option" proposal for the elimination of all INF, Leonid Brezhnev vigorously rejected the offer as totally inequitable.

Between 1985 and 1986, on the other hand, the Soviet Union agreed, at least in principle, to large-scale reductions (about 40 to 50 percent) in strategic weapons, and it had accepted massive INF reductions (from over 1,300 to 100 warheads),[4] tantamount to accepting the "zero-option" it had rejected five years earlier. It also trumped the U.S. proposal for 50 percent reductions in strategic nuclear forces by proposing, in January 1986 and again at the Reykjavik summit, the total elimination of nuclear weapons. And it trumped the U.S. proposal for collateral constraints on short-range INF systems by proposing to eliminate these forces as well: the "double-zero" option.

In sum, through a mix of new blood, sophisticated operational savvy, unexpected openness, and diplomatic aggressiveness, the Soviets have seized hold of the major elements in the Soviet-American foreign policy and arms control agenda, outmaneuvered its prime adversary in the public arena, and forced the United States into a largely reactive, defensive mode.

Soviet Motives and Objectives

If one can conclude that the Soviet Union is indeed interested in more than simply embarrassing the Reagan administration, what might be the motivating factors behind this interest in exploring the further reaches of arms control? There are, it would seem, at least four factors driving current Soviet policy in this area that deserve exploration. First, there is a significant body of evidence accumulating since at least the mid-1970s that the Soviet Union has been seriously questioning the utility of nuclear weapons for theater warfighting. Arguments supporting this change in Soviet attitudes toward nuclear weapons have been based on a careful analysis of Soviet doctrinal literature by Mary Fitzgerald and on the restructuring of military forces by Michael McGwire. They note such authoritative statements as that of Marshal N. V. Ogarkov, who considers limited nuclear options impossible in practice and likely to lead to "a catastrophe that can call into question the fate of life itself on the whole earth."[5]

Chief of the General Staff Marshal S. F. Akhromeyev, using U.S. doctrine as a foil for discussing projected Soviet doctrine, wrote that "'the inevitability of a retaliatory nuclear strike and its catastrophic consequences' have convinced the probable opponent to concentrate on developing conventional weapons that are characterized by greater effectiveness in yield, range, and accuracy. Methods of conducting military action with automated, precision-guided conventional weapons are also being improved. Soviet military science has not ignored these trends, he continued, and 'takes them into account in the training and command and control of troops.'"6

It is also possible to trace the change in Soviet attitude toward nuclear weapons through the evolution in their arms control negotiating position. For example, even knowledgeable observers often overlook the fact that in 1979 the Soviet Union agreed to limit its strategic nuclear forces to 2,400 launchers, to reduce those to 2,250 within one year, and committed itself to pursue further reductions. In 1982 the Soviet Union proposed a limit of 1,800 on strategic delivery vehicles—this was before the SDI program had been announced by the United States and was coincidentally the same figure the Soviet Union had rejected when proposed by the Carter administration in 1977—and then had reduced this level to 1,250 (Soviet) and 1,600 (U.S.) delivery vehicles by mid-1985.7 The same sort of evolution in the Soviet position took place in the INF discussions.8

Second, the Soviet Union has exhibited an evident desire to moderate the military and technological competition with the United States. The Soviets for some time have been quite explicit about their technological—and strategic—concerns, particularly as manifested by the latest twist in the arms spiral: the SDI program. It is quite clear that the Soviet Union considers that SDI could lead to high-tech breakthroughs in the conventional military sphere. Ogarkov took note of this development when he noted that "the rapid development of science and technology in recent years creates real preconditions for the emergence in the very near future of even more destructive and previously unknown types of weapons based on new physical principles. Work on these new types of weapons is already in progress in a number of countries, for example the US. Their development is a reality of the very near future, and it would be serious mistake not to take account of this right now."9

The Soviets also believe that SDI could lead to new and highly specialized offensive weapons and improve U.S. ability to operate in and threaten the Soviet Union from space. Akhromeyev, for one, has claimed that "the weapons envisioned by the SDI program [for example, lasers and other directed energy weapons] are strike weapons, with which the US hoped to 'blind' the other side, make it deaf and dumb, catch it unaware and deny it any possibility of retaliating against a nuclear attack."10

The Soviets also fear that SDI would lead to destabilizing developments in the strategic situation. In the same statement noted above, Akhromeyev argues that "they [the United States] are adding to the strategic offensive potential and shaping it up for a first strike with the hope of impunity."[11] And SDI will require additional resources to accelerate a counterpart Soviet SDI program. Gorbachev made this point explicitly in his press conference after Reykjavik: "The US wants to exhaust the Soviet Union economically through the build-up of sophisticated and costly space weapons."

SDI also will require additional resources to increase the number and survivability of Soviet offensive forces. Akhromeyev has noted that "if no ban [on space weapons] exists, an unchecked race will start ...nothing will remain for us but to adopt counter-measures in the field of both offensive and other, not excluding defensive, armaments, including those based in outer space."[12] And SDI will require additional resources to attend to ASAT and ATBM countermeasures. Oleg Bikov, vice director of the Soviet Union's Institute of World Economy and International Relations, has taken note of the similarity between SDI and ASAT technology, stating that it would be tempting to employ spaced-based defense against the Soviets' satellites.

In addition, SDI will require the Soviet Union to concentrate on critical technologies, such as computers and sensing systems, in which the United States holds a clear (and increasing) advantage. At Reykjavik, Gorbachev noted that "the US Administration...is confident of US technological superiority and is hoping to achieve, through SDI, military superiority."[13]

A third factor affecting Soviet arms control policy is a desire to revise the image of the Soviet Union that developed in the late 1970s and early 1980s based on such public relations disasters as SS-20, Afghanistan, Krasnoyarsk, the Geneva walkout, and the KAL shootdown. Gorbachev's intention is to assume a forceful, forward, pro-arms control posture and engage the United States in its chosen arena of public diplomacy. There is abundant evidence of this goal, such as Gorbachev's speech at the February 1987 disarmament conference in Moscow, which contains such statements as:

> Since Hiroshima and Nagasaki, war (at any rate, world war) ceased to be a continuation of politics by other means. Nuclear war would incinerate the architects of such a policy, too; [or]

> The Reykjavik meeting...approached the issue of reducing nuclear arsenals in an entirely new conceptual key, as a political and psychological problem rather than just a military and technical [one]....When both sides agreed at Reykjavik

to make deep cuts in their nuclear arsenals and then eliminate them entirely, they virtually recognized that nuclear weapons can no longer effectively guarantee security.

This speech, as well as the entire conference, was only one in a series of Soviet moves (for example, the July 1985 testing moratorium) to take the high ground in the battle for a better public image, most of which date from Gorbachev's assumption of office.

The USSR also wishes to stimulate critical, divisive reactions to the United States and its policies, and to exploit the incoherence of the U.S. position. This fourth objective has been very much in the news as a result of the February 1987 Soviet proposal to delink a "zero" INF agreement from an overall strategic settlement. The NATO allies, for differing reasons, were in varying states of dismay and disarray over the possibility of actually eliminating INF from Europe. They saw political, strategic, military, and economic problems in a "zero" INF agreement, with the most outspoken comment coming from the French defense minister who called it a "nuclear Munich."

No less an analyst than Henry Kissinger has argued that "the removal of American and Soviet medium-range missiles from Europe leaves unimpaired the Soviet ability to devastate Europe with short-range missiles and ICBMs. It eliminates the American ability to retaliate from Europe. It thus magnifies European fears that the United States might not respond to a nuclear attack confined to Europe, much less to a conventional one. With such an agreement, the Soviet strategy to decouple the defense of Europe from that of the United States will gain momentum."[14]

In addition to the criticism of the allies and the U.S. foreign policy establishment, Congress, in a devastatingly critical report on Reykjavik released in April 1987 by the Defense Policy Panel of the House Committee on Armed Services, concluded that "zero INF does not help (Allied) cohesiveness" and recommended that the United States "not insist on zero INF." This is precisely what did result at the Washington summit, and we can expect to witness some of the political fallout from a "global zero" INF accord during the U.S. INF ratification hearings and during debates in the councils of NATO.

The other areas wherein the Soviet Union has attempted to generate divisive reaction are SDI and the test moratorium. In the first case the allies attempted to circumscribe the SDI program (for example, Geoffrey Howe and Margaret Thatcher) and to forestall adoption of the reinterpretation of the ABM Treaty. More recently, West German Chancellor Helmut Kohl expressed concern that a unilateral U.S. decision to adopt the reinterpretation would derail the strategic arms negotiations. Canadian External Affairs Minister Joe Clark's letter to

Secretary of State George Shultz likewise suggested that Canada would not support the deployment of "near-term" BMDs or the more permissive interpretation of the ABM Treaty. Furthermore, Australian Prime Minister William Hayden remarked to Ambassador Edward L. Rowny (during the latter's visit to Canberra) that the successful conclusion of agreements providing for radical reductions in strategic nuclear forces depended on both sides' confidence that the ABM Treaty remained a reliable barrier to the pursuit of deployable wide-scale BMDs.

In the case of the testing moratorium the Soviets generated some resonance on this issue among segments of Western publics and among the nonaligned and Third World nations. However, they failed to capture elite opinion or to provoke any overwhelming condemnation of the United States for continuing testing from either its allies, Congress, or the establishment.

Outcomes

What can be made of the strategic dialogue of the mid-1980s? If the Soviet Union is indeed moving away from nuclear war-fighting options and is anxious, for various domestic as well as foreign policy reasons, to moderate the scope and pace of the competition with the United States, then we are likely to see a series of interwoven outcomes.

First, the Soviets will continue their efforts to constrain SDI. In terms of the challenge it poses to the economic and military plans of the Soviet Union, this anti-SDI effort is certain to remain one of the most prominent features in the Soviet-American strategic landscape. A second outcome is also certain: that there will be no major arms control settlement on strategic offensive systems *unless* and *until* assurances are in place concerning the future of the ABM Treaty and some constraints are placed on the SDI program.

Nonetheless, as a third outcome, one can expect continued Soviet efforts to engage the United States in other aspects of arms control, with limited success possible primarily at the margins. For example, we have seen the successful conclusion of the INF negotiations; the establishment of modified crisis control centers;[15] and the continuing negotiations on confidence-building measures, nuclear testing, and chemical arms. In this connection, a most vexing decision for the Soviet Union, and one that seems to have been made in February 1987, was whether to retain the linkage between strategic issues and INF and remain empty handed, or break off INF from the overall package and build pressure against SDI by achieving some success in a secondary area. A continuation of this same policy—that is, maintaining at least the perception of arms control momentum to help constrain SDI—seems to be behind the Soviet pledge at the Washington summit to seek a START treaty by the next superpower meeting.

Fourth, as long as the United States is perceived to be the nation threatening to abrogate accords (that is, SALT II and the ABM Treaty), there will be a low likelihood of "provocative" Soviet moves in the near future—through the balance of the Reagan administration and into the early part of the next presidency. This nonprovocative policy, including withdrawal from Afghanistan, represents a major change in Soviet international behavior and a much more subtle approach to its adversarial relationship with the United States. This new approach is directly attributable to a significantly more sophisticated Soviet leadership.

A fifth consequence of the strategic dialogue has been, and will be, a heightened role for third parties—such as Congress, the allies, and public opinion—in the Soviet-American relationship. This may be a transitory phenomenon brought about because the Reagan administration undermined confidence in the United States and generated an unprecedented amount of criticism for its policies and process. Allied reactions played a role in sharpening the SDI debate, in delaying for one year the overthrow of SALT II, and in forestalling the adoption of the ABM Treaty reinterpretation. The allies also played a role in the evolution of the U.S. INF position, from the initial German demand for deployment to their subsequent requirement for concurrent constraints on short-range systems. Congress, too, has been increasingly active in the arms control area and is likely to be the force—through budget limitations on military programs or direct challenges to administration actions—that determines whether and how the strategic relationship with the Soviet Union will evolve after Reagan and into the 1990s.

Less clear is how the United States will approach post-Reykjavik arms control issues in the wake of the Iran-contra affair and the waning days of the Reagan administration. It seems clear that, until January 1987, the administration was intent on overturning the ABM Treaty and with it the chances for any arms control in this decade. However, this effort seems to have peaked, and a combination of stiff resistance from Congress, budgetary constraints, scientific skepticism, vigorous and voiced concern from the allies, weakened credibility from a major domestic scandal, and Soviet flexibility on INF turned the tide during 1987. Thus, at this writing, it seems less likely that the Reagan administration will succeed in actually implementing its tortured reinterpretation of the ABM Treaty and in enlisting congressional support for a move toward early deployment of an ABM system.

What also remains problematic is whether the Reagan administration, which clearly would like to register a major foreign policy accomplishment in its last year, can organize and discipline itself sufficiently to achieve a START agreement with the Soviet Union in the time left to it. Even though the INF negotiations did succeed, it was not so much because the Reagan administration sought arms control but because it had arms control thrust upon it. The advent of a new U.S. administration, it is hoped, will give us the opportunity to move from a policy of arms control by inadvertence to one of arms control by design.

Notes

[1] Lee Hamilton, "Soviet Compliance and the Future of SALT," *Arms Control Today* 16, no. 5 (July-August 1986): 3–5.

[2] Kinetic-kill vehicles, sometimes referred to as "smart rocks," involve the least uncertain of SDI technologies—tiny, satellite-launched projectiles that impact enemy missiles.

[3] *Nuclear Arms Control: Background and Issues* (Washington, DC: National Academy Press, 1985), pp. 191–92.

[4] The Soviet Union had agreed to eliminate even these 100 warheads by mid-1987.

[5] See, for example, Mary Fitzgerald, "Marshal Ogarkov on the Modern Theater Operation," *Naval War College Review* (Autumn 1986): 6-25 (quote is on p. 7). Equally interesting on this subject is Michael McGwire, *Military Objectives in Soviet Foreign Policy* (Washington, DC: Brookings Institution, 1987); and McGwire, "Why the Soviets Want Arms Control," *Technology Review* 90, no. 2 (February-March 1987): 36–45.

[6] Fitzgerald, "Marshal Ogarkov," p. 20.

[7] The difference between the U.S. and Soviet levels resulted from the inclusion of INF systems in the U.S. total. For a fuller discussion of the evolution of Soviet policy toward strategic reductions see Jack Mendelsohn (co-authored with J. Rubin), "SDI as Negotiating Leverage," *Arms Control Today* 16, no. 9 (December 1986): 6-9.

[8] For a discussion of the evolution of the Soviet position toward INF see Jack Mendelsohn, "Wending Our Way to Zero," *Arms Control Today* 17, no. 4 (May 1987): 4-9.

[9] N. V. Ogarkov, interview, *Krasnaya Zvezda*, May 9, 1984.

[10] S. F. Akhromeyev, interview, *Stern*, November 27, 1986.

[11] Ibid.

[12] S. F. Akhromeyev, interview, *Pravda*, October 19, 1985.

[13]Press conference (Reykjavik), October 12, 1986, transcript provided by Soviet embassy, in "News and Views from the USSR," *Mikhail Gorbachev's Press Conference*, October 14, 1986, p. 7.

[14]Henry Kissinger, as quoted in *Newsweek* 109, no. 9 (March 2, 1987): 39–47. See also the *Washington Post*, March 8, 1987.

[15]In September 1987 the United States and the Soviet Union agreed to establish nuclear risk reduction centers.

9

Marching to a Different Drummer: U.S. and Soviet Interventionism in the Third World

Michael T. Klare

It is widely believed that the United States and the Soviet Union are engaged in a determined and continuous competition for influence and power in the Third World. When one nation steps up its efforts in this struggle, the other is assumed to follow suit reflexively, producing a global tug-of-war between Moscow and Washington for control over strategic Third World areas.[1] In fact, this image has constituted a dominant motif of the Reagan era, impelling a major buildup of U.S. "power projection" capabilities—that is, forces designed for military intervention in distant areas. While this analysis enjoys considerable popularity in Washington, it does not accurately portray U.S. and Soviet behavior in the Third World. Indeed, as will be demonstrated in this chapter, the interventionary policies of the two superpowers are frequently "out of sync" with one another, reflecting divergent concerns, goals, and priorities. To obtain an accurate assessment of the interventionary policies of the two superpowers, it is useful to consider the major shifts that have occurred in U.S. and Soviet policy toward the Third World since 1970.

The United States: From Richard Nixon to Jimmy Carter

By any measure the Vietnam War was the high-water mark of U.S. military involvement in regional Third World conflicts—involving at its peak the commitment of some 550,000 U.S. troops and a significant concentration of American air and naval power. Vietnam also dominated the strategic thinking of the U.S. military establishment for a generation, beginning in 1962 when President John F. Kennedy embraced the doctrine of "counterinsurgency" as the favored U.S. response to "wars of national liberation" in the Third World.[2]

Given the degree of political and military mobilization engendered by the Vietnam War, it is not surprising that, in the wake of U.S. defeat, the American people were so determined to prevent another such fiasco. In consonance with what is called the "Vietnam syndrome," the U.S. public imposed a number of significant restraints on American interventionism abroad. Among these restraints were the abolition of conscription; a significant reduction in the U.S. defense budget; tight controls on U.S. military aid and training abroad; and, most importantly, the War Powers Act of 1972, which prohibits the extended deployment of U.S. combat forces abroad without congressional authorization.[3] Some of these measures have been loosened since 1972, and certainly we see a harsher public attitude regarding acts of terrorism. On the whole, though, we find that the Vietnam syndrome is alive and well today, imposing all kinds of retraints on U.S. policymakers that will be discussed later.

The existence of the Vietnam syndrome, however, did not entirely discourage those policymakers who sought to enhance U.S. power and influence in the Third World. To get around the impediments described above, Henry Kissinger and his colleagues devised what can be called the "post-Vietnam strategy" of indirect intervention. This strategy eschewed the direct use of U.S. combat forces in regional Third World conflicts but employed other means for exercising U.S. power. In particular, this strategy entailed: 1) the extensive use of arms transfers and military aid to bolster the defense capabilities of friendly Third World nations (the policy we know as the Nixon Doctrine); 2) the extensive use of covert operations to manipulate the political environment of selected Third World countries (this being most evident in the U.S. campaign to undermine the Allende regime in Chile in 1971–73); and, 3) the cultivation of surrogate gendarmes to guard U.S. interests in critical Third World areas (the most important such surrogate being Iran under the shah). Together, these measures constituted the major thrust of U.S. policy toward the Third World in the immediate post-Vietnam period.[4]

One cannot say, therefore, that interventionism disappeared entirely from the repertoire of U.S. policy in the 1970s. But there certainly was a decreased level of direct military involvement in Third World conflicts, as exemplified by the U.S. failure to intervene in the Angolan civil war of 1975–76 (in which U.S. involvement was precluded by the Clark Amendment to the defense appropriations bill for FY 1976), in Iran during the collapse of the shah in 1978–79, and in Nicaragua during the overthrow of Anastasio Somoza in 1979.

If the most prominent legislative expressions of the Vietnam syndrome were the War Powers Act and the Clark Amendment, its most decisive expression in institutional terms was the reorientation of the

U.S. military establishment, especially the army, to an almost total preoccupation with preparation for a war in Europe. During the Vietnam War, America's NATO-based units had been denuded of key forces, cadre, and weapons, significantly degrading U.S. military strength in Europe. After the war the pendulum swung completely in the opposite direction, with Europe receiving the full thrust of U.S. attention while counterinsurgency was largely ignored.[5]

This European focus was attractive to the military for a variety of reasons: it was easy to sell to Congress because it had no taint of Vietnam and hinged on opposition to a traditional enemy, the USSR; it required a vast modernization of U.S. ground and air capabilities, since one cannot fight the Russians in Europe with Vietnam-oriented equipment (producing lucrative contracts for the U.S. defense industry and thereby satisfying important domestic constituencies); it favored an "old school" style of military management (that is, one that favored the tank generals of World War II experience rather than the counterinsurgency experts of Vietnam fame); and it simplified military recruiting in an all-volunteer setting (West Germany being a much more attractive posting than Vietnam). For all of these reasons, preparation for a European conflict became the central concern of U.S. defense planning in the mid-1970s. This, in turn, entailed a buildup of heavy mechanized forces (at the expense of light infantry and the Special Operations Forces [SOF]) and the modernization of U.S. tactical nuclear weapons capabilities, leading ultimately to the 1979 decision to deploy cruise and Pershing II missiles in Western Europe.

In line with this tilt toward Europe, the Third World was largely pushed to the periphery of U.S. strategic thinking. Accompanying this decline in the perceived significance of the Third World was a substantial contraction of America's SOF—the army's "green berets," the navy's SEALs, and the air force's special operations squadrons—and other capabilities for "unconventional warfare" in the Third World. "One of the most serious and far-reaching casualties of Vietnam," counterinsurgency specialist Neil C. Livingstone wrote, "was America's special operations/unconventional warfare capability." Counterinsurgency and unconventional warfare became "dirty words," Livingstone observed, and "much of what was learned in Vietnam about fighting low-intensity conflicts was discarded, shredded, or simply forgotten."[6]

The Soviet Union: From Leonid Brezhnev to Mikhail Gorbachev

If the early 1970s was a time when the U.S. military was turning from the Third World to Europe as the main focus of its strategic thinking, it was also a time when the Soviet Union was making an opposite shift, turning to the Third World with considerable zeal after a period of relative disinterest. There was an earlier period of deep Soviet involvement in the Third World, during the Khrushchev and early Brezhnev periods (roughly from 1954 to 1968). This earlier interventionist thrust began with the first significant deliveries of Soviet arms to the Third World (1955–56), and the first deployments of Soviet military technicians and advisory personnel. It was exemplified in the close Soviet relations with Gamal Abdul Nasser in Egypt, Achmed Sukarno in Indonesia, Mohammed Ben Bella in Algeria, and other radical nationalist leaders. In recalling this earlier period, however, it should be remembered that Soviet arms transfers were not backed by direct Soviet military involvement in the Third World, and that, in fact, the Soviet Union found itself quite powerless to affect the outcome of the 1956 war in Suez, the fall of Patrice Lumumba in the Congo in 1960, or the June 1967 conflict in the Middle East. Indeed, these events exposed the general inadequacy of Soviet capabilities for long-range power projection in the Third World: the USSR had no aircraft carriers, a limited intercontinental airlift capacity, and only a small force of naval infantry for distant operations. This earlier period of Soviet interventionism ended in the late 1960s with significant Soviet setbacks in Algeria, the Congo, Indonesia, and elsewhere in the Third World.[7]

At first, Nikita Khrushchev's successors were disinclined to risk further ventures in the Third World. By the early 1970s, however, they began to envision a new extension of Soviet power and influence in the Third World. Several factors led to this shift in outlook:[8]

1) The achievement of nuclear parity with the United States provided Moscow with the confidence that it could engage in overseas risk-taking without inviting a U.S. nuclear response.

2) As a result of no. 1, and with the general maturation of Soviet military power, Soviet leaders believed that the USSR had come of age as a superpower and therefore was entitled to the same sort of great-power interventionary rights in the Third World that was long the exclusive privilege of the West. (This phenomenon was often described in Soviet texts as a shift in the global "correlation of forces" from West to East.[9]) This perception was accompanied by a new Soviet desire to manifest its global power and prestige through the acquisition of new allies and clients in the Third World.

3) As a result of the Vietnam syndrome the Soviets assumed that there was a diminished likelihood that the United States would come to the aid of shaky clients in the Third World. This factor

figured most prominently in the case of the former Portuguese colonies, which became independent in 1975. Prior to Vietnam the United States had aided Lisbon in its efforts to crush the various independence movements in its colonies. With the withdrawal of U.S. aid at the end of the Vietnam War, and with the evident U.S. reluctance to become involved in regional Third World conflicts, it became apparent that the Portuguese counterinsurgency effort would surely fail. This, in turn, prompted Portuguese military officers to overthrow the Salazar dictatorship, resulting in the long-overdue collapse of the Portuguese Empire and the emergence of Soviet-backed Socialist regimes in Angola and Mozambique. (I stress "long overdue," because much subsequent U.S. literature on Soviet involvement in Africa has portrayed Moscow's gains there as the product of a determined Soviet drive to alter forcibly the status quo, whereas in fact the critical events were not the result of Soviet behavior but rather followed the final collapse of a decaying and anachronistic nineteenth-century European empire.)

4) Incipient Soviet capabilities for long-range power projection in the Third World emerged. These capabilities included new military transport aircraft (the An-22 Cock and Il-76 Candid), the Soviets' first air-capable combat vessels (the *Moscow*-class helicopter carrier and *Kiev*-class VTOL carrier), the Soviets' first oceangoing amphibious assault ships (notably the *Ivan Rogov* class), and expanded Soviet naval infantry forces. The decision to acquire these assets was probably made in the mid-1960s, following the Cuban missile crisis of 1962 and the Arab-Israeli War of 1967, when the deficiencies in Soviet conventional capabilities were brought to the fore; nonetheless, their emergence at this time endowed Moscow with a new capacity for long-range interventionary operations—an advantage that became visible during the 1975–76 civil war in Angola and the 1977–78 fighting in Ethiopia.[10]

For these reasons a dramatic increase in Soviet political and military involvement in the Third World was witnessed from the mid- to late 1970s. This outreach was accompanied, moreover, by an effort to forge new instruments of power in friendly Third World countries to prevent any recurrence of the losses experienced in the late 1960s. In particular, Soviet officials sought to establish Marxist-Leninist vanguard parties in these nations, believing that such formations would prove more stable than the one-man leadership model of the earlier period.[11]

If Vietnam was the high-water mark of U.S. interventionism in the post-1945 era, then the 1979 Soviet entry into Afghanistan with combat forces was the high-water mark of Soviet interventionism. Until

Afghanistan, Moscow operated in the Third World with an undisguised sense of confidence and resolution, accompanied by a willingness to assume risks that had not previously been characteristic of Soviet behavior. After Afghanistan, however, a shift is seen in Moscow's thinking on Soviet involvement in the Third World—at first tentative, under Leonid Brezhnev, and then more pronounced under his successors. Since Afghanistan we have seen no further instances of Soviet risk-taking on any significant scale, and a new attitude regarding the "correlation of forces."

Soviet analysts no longer avow that political and military factors favor the Soviet Union in the Third World, and they are willing to concede that the USSR may face the further erosion of its Third World alliances as once-Socialist regimes adopt the "capitalist road" to development. This shift has been accompanied by a slowdown in the expansion of Soviet power projection capabilities (only two vessels of the *Ivan Rogov* class have been produced, and there have been no other improvements in the amphibious area) and by considerable restraint in Soviet arms transfers to the Third World (hence, Moscow has not sold any MiG fighters to Nicaragua and has limited its arms transfers to North Korea). This shift was also reflected in a new flexibility in the Soviet bargaining position on a pullout from Afghanistan, suggesting that Moscow would be willing to accept a coalition government in Kabul.[12]

Soviet scholars have identified several factors to explain this "post-Brezhnev reassessment of the Third World":[13]

1) The unexpected vehemence of the U.S. reaction to Soviet adventurism in the Third World. Soviet leaders were at first peeved when U.S. leaders complained about Soviet efforts to "take advantage" of détente by expanding its dominion in the Third World, since Moscow's interpretation of détente implied the recognition that, as a coequal superpower, the Soviet Union had the same rights and privileges in the Third World as did the West, including the right to behave in an interventionary manner. However, once it became apparent that Soviet opportunism in the Third World could invite threats to more fundamental security interests—for example, through nonratification of the SALT II Treaty and accelerated U.S. military aid to China—Soviet leaders reassessed their priorities and began to put more emphasis on improving their relations with Washington while moderating their expansionary drive in the Third World.[14]

2) Acknowledgment of the strains placed on the Soviet economy by the open-ended expansion of the Soviet domain in the Third World, coupled with a new emphasis on modernization of the Soviet military and industrial capabilities. Both of these factors

argue against further risk-taking in the Third World. In fact, General Secretary Mikhail Gorbachev has explicitly said that the best way for the Soviet Union to help the Third World is for the USSR to get its own economic house in order, which is not a very subtle way of saying "don't count on us for expanded military or economic assistance." It is also important to note that recent Soviet gains in the Third World, for the most part, have not involved wealthy or resource-rich nations; instead, they have generally involved impoverished nations that require considerable Soviet assistance.[15]

3) The belated recognition that the anticolonial, anti-Western attitudes that have long afflicted the United States and its allies can also apply to the Soviet Union and its allies. Surely, the high degree of indigenous resistance to the Soviet occupation of Afghanistan must have come as something of a shock to Moscow, leaving aside the role played by China, Saudi Arabia, Pakistan, and the United States in aiding the Muhjahidin. The Soviet Union also has discovered that it can be extremely difficult to consolidate power in divided Third World nations such as Angola, where tribal as well as political fissures threaten the stability of the MPLA regime. Sustaining such regimes has absorbed a significant allocation of Soviet military resources and has clearly discouraged Moscow from taking on any additional military commitments in the Third World.[16]

For all these reasons, we have witnessed a general Soviet retreat from the activist policy of the post-Vietnam period. This does not mean a total withdrawal from the Third World: in those regions where the USSR has made a real commitment—in countries such as Ethiopia, Angola, and Vietnam—there has been a stepped-up effort by Moscow to overcome internal threats.[17] Nevertheless, it does not appear likely that we will see any vigorous Soviet efforts to acquire new clients and dependencies in the Third World, nor is it likely that we will see any more "Afghanistans"—that is, instances of direct Soviet intervention to preserve a radical Third World regime.

The United States: From Jimmy Carter to Ronald Reagan

If the Soviet Union appears to be turning away from interventionism in the Gorbachev era, we once again witness a corresponding flip-flop on the U.S. side, with the Eurocentric posture of the Nixon-Ford-Carter era giving way to a new emphasis on military intervention in the Third World. This shift first became apparent in mid-1979, prior to

the Soviet invasion of Afghanistan and the ascendancy of President
Ronald Reagan. It is important to emphasize this chronology because it
is common in U.S. literature to view this shift as an after-the-fact
Reagan administration response to Soviet action. In fact, the key pre-
cipitating event in this reversal was the fall of the shah of Iran in
January 1979. The shah was the principal U.S. "surrogate" in the Third
World and, with his demise, the entire edifice of the post-Vietnam
strategy collapsed as well. Moreover, his fall occurred at a time of growing U.S. dependence on the oil and mineral resources of the Third
World, thereby intensifying the shock waves produced by the Iranian
revolution.

The revolution in Iran and the perceived threat to U.S. oil supplies
led many U.S. policymakers to call for a more activist military stance in
suppressing Third World upheavals. "The tide that swept back U.S.
intervention in Vietnam, Cambodia, and Angola could now be turning
the other way," the *Washington Post* observed. "Strong pressures are
beginning to build up that could pave the way for a return to a more
interventionist policy, based on a military presence, to guarantee U.S.
access to foreign energy supplies." [18]

In response to these pressures and the collapse of the shah, the
Carter administration undertook a major review of U.S. strategy in the
Persian Gulf and the Third World generally. What emerged from this
review was a consensus that critical U.S. interests in the Third World
were at risk and that the United States should take stronger action to
protect these interests. Subsequently, at a series of secret National Security Council (NSC) meetings in June 1979, this consensus was translated
into several key presidential decisions: 1) a commitment to use American military power to protect key economic resources, especially oil, in
the Third World; 2) the activation of the Rapid Deployment Forces
(RDF), an assortment of units from all four military services earmarked
for intervention in the Third World; 3) the acquisition of new basing
rights in the Indian Ocean area (notably in Oman, Kenya, and Somalia)
and the expansion of the existing U.S. naval base at Diego Garcia; and
4) the permanent deployment of a carrier battle group in the Indian
Ocean.[19]

These decisions were made prior to the onset of the Iranian hostage crisis in November 1979 and the Soviet invasion of Afghanistan in
December, but they were not openly announced to the American public
until early 1980 when President Jimmy Carter, in his State of the Union
address, affirmed Washington's readiness to use military force to protect
Persian Gulf oil supplies. "Let our position be absolutely clear," Carter
told a joint session of Congress on January 23. "An attempt by any
outside force to gain control of the Persian Gulf will be regarded as an
assault on the vital interests of the United States of America, and such

an assault will be repelled by any means necessary, including military force."[20] This announcement, soon known as the Carter Doctrine, continues to govern U.S. military action in the Persian Gulf today.

These moves, though, were not sufficient to overcome public dissatisfaction with the president's performance during the Iranian hostage affair and other international crises, and so Carter lost to Reagan in the 1980 election. Reagan has since moved much further toward implementing a policy of renewed interventionism. However, much of what he has done, especially with respect to the RDF and the expansion of U.S. power projection capabilities, was initiated by Carter during his last months in office.

Although Reagan certainly owes a debt to the interventionary buildup initiated by Carter, there is no question that he has placed much more emphasis on the use of force to advance U.S. foreign policy objectives in the Third World. In early policy declarations, Reagan denounced the Vietnam syndrome as "a temporary aberration" and vowed to enhance America's capacity for intervention abroad.[21] The multibillion dollar military buildup launched by the Reagan administration in 1981 placed special importance on the expansion of U.S. power projection capabilities, particularly the army's special forces, the navy's carrier and amphibious fleets, and the air force's long-range airlift units.[22] In defending this buildup, Defense Secretary Caspar Weinberger declared in 1981 that "we and our allies have come to be critically dependent on places in the world which are subject to great instability," and therefore we must "urgently [develop] a better ability to respond to crises far from our shores, and to stay there as long as necessary."[23]

This buildup has been accompanied, moreover, by a conspicuous readiness to use force in overseas conflict situations. Since assuming office, Richard Halloran of the *New York Times* has observed, "President Reagan has clearly stepped into the front ranks of those American Presidents who, since World War II, have been willing to employ military force as an instrument of national policy." Often disregarding the cautionary advice of his military advisers, Reagan has deployed U.S. troops or advisers in Lebanon, Grenada, and Central America; authorized air strikes against Libya; and sent a powerful naval fleet into the Persian Gulf. Such action, Halloran wrote, "has put Mr. Reagan in a league with President Truman, who sent forces to fight in Korea, and Presidents Kennedy and Johnson, who led the United States into the war in Vietnam."[24]

Today, the revived U.S. commitment to interventionism is largely encapsulated in the doctrine of "low-intensity conflict," or LIC as it has become known in military circles. In basic terms, LIC merely connotes the low end of the "spectrum of violence," embracing terrorism, guerrilla war, counterinsurgency, ethnic and border conflicts, "police" actions, and other engagements that fall short of full-scale combat between modern armies. But, under Reagan, LIC has taken on a much broader meaning, entailing a new policy of military intervention in the Third World. Indeed, U.S. military strategists now speak of the doctrine of low-intensity conflict, and new military manuals, tactics, and forces have been created in accordance with this doctrine.[25]

This new doctrine can be defined by four basic characteristics:

An extremely pessimistic assessment of the world military situation. In this assessment, American interests are seen as being vitally threatened by the growing violence and disorder of the Third World. No one has stated this with more urgency than Lieutenant Colonel Oliver North, who told the Select Committee on the Iran-Contra Affair in 1987 that covert warfare of the sort he managed at the NSC is essential because "this nation is at risk in a dangerous world."[26] The increase in international disorder is occurring, moreover, at a time when the United States is seen as growing more dependent on Third World markets and sources of raw materials. While most local conflicts are assumed to have their roots in the social, political, and ethnic divisions that are endemic to Third World areas, the Soviet Union is seen as a global predator ready to seize on and exacerbate any disturbance in order to undermine the power and interests of the West.[27]

A commitment to intervention. In response to the growing world turmoil, LIC theorists argue that the United States must use its military power in a preemptive, spoiling mode to break up and destroy nascent centers of insurrection early, while our enemies are weak rather than to wait until later when our adversaries have grown stronger and can threaten us in a more serious way. This approach was laid out by Secretary of State George Shultz at the Pentagon's 1986 conference on LIC:

> Americans must understand...that a number of small challenges, year after year, can add up to a more serious challenge to our interests. The time to act, to help our friends by adding our strength to the equation, is not when the threat is at our doorstep, when the stakes are highest and the needed resources enormous. We must be prepared to commit our political, economic, and if necessary, military power when the threat is still manageable and when its prudent use can prevent the threat from growing.[28]

This outlook is deeply embedded in LIC doctrine and underlies the current expansion of America's power projection capabilities.

In protecting its interests the United States will not employ defensive means alone but will take the offensive against radical anti-Western regimes. This commitment is the essence of the Reagan Doctrine, with its call for U.S. aid and assistance to anti-Communist insurgents in the Third World. The doctrine was first given formal enunciation in February 1985 when Reagan pledged, in his State of the Union address, to aid the "freedom fighters" who are battling pro-Soviet regimes "on every continent, from Afghanistan to Nicaragua."[29] Support of this kind has been provided to the contras in Nicaragua, the Mujahidin in Afghanistan, the forces of UNITA in Angola, and possibly to other insurgent formations.[30] Such efforts are seen both as a way of weakening America's adversaries in the Third World and of shifting the global "correlation of forces" in America's favor.[31] (It should be noted that this drive, more than anything else, precipitated the Iran-contra arms scandal of 1986–87, for it was North's quest for funds for the contras that led him to persist in clandestine arms sales to Iran long after it became apparent that other administration goals—the release of American hostages and a "strategic opening" to Iran—were not going to be attained.[32])

To conduct LIC operations successfully in a perilous world, the United States requires "special" forces with a proficiency in low-intensity warfare. Because a low-level contingency can occur at almost any moment at any spot on the earth's surface, the United States needs light, mobile, quick-reaction forces that can be rushed to distant war zones and used to crush opposition forces before they can achieve notable success. "The low-intensity battlefields of the future," Colonel James B. Motley of the U.S. Army wrote, will require "more strategically responsive and flexible forces organized to respond to a broad spectrum of combat operations and a wide array of contingencies."[33] This, in essence, is the justification for the activation of four new light infantry divisions by the army, and the acquisition of new airlift and sealift capabilities by the air force and the navy. And because many low-intensity conflicts generally emerge out of the political and social schisms of underdeveloped Third World countries, Pentagon doctrine holds that America's LIC warriors must be skilled at political and psychological warfare, hence the expansion and "revitalization" of the SOF.[34]

These four precepts constitute the underlying principles of current LIC doctrine. In strictly operational terms the doctrine envisions five distinct "mission areas" for U.S. military forces: 1) *counterinsurgency*, or U.S.-backed counterguerrilla operations of the sort now being practiced in El Salvador and the Philippines; 2) *proinsurgency*, or the Reagan Doctrine; 3) *peacetime contingency operations*, or "police" actions of the sort employed in the 1983 invasion of Grenada and periodic U.S. clashes with Libyan planes and ships in the Gulf of Sidra; 4) *terrorism counteraction*, or the use of military forces to deter, prevent, or punish terrorist activities; and 5) *antidrug operations*, or the use of military force to interdict the flow of illegal narcotics into the United States or to suppress the production of narcotic substances abroad.[35]

All of these activities entail a significant "role expansion" for the U.S. military, pushing it into fields once reserved for diplomatic, police, and customs personnel; all, moreover, entail a significant risk of escalation. Counterinsurgency can lead to direct U.S. involvement in a counterguerrilla war if local government forces collapse in the face of superior insurgent capabilities, as in Vietnam in 1965; proinsurgency can invite U.S. intervention to defend a U.S.-backed insurgent group that faces defeat on the battlefield, as can occur in Nicaragua at almost any time; and peacetime contingency operations or antiterrorist/antidrug operations could precipitate a regional conflict of unforeseeable breadth, duration, and intensity. While it is impossible to predict when and where such escalation will occur, the broad sweep and aggressive nature of LIC doctrine suggest that it is just a matter of time before one or another of these military initiatives will lead to a full-scale U.S. involvement in a regional Third World conflict.

A World Out of Sync

It would appear from the foregoing analysis that the two superpowers are perennially out of sync in their policies on military intervention in the Third World. While conventional wisdom has it that each superpower's moves in the Third World are a direct response to some action by its opponent (as if the world is a giant chessboard, with Washington and Moscow deciding the fate of entire nations in their continuing competition for global power and prestige), history suggests that the United States and the Soviet Union both follow their own independent script in the Third World, responding as much to internal pressures and parameters as to the moves of the other superpower. Thus, the United States is now stepping up its military involvement in the Third World, even though the Soviet Union appears to be curtailing its involvement. Furthermore, it is now abundantly evident that a wide variety of Third World forces and movements—among them, Islamic fundamentalism in the Middle East, liberation theology in Latin America, and "people power" in the Philippines and Korea—plays a wholly autonomous role in international affairs.

What policy implications can we draw from this? One can approach this question from several directions: What does it mean for the United States individually? What does it mean for North-South relations? What does it mean for Soviet-American relations? For the United States the future is likely to entail a greater preoccupation with developments in the

Third World, coupled with diminished anxiety over the Soviet military threat in Europe. This will involve a growing concern with international terrorism, guerrilla warfare, threats to strategic raw materials, and regional conflict in general. Accompanying this concern will be stepped-up efforts to enhance America's interventionary capabilities, particularly the SOF, the navy's carrier and amphibious fleets, and the army's light-infantry divisions. It is also likely to entail an increased risk of U.S. military involvement in regional Third World conflicts.

In the area of North-South relations, we are likely to experience a growing polarization between the "haves" and "have-nots," as the affluent nations prove less forthcoming in economic aid and trade benefits for the less developed countries, and as Third World agitators become more extreme in their condemnation of Western capitalist society. As a result, we are likely to witness a growing number of terrorist incidents, social upheavals, and guerrilla wars on one side, and punitive raids, "police" actions, and counterinsurgency campaigns on the other.

Finally, in the area of Soviet-American relations, the prognosis is for a significant reduction in tension, possibly accompanied by new strategic arms reductions agreements. The thaw in East-West relations could then lead to a condition of entente, if Washington and Moscow respond to intensified Third World violence with cooperative conflict-control activities such as arms embargoes, diplomatic pressures, or joint peacekeeping operations. On the other hand, intensified U.S. involvement in regional Third World conflicts could lead to renewed antagonism toward the USSR, if Moscow is seen as the principal patron of Third World aggressors. Even more worrisome, it could lead to a future Soviet-American confrontation if the Soviets feel compelled to come to the aid of a client regime that is threatened by U.S. military action. This is the greatest peril of all because it is precisely this sort of situation—a mutual superpower involvement in a regional Third World conflict—that is most likely to ignite a global nuclear holocaust.[36]

In sum, the future seems to hold both some hopeful developments (gradual Soviet disengagement from Third World conflict situations, along with a thaw in Soviet-American relations) and some rather disturbing developments (an increase in North-South antagonisms, a growing risk of U.S. involvement in regional Third World conflicts, and an attendant risk of East-West confrontation). It follows from this that, if we are to enhance the potential for international peace and stability, we should work to facilitate the hopeful trends and try to reverse the more worrisome trends. In doing so we need to pay greater attention to the purely indigenous causes of strife in Third World areas and not assume that every outbreak of conflict is a manifestation of Soviet-American rivalry. Because Third World conflicts "may be more likely to engage the superpowers in dangerous confrontation than the intersection of their interests in Europe," Marshall D. Shulman of Columbia University has affirmed, it is essential that we not allow "the East-West competitive aspect of local conflict situations to obscure our understanding of the local circumstances involved" in each such incident.[37]

Notes

[1]For examples of this perspective see Noel C. Koch, "Cockpit of Conflict," *Defense/86* (March-April 1986): 35–47; Fred C. Ikle, "Taking Sides in Small Wars," *Defense/86* (March-April 1986): 7–13; and Francis J. West, "Defense and Security beyond Europe," *Defense/83* (May 1983): 9–20.

[2]For discussion see Douglas S. Blaufarb, *The Counterinsurgency Era* (New York: Free Press, 1977); and Michael Klare, *War without End* (New York: Knopf, 1972).

[3]For discussion see Michael Klare, *Beyond the "Vietnam Syndrome"* (Washington, DC: Institute for Policy Studies, 1981), chap. 1.

[4]Ibid. See also Stephen E. Ambrose, *Rise to Globalism*, 4th rev. ed. (New York: Penguin, 1985), chaps. 3–15.

[5]This shift is perhaps best reflected in the statements and articles published in the annual "Army Green Book," every October issue of *Army* magazine (published by the Association of the U.S. Army).

[6]Neil C. Livingstone, "Mastering the Low Frontier of Conflict," *Defense & Foreign Affairs* (December 1984): 9.

[7]For discussion see Francis Fukuyama, "Military Aspects of U.S.-Soviet Competition in the Third World," in Marshall Shulman, ed., *East-West Tensions in the Third World* (New York: W. W. Norton, 1986), pp. 199–202; Mark N. Katz, *The Third World in Soviet Military Thought* (Baltimore: Johns Hopkins University Press, 1982), chaps. 1–2; and Rajan Menon, *Soviet Power and the Third World* (New Haven: Yale University Press, 1986), pp. 4–8.

[8]These factors are discussed at greater length in Fukuyama, "Military Aspects," pp. 202–7; Katz, *Soviet Military Thought*, chaps. 3–4; and Menon, *Soviet Power*, pp. 8–17.

[9]For discussion of the Soviet view of the "correlation of forces" see Menon, *Soviet Power*, pp. 22–33.

[10]For an assessment of Soviet power projection capabilities, see ibid., pp. 90–149. For detailed information on the buildup of these capabilities see John M. Collins, *U.S.-Soviet Military Balance, 1960–80* (New York: McGraw Hill, 1980).

[11]For discussion see Fukuyama, "Military Aspects," pp. 203–7; and Menon, *Soviet Power*, pp. 33–60.

[12]For discussion see Francis Fukuyama, *Moscow's Post-Brezhnev Reassessment of the Third World*, RAND Report no. R-3337-USDP (Santa Monica: RAND Corporation, 1986); Jerry Hough, "The Revolutionary Road Runs Out," *Nation* (June 1, 1985): 666–68; and Menon, *Soviet Power*, pp. 53–60. On Afghanistan see *New York Times*, September 5, 7, 1987.

[13]For example, see Fukuyama, *Moscow's Post-Brezhnev Reassessment.*

[14]Ibid., pp. 23–27.

[15]For discussion see Fukuyama, *Moscow's Post-Brezhnev Reassessment,* pp. 16–23; and Menon, *Soviet Power,* pp. 53–60.

[16]For discussion see Fukuyama, *Moscow's Post-Brezhnev Reassessment,* pp. 27–39; Katz, *Soviet Military Thought,* pp. 145–50; and Mark N. Katz, "The Soviet Union and the Third World," *Current History* (October 1986): 329–32, 339–40.

[17]See Fukuyama, *Moscow's Post-Brezhnev Reassessment,* pp. 47–75.

[18]Jim Hoagland, *Washington Post,* June 3, 1979.

[19]See ibid., June 22, 1979; and *New York Times,* June 28, 1979.

[20]Cited in *New York Times,* January 24, 1980.

[21]See Reagan's remarks at West Point on May 27, 1981, as reported in *New York Times,* May 28, 1981.

[22]See Stephen D. Goose, "Low-Intensity Warfare: The Warriors and Their Weapons," in Michael Klare and Peter Kornbluh, eds., *Low-Intensity Warfare* (New York: Pantheon, 1988).

[23]Remarks before the American Newspaper Publishers Association, Chicago, IL, May 5, 1981 (U.S. Department of Defense transcript).

[24]Richard Halloran, "Reagan as Military Commander," *New York Times Magazine,* January 15, 1984, pp. 24–25.

[25]For discussion see Michael Klare and Peter Kornbluh, "The New Interventionism," in Klare and Kornbluh, *Low-Intensity Conflict.* See also Sarah Miles, "The Real War: Low Intensity Conflict in Central America," in *NACLA Report on the Americas* (April-May 1986): 18–48; and Marc S. Miller, "Ambiguous War: The United States and Low-Intensity Conflict," *Technology Review* (August-September 1987): 60–67. For a compendium of Pentagon views on low-intensity conflict see *Proceedings of the Low-Intensity Warfare Conference* (Washington, DC: Department of Defense, 1986).

[26]*Taking the Stand,* the testimony of Lt. Col. Oliver L. North (New York: Pocket Books, 1987), p. 12.

[27]For a clear expression of this view see Neil C. Livingstone, "Fighting Terrorism and 'Dirty Little Wars,'" in William A. Buckingham, Jr., ed., *Defense Planning for the 1980s* (Washington, DC: National Defense University Press, 1984), pp. 165–96. See also Ikle, "Taking Sides."

[28]Remarks before the Low-Intensity Warfare Conference, Washington, DC, January 15, 1986, from transcript in *Proceedings,* p. 10.

[29]Cited in *New York Times,* February 7, 1985.

[30]See Patrick E. Tyler and David B. Ottaway, "Reagan's Secret Little Wars," *Washington Post National Weekly Edition,* March 31, 1986, pp. 6–7. See also "The Reagan Doctrine," *Los Angeles Times,* August 31 and September 1–2, 1986.

[31]For discussion see William R. Bode, "The Reagan Doctrine," *Strategic Review* (Winter 1986): 21–29; Michael Ledeen, "Fighting Back," *Commentary* (August 1985): 28–31; and George P. Shultz, "New Realities and New Ways of Thinking," *Foreign Affairs* (Spring 1985): 705–21.

[32]See *The Tower Commission Report,* the full text of the president's special review board (New York: Bantam Books and Times Books, 1987). See also *New York Times,* September 18, 1987.

³³Col. James B. Motley, "A Perspective on Low-Intensity Conflict," *Military Review* (January 1985): 9.

³⁴See Goose, "Low-Intensity Warfare." See also Michael Klare, "The Interventionist Impulse: U.S. Military Doctrine for Low-Intensity Conflict," in Klare and Kornbluh, *Low-Intensity Warfare.*

³⁵Current U.S. doctrine for low-intensity conflict is spelled out in U.S. Army Command and General Staff College, *Low-Intensity Conflict,* Field Circular 100-20 (Fort Leavenworth, KS, 1986). See also Klare, "The Interventionist Impulse."

³⁶For discussion of this risk see Joseph Gerson, ed., *The Deadly Connection: Nuclear War and U.S. Intervention* (Philadelphia: New Society Publishers, 1986).

³⁷Marshall D. Shulman, "Overview," in Shulman, *East-West Tensions,* pp. 5, 17.

10
Reflections on the Superpowers' Relations with Their Allies

Jane L. Curry

"Superpower" is the label that equates the United States and the Soviet Union. Both countries have sought to be known by such a label, and both have awarded it to themselves. With this they have implied that all other nations' concerns pale in insignificance. Decisions or issues between the two come to be seen not as problems or agreements between the two nations but as "international agreements."

The notion of superpower has become more than a source of self-definition for the Soviet Union and the United States. In the postwar world, it also has developed into a prime mode of scholarly understanding of international relations. Concepts such as coalitions and multinational alliances have faded. Concerns of international law and organization, too, have been pushed aside; instead, questions of bloc relations and superpower leadership have become major issues. The Yalta Agreement, and not the formation of the United Nations, is presented as the basis of the new postwar world.[1]

During the last decades, however, these superpower self-definitions and scholars' images increasingly have become distorted visions of politics and international realities. In retrospect, the notion of superpower has been a distorting prism since the day it was conceived. Neither the United States nor the Soviet Union is, or has ever been, clearly superior to the small and middle-sized nations in the world—the basis for their claimed positions as superpowers. Nor do they, or have they had, the real recognition of their superiority from their "subordinates." Finally, the hegemony of these superpowers over the nations in their blocs has weakened perceptibly. Eastern and Western Europe have drawn together, while superpowers, since the 1960s, have begun to pull at "each others' allies." This shift, most visible from the early days of détente, has removed the last special characteristic of "superpowerness" and has rendered the division of the world into "theirs" and "ours" less than tolerable for the Europeans themselves.

What remains is the superpowers' own public insistence of their "specialness" in the face of another reality: the only unique hold of the superpowers is their dominant and threatening nuclear power. The scholarly focus on superpower concerns remains evident as well. Yet, leaders and opposition of Western Europe, and leaders and dissenters of Eastern Europe, have all pointed out that neither the United States nor the USSR exercises the control they once did over their allies' resources in military issues, socioeconomic policies, or ideological positions.[2] Frustration among European nations with controls and the self-serving nature of superpowers' policies have surfaced with a pressure built up from nearly forty years of unwilling subordination.

Reexamined here will be the notion of superpower relations and "bloc management" at a time when Europeans are questioning the superpowers' dominance and are looking more and more to each other for sustenance. In doing so, this analysis responds to the increasing European exchanges between East and West on their joint problems and realities, while comparing the dominance of the superpowers without focusing on the manner of that control. That the Soviet Union has been far more repressive and heavy-handed than the United States with its allies goes without saying. There is already an extremely rich literature pervading all the fields of international relations on all aspects of Soviet-East European relations and American-West European relations.[3] For the purpose of this comparison, the virtues and vices of the control one or the other system maintains over its allies, and the demands that are made, are set aside. Instead, the nature and effect of superpower behavior on the relations between nation-states, and how the small and medium-sized nations of both NATO and the Warsaw Treaty Organization have reacted to their controls, will be investigated. In these reactions, similarities far outweigh the differences between East and West. Comparison of these relations is not done just for curiosity but, rather, as a means to understand the problems and perspectives of this postsuperpower world.

The superpower world was one in which the United States and the Soviet Union "called the tune" for their individual blocs of allies.[4] The postsuperpower world finds Soviet-American relations still paramount, but their individual allies no longer "dance in unison" (or appear to dance in unison) only to their superpower's tunes. Instead, partners are exchanged from one line to the other, and each state eschews playing a part in some grand design of either side. Allies of both superpowers behave in ways that reflect both resentments over their subordination and the economic growth that has made Eastern and Western Europe in some ways stronger economically than either the Soviet Union or the United States.[5] The coming of age of the postwar generation in Europe also has contributed to a postsuperpower world. A generation has come to power in all of Europe that has no memory of being liberated by anyone, with none of the fear or gratitude their elders had exhibited toward Soviets and the Americans, who seemed, to those involved, to have brought the war to an end. Finally, the superpowers themselves have forced their European birds to "fly on their own." For both the United States and the USSR the maintenance of a loyal alliance has become too costly, imposing constraints on the actions of both superpowers in actions outside Europe.

The 1950s and 1960s: The Era of the Superpowers

The roots of the present changes lie in the historical context of super-power relations with their European allies. This historical context was a matter not only of the emergence of two giant powers holding down those around them at the end of the war but also the drawing of an "iron curtain" across Europe. For European nations on either side, that curtain was as much an "iron corset" as it was a dividing line. However, it was also a demarcation of "theirs" and "ours," across which no nation was to step.

East Europeans, with leaders brought in from, or supervised by, the Soviet Union, and with Soviet troops stationed on their soil, knew that their political existence was dependent on Soviet tolerance. Those in the leadership and in the population who had the nerve to call for national interests to be considered found themselves in prison camps or convicted of the capital crime of "nationalism."[6] In 1956 the lesson was brought home as Soviet troops put down Hungary's momentary flirtation with national interests and independence. The East Europeans also knew, as their products and machinery were shipped to the Soviet Union while local plants were taken over as "joint enterprises," that their economies were no longer their own.[7]

For the West Europeans the realities and the messages were far less brutal, but they were no less real. Although U.S. troops returned to their bases and limited their presence to the American sector of Germany, their dominance was still felt. Marshall Plan aid "saved" Western Europe and allowed it to stand on its own feet. It also set priorities for Western Europe. American money and investment underlay most of what occurred in Western Europe and, although there was not the "raping" of the econ-omy perpetrated by the Soviets in Eastern Europe, the ultimate economic gain was made by American interests.[8] American media and fashion swept Europe. Even the political leaders of Western Europe, as they dealt with domestic Communist parties, were limited in their options by what American sensibilities would tolerate—a toleration, as the Europeans soon realized, that excluded both Communist party members sitting in the cabinets of America's NATO allies and criticism of the "American way."[9]

For Americans and Soviets, exercising control within their own world of allies provided an ideological justification for domestic conditions. For the United States, Western Europe's loyalty was proof that World War II had been a war that was right, and that Americans' sacrifices had been appreciated. Furthermore, Europe's devotion enhanced, for Americans, the glory of the 1950s, when the United States had basked in victory and an economic boom. The first two postwar decades seemed even more golden to Americans since the devotion of the British and the French—once America's colonial masters—enhanced our new vision of ourselves as the world's chosen people. From the other side the existence of Soviet satellites in Eastern Europe not only fueled the flames of national paranoia (played out in Senator Joseph McCarthy's red-baiting) but also made our first forays into foreign aid far more credible.

For the Soviet Union, on the other hand, Eastern Europe also legitimized the horrible losses of World War II. It was a *cordon sanitaire* keeping the homeland safe from Western incursions as well as evidence that Marxism could fulfill its destiny of fostering world revolution. The existence of opponents to Soviet dominance of Eastern Europe and, even more, the presence of NATO's armed camp in Western Europe were further justifications for Joseph Stalin's purges and the terror imposed on East European societies.

The ideological dominance of both the Soviet Union and the United States was not accepted by the Europeans. As their recoveries from the war progressed and their attention increasingly was devoted to their own interests, superpower ideological dominance became less tolerable. By the 1960s, East and West Europeans began to rediscover and reemphasize their national histories, which had been washed aside in the tide of Soviet and American dominance. East Europeans have had much greater difficulty in uncovering their own pasts than have the West Europeans: Soviet monitoring of the East European media and domestic censorship made honest histories dangerous to research and write. Nevertheless, oral tradition, family discussions, dissident media, and gradual pressure on the leaders combined to make the reemergence of national traditions and history possible. Remembering their cultural leadership over the "upstart American colonies" and the backwaters of Russia made the Europeans even less inclined to continue to be Russianized or Americanized. For the Poles and Romanians these sentiments were amplified by their ancient histories of bitter battles with the Russians.

The military benefit of geographical blocs of dependent allies was considerable for both superpowers. It was possible for the United States and the USSR to reduce or control their military commitments and risks. Battle plans assumed that both countries would be shielded from the devastation of ground war because the primary battle would be on their allies' territory—from the Atlantic to the Bug River. Both Soviet and American planners saw the troops of their allies in Eastern and Western Europe as cost free, or at least less costly to use than their own men. Therefore, they referred to the principle of "shared military responsibility," even as they have refused to share control over the supreme command or to give up their dominance in the production and deployment of weapons.

Beyond the savings of what were to be shared military costs and a distancing of battlefields from their soil, the two superpowers have tried to weave their European allies into larger military alliances to avoid being brought into someone else's war. When East Germany began to block entrances and roads to West Berlin in the early 1970s, or when the French and English fought over the Suez Canal, the Soviets and Americans therefore distanced themselves.[10] They either disavowed their allies' actions or tried to torpedo them. On the other hand, when the United States fought in Vietnam or stationed "peacekeeping forces" in Lebanon, and when the Soviet Union involved itself in Angola or invaded Afghanistan, both expected their allies either to send troops or, even better from the superpowers' perspective, to serve as their surrogates.[11] When no amount of pressure could bring this about, the superpowers have tried to extract silent but loyal affirmation.

For the Europeans the superpower umbrella initially was worth the tradeoff of troops for power. In the years after World War II they wanted to dispense with all their international commitments and were content to let the United States or the Soviet Union involve themselves. In the initial days of East European Stalinism, and the repression that followed Hungary's and Czechoslovakia's ill-fated attempts at a democratized socialism, the enemy of the other side loomed large as well. To be protected by one's superpower was valuable.

The growth of conflicts over nuclear warfare changed all of this. As nuclear warfare between the United States and the Soviet Union clearly became an option that also would rain destruction on Europe, the superpower umbrella became dangerous. Nuclear nonproliferation treaties between the superpowers and the insistence of the superpowers on controlling "their" nuclear technology made it all too clear to the Europeans that the umbrella only covered them once the superpowers were covered. For this leaky coverage, over which they had no control, the costs grew far higher than the military savings.

Neither did Europeans benefit economically from their ties to superpowers in the 1950s and 1960s. For all the benevolence of the Marshall

Plan, America was a prime beneficiary. We were ensured markets for our technology and sources for cheap goods to fill gaps in our own production. American firms, by and large, owned the patents and organized European industries, directly or indirectly, into multinational corporations whose shareholders and corporate offices were in New York City, not in Paris, Bonn, or London. When investment was made in European products it was for Volkswagens, which were too cheap for American workers to produce, and for the purpose of helping direct competitors of American products. The economic growth that the Marshall Plan encouraged was an insurance plan that Western Europe would be able to stand on its own feet, be our market, and not need our assistance.

For the Soviet Union, Eastern Europe was a base on which to construct its own economy. The Soviet Union did not give aid to Eastern Europe, nor was it willing to have it receive aid from the United States. In fact, it forbade Eastern Europe to receive aid from the Marshall Plan when it was offered. Instead, the Soviet Union took over $10 billion in reparations from "its" zone of Germany. Soviet soldiers transported factories and machines from the states they "liberated" in Eastern Europe back to the Soviet Union.[12] Like classic colonial powers the Soviets appropriated the raw materials of Eastern Europe with little regard for the domestic needs of the East Europeans. And, in the wake of the Soviet military presence, they established joint companies, majority-owned by the Soviet Union, to produce goods that East European states could produce better and cheaper than they could. Finally, by imposing the ruble standard on all of their allies, the Soviets assured themselves a market for their goods. After all, since their currencies were no longer exchangeable with those of the Western world, the East Europeans were cut off from their own old trading partners.

As Eastern and Western Europe developed, these economic nets strangled their growing economies. In both East and West the power of the Soviet Union and the United States left European economies seriously askew. Economic decisions on what to produce and how to produce it, as well as on the economic structures in Eastern Europe and, less directly, in Western Europe, were made in terms of the needs of the superpowers rather than the needs of each autonomous nation's populations and economies.[13] The dollar and ruble curtain, moreover, kept West and East apart even as they were natural trading partners. As Western Europe industrialized, it needed the agricultural goods Eastern Europe produced best and most cheaply. Meanwhile, East European industries were scaled so that the less advanced and smaller scale technology of Western Europe was more appropriate and cost-effective for them to use. Ultimately, the natural attraction was for Europeans, East and West, to trade with their European bedfellows rather than with their superpower bosses—a pull that was steadily resisted by the superpowers until the 1970s when the rules changed and the superpowers no longer had the same needs for "colonies."

The 1970s: The Beginning of the European Era

By the 1970s the Europeans bridled at the pull of the superpowers' reins. They bolted even as both the Soviet Union and the United States were loosening their hold. For all of the European states, "Europeanization" was the agenda of the decade. It was suggested by their superpower leaders and moved far forward on their own initiatives. By the 1970s the fears and wounds of the war had healed. Even as East Germany tried to block the Soviet Union's settlement with West Germany, and West German politicians kept the illusion of the unification of all of Germany alive as a faint dream, German revanchism was no longer a threat nor was there any real hope of turning back the clock for those who had lived through the postwar transformation of Europe. European "baby boomers" came into leadership roles in the 1970s. With the specter of World War II gone and the horrors of Stalinism disclaimed by the Soviets themselves, Europeans on both sides pushed open the borders so they could see family and friends on the other side of what had come to be a true "iron curtain" dividing peoples.

Both sides looked back to their common European heritage. The East Europeans moved as they could with the expansion and contraction of cultural limits as various eras of de-Stalinization came and went in Eastern Europe. The West Europeans pushed to shake off the tentacles of American culture that had taken hold of their media soon after the war. The traditional links between the Germanies, or between Hungary and Austria, Poland and France, and Czechoslovakia and Austria, were reconstituted. Quality was found in the classics of France and Britain and not in the "new" culture of America or Russia. All of this meant that, on the stages, in the galleries, and in the classrooms of both Europes, it was European cultural figures and not the "Asiatic hordes of Russia" or the New World frontier of America that was the focus.[14] Even the brutal crushing of Czechoslovakia's "socialism with a human face," looking as that face did to the West and not the East, did little to encourage this "reenlightenment."

Pressures for independence from the superpowers also came as a result of changes in the domestic realities of both Eastern and Western Europe. A new generation of leaders was coming into power. No longer were the leaders of the states of Europe protégés of either the United States or the Soviet Union as their first generation of powerholders had been. No longer were the leaders of the states in Europe good leaders because they were clear of wartime connections or, for the East Europeans, because they had some veneer of "nationalism" earned either by dint of their past or their ability to extract concessions from the Soviet Union. The Willy Brandts, Charles de Gaulles, and Edward Giereks of Europe rose to power on their own. Their bases of authority and legitimacy were their own, and they did not want, nor did they need, Soviet or American tutelage. They wanted to make their own foreign and domestic policy and were unaccustomed to consulting the Soviets or the Americans. After all, they owed less to the superpowers than had their predecessors, and generally had fewer personal links to them.

Ironically, these winds of change even spread to the long-time Soviet loyalists in the leadership of Hungary, Bulgaria, East Germany, and Czechoslovakia. These men had been in power for so long that they had outlived their Soviet mentors. No longer did they feel indebted to anyone. For them and their countries the Soviet Union was nothing more than a trying burden on many issues. By the end of the 1970s they, too, were trying their wings and pushing for a new foreign policy.[15]

At home, East and West Europeans no longer feared their domestic opponents to the same degree as they had as they were establishing themselves. Dissenters on both sides ceased to call for the overthrow of their systems and began, instead, to talk of modifications and reforms in their nation's politics and policies. The Communist parties of Western Europe no longer claimed loyalty to the Soviet Union. Instead, they spoke of themselves as Eurocommunists—fighters for the rights of workers in multiparty democracies. In doing this they eschewed revolution.

On the other side of the divide, few dissidents of Eastern Europe saw any hope of breaking totally with the Soviet Union. Creating systems like those in Western Europe was clearly beyond hope, and, as the East Europeans came closer to Western Europe, these alternatives looked less attractive than they had from across the Iron Curtain. Many dissidents saw East European populations as being satiated with the relative economic prosperity of the 1970s and surviving with hopes dimmed by the tragedy of the 1968 Soviet invasion of Czechoslovakia that ended the Prague Spring and its "socialism with a human face." As a result, they increasingly called not for rejecting communism but for improving it. However, their calls had little resonance in East European societies until Solidarity erupted in Poland in August 1980. As West European leaders breathed easier with declarations of Eurocommunism, East European leaders everywhere but Romania and Czechoslovakia increasingly saw dissidents as mere safety valves.

In the 1970s all this was encouraged by the faces that the superpowers put to the rest of the world and by the pressure that they placed on

European states to be politically and economically self-sufficient. From the outside the leaders of both superpowers in the 1970s and 1980s had little authority. Until Mikhail Gorbachev came to power as the first of an untested new generation, the Soviet Union had been led by a dottering gerontocracy. As outsiders and insiders speculated on the physical demise of Leonid Brezhnev, Yuri Andropov, and Konstantin Chernenko, American leaders' peccadilloes left them with little authority in Europe. Their foreign policy predilections hardly made the Europeans feel secure. To them, American anticommunism led to overly harsh and provocative screams of danger in the Middle East and in Asia, where the United States saw the Soviet Union's hand in every threatening event. Soviet bumbling was no less worrisome and costly for the East Europeans, who were bearing more than they could afford of the burden of aid for the Third World and the push for Western aid and technology.

Even more unsettling for Europeans on both sides was the all-too-clear message that Americans and Soviets would not engage in nuclear self-control, preferring instead the "solution" of nonproliferation. The Soviet Union and the United States had agreed tacitly not to restrain themselves, while keeping the rest of the world out of the nuclear game. The danger of all this was not lost on the populations of East and West Europe, for whom the risks of following American or Soviet initiatives into the Third World, or relying upon them as guardians, were great. Soviet and U.S. nuclear weapons were being deployed on their allies' soil, so that these targets were far from either superpower's home territory. Such a situation, however much the European states ultimately had to tolerate it, could not remain viable. Because of the Europeans' vulnerability as nuclear targets, and the reluctance of the superpowers to be targets themselves, European leaders were pushed by their populations to act with greater autonomy in an effort to modify the terms of Soviet and American nuclear weapons policy.[16]

Within limits, such European interests and autonomy could have fit well into Soviet and American views of the world. Indeed, through the 1970s both the United States and the USSR had tried to use their small and middle-sized allies to affect the limit of the other superpower and to reduce their own international costs. The Soviets sought détente with West European nations in order to weaken America's global position by breaking up its alliances. They also used Western Europe as a funnel for much-needed Western technology and trade—keyed as both were in American policy not to realpolitik but to America's domestic political concerns and to the nebulous slogan of human rights.[17]

East European states also were useful pawns for the Soviets. Instead of conceding on domestic human rights concerns, they pushed their East European allies to be the stages for concessions so that their own soil could be protected from the instability that reform often brought with it. And, since the United States tended to treat Eastern Europe as a part of the Soviet Union, change in Poland or Hungary was, for America, virtually the same as change in the Soviet Union.

The Soviets also encouraged their East European allies to step out and "dance with the West Europeans" to increase the eastward flow of high technology to industries that were closely tied to Soviet counterparts. After all, Western states were far less restrictive about licenses and equipment being shared with those "somewhat independent" East European states of Hungary and Poland, to say nothing of East Germany with its special relationship with West Germany. At the same time, the USSR required that its allies support and, in the case of the East Germans, participate in Soviet Third World adventures.[18] By doing this the Soviets kept their hands far cleaner and made their incursions more "explainable" to those in the United States who wanted to protect the goals of détente.

The Americans reached out to Poland and Hungary in response to the softening of the hatred for Communist regimes by the Polish and Hungarian lobbies. In the Nixon years they moved gingerly to set up links with the leaders of Eastern Europe, with the faint hope of weakening the Soviet bloc itself. In addition, American banks—and even more their West European fellows—awash in petrodollars in the 1970s looked to Eastern Europe and the Soviet Union as the last great frontier of guaranteed markets and borrowers. To Eastern Europe and the Soviet Union, they extended all the loans they could on the assumption that the Soviets would have the resources and largess to cover any of the debts of their East European satellites or the mistakes and overcommitments of their own planners.[19]

The 1980s: The Superpowers' Agenda

That Europeans have adopted a new posture in world affairs has made evaluating political decisions far more complex for both the Soviet Union and the United States. Their decisions, however they were calculated, have failed to provide the gains hoped for by either superpower. At the very least, East European nations and their supposed Soviet underwriters were not the reliable borrowers and unending markets that American and West European bankers had sought; neither were these countries the cost-free funnels for foreign technology that the Soviets had desired. As Poland dramatically illustrated, East European states and their debts could be equally burdensome to both East and West. And, although the political and economic links that had been forged across what was once an iron curtain complicated the Soviets' relations with their allies, the presence of these links ultimately did not protect Solidarity from repression or "liberate" Eastern Europe from the Soviet net. The Soviet Union saw to it that, as East Europeans reached out to the West, their economies were actually more and more interdependent with those of the rest of the Soviet bloc. On the other hand, while West Europeans had long spoken loudly of their independence from America, when the United States decided to deploy more nuclear weapons in Western Europe in 1974, public protests and Soviet bait ultimately did nothing to block that decision and their placement.

Still, even as the United States and the Soviet Union have continued to hold sway over their European allies, none of their victories has been simple or without cost. In the 1980s both the Soviet Union and the United States have found themselves losing more and more control over their allies who increasingly sport their "Europeanness" against the pressures of the superpowers. The result has been, for both the Soviet Union and the United States, that the cost of the support of the European allies has risen. With the Europeans seeing themselves as nations with common interests if not common ideologies, the superpowers often are able to reach public agreements with each other far more easily than they are able to obtain concessions from their European allies.[20]

Ironically, although East Europeans have behaved far less independently than West Europeans, the cost of their attempts at autonomy has been higher for the Soviets than the costs to the United States of West European independence. For all the similarities in the superpowers' expectations of their "Europes," Americans have invested economically and politically in Western Europe.[21] The West Europeans' satisfaction with democracy, if not with the United States, is far greater than that of the East Europeans with communism and the Soviet Union. Furthermore, American attacks on Soviet dominance in Eastern Europe and demands for open borders have been largely rhetorical. Ethnic lobbies in the United States have limited the flexibility of our relations so that high-level and visible relations with East European governments— regardless of the positive effect of such contacts—often have been seen as "being tainted red." Working with dissidents is both potentially harmful for them and often questioned by those very same ethnic actors. As a result, Americans have moved gingerly toward increased contacts and links with Eastern Europe, in contrast with the direct and widespread Soviet efforts in the West. Moreover, because we are an ocean away and took on the role of "world power" when the European colonists were forced out of the Third World, America's international success and failure and its displays of power have been in the Third World, not Western Europe.[22] Eastern Europe has remained the Soviets' prime area of concern and front line.

For the Soviets, all of these changes are much closer to home. Soviet economic involvement with Eastern Europe has been bent on linking Eastern Europe and the Soviet Union together through the Council for Mutual Economic Assistance. Economic problems in one East European state thus mean far more than a trade war or currency problem. These economies are, after all, deliberately interdependent. Not only are they all on the ruble standard, they also are intimately linked through industrial designs that ensure the use of Soviet oil and the compatibility of one nation's production with other bloc nations' products or markets. This often means, as was the case when the Polish economy started to unravel in 1980, that the assembly lines in Moscow and Leipzig soon began to stand idle. Also, since Western banks and governments have tended to regard Eastern Europe and the Soviet Union as interchangeable, it follows that economic problems that affect one East European country often create international credit difficulties for even the best tended economies in the Soviet bloc.

Challenges to the "Communist way" in Eastern Europe have raised questions about the Communist way not only in Poland or Czechoslovakia but also in the Soviet Union. Indeed, testing political and ideological limits, and questioning the system of Communist party rule in Eastern Europe, is more of a threat to the Soviet's dominance over its own people than any Western pressure or propaganda.

Soviet Sacrifices

For the Soviet Union, recognition alone in Western Europe has been a valuable prize. To achieve such ends they have been willing to make compromises with their East European allies and concessions to the West European states they are wooing. The USSR's effort is certainly not to bring additional states into the Soviet bloc but, rather, to promote a decoupling of Europe from the United States on a move toward a "European" identity. This complex of Soviet compromises began during the early 1970s as détente with the United States was in full swing and has accelerated in the Gorbachev era.

In very tangible respects the Soviet leadership's credibility depends on improving its ties with Western Europe. As their economic growth declined, Soviet leaders tried to use the prestige of François Mitterrand or Helmut Kohl's "red carpet" as symbolic replacements for commodities no longer on the shelves in Russian stores. This visible respect and the deference of West European leaders to the Soviet Union, once the plague of Europe, took on special significance in the 1980s as détente with the United States undeniably soured.

Soviet economic failures have created additional pressures for improvements in Moscow's relations with Western Europe. To provide even minimal gains for its population the new Soviet leadership knows that the growth of military expenditures must be slowed. It also recognizes that it needs new technology and money to improve Soviet industry and provide the consumer goods that Soviets are beginning to demand.

For the Soviets, Western Europe is the linchpin. Politically, the Soviets count on Western Europe to push a bellicose United States into arms reduction and to control treaties so they can slow the growth of their own budget for arms. They also have turned increasingly to Western Europe as their prime source for new industrial technology and as markets for their best goods. In doing this they know West European countries are more reliable partners than the United States and far more useful than either the troubled economies of Eastern Europe or those of the "needy" nations of the Third World. For West European states like Austria and West Germany, trade with the Soviet Union is a far more significant part of their overall commerce than the minuscule trade in nonagricultural products between the United States and the Soviet Union. Even in the area of agriculture the prohibition against sales of American grain to the Soviet Union after the USSR's invasion of Afghanistan hurt America's grain belt enough that President Ronald Reagan, notwithstanding his anti-Sovietism, ended the sanctions. For neither side, however, were grain sales more than convenient plugs for faltering economies. The Soviets are thus aware that West Europeans need the USSR more than the Soviets need the United States, and that the West Europeans are less inclined to use economic relations as a battering ram to force political concessions. Their experience with the Americans has taught them that we regard trade as a weapon with which to coerce societies to be acceptable to us.

For this European support, however, the Soviets are paying dearly in economic terms as well as through once unthinkable political and ideological concessions.[23] Their willingness to pay and the visible movement made by Gorbachev toward Western Europe and its interests are ample evidence of the important benefits Western Europe offers the Soviet Union.

Since the mid-1970s the Soviets have emphasized their European-ness. No longer do they bridle at the notion that Europe extends all the way to the Urals. In doing this the Soviets focus on the culture and concerns they share with Western Europe. They also stress that American nuclear weapons in Western Europe, and Soviet nuclear weapons in Eastern Europe and the USSR, will be instruments of destruction for

European targets. In other words, the next war will be a European-Soviet tragedy, while America is simply oceans away. Regardless of how accurate this scenario might be, it is nevertheless a powerful Soviet appeal to West European audiences.

In drawing closer to Western Europe the Soviets have accorded more attention to Europe. Gorbachev has exchanged visits with, and courted, most of the major leaders of Western Europe. "International" conferences that are peopled largely with West Europeans have been held by the Soviets. Even as the United States and the Soviet Union have tussled over exchanges and cultural ties, the Soviets have moved ahead at full speed in these areas with Western Europe.[24] Backing these symbolic public moves, the Soviets have shaken up their own foreign policy apparatus. Specialists on the Third World and other Communist states have been set aside in favor of those persons who are most knowledgeable on not only the United States but also on Western Europe and the very "European" issue of arms control.[25]

The Soviets also have reduced their expectation of Western Europe. In the 1980s they have made it clear that they will no longer demand an end to NATO and the Common Market, once treated as hostile to the Soviet Union. Instead, the Soviets are willing to negotiate with both NATO and the Common Market as international partners. Old loyal Communist parties and their leaders in various countries have been cast off in favor of cozy relations with all kinds of governmental officials.[26] Quite simply, international communism has fallen from the agenda.

As they have done this, the Soviets both pushed and permitted the leaders of Eastern Europe to play a part. They have spoken about their own Europeanness and their greater ties with the West European community than with the Soviet Union or the United States. Remarkably, those who have joined the Hungarians and Poles in this revived European identity are the Soviet loyalist leaders: Todor Zhivkov from Bulgaria, Gustav Husak of Czechoslovakia, and Erich Honecker of East Germany.

For the Soviets, however, this initial posturing has had a cannonball effect: symbolic affirmations of Europeanness turn rapidly into real East and West European moves to form these links. Gains of West European independence from Washington are mirrored by increases in East European autonomy from Moscow. The Soviets have cherished, and perhaps helped foster, an antinuclear movement in Western Europe geared toward getting American nuclear weapons out. The same antinuclear movement, in some cases, has simultaneously called for both the removal of nuclear weapons and the observance of human rights. Its flame also has been taken up by East Europeans. Because of the links between East and West, the old instant repression has not been possible.

More concrete gestures by the Soviets have been made in the Gorbachev era. Arms control proposals on medium-range nuclear weapons no different from those long demanded by the Europeans, and rejected earlier by the Soviets, have been successfully negotiated, while other proposals on long-range weapons acceptable to many Europeans have been put on the table. These are major public concessions on once sacred Soviet interests, whether or not they are accepted by the American side. Furthermore, the Soviets are paying a hefty price to keep trade going with Western Europe. They often have been willing to lose money in the short run to preserve trade. Finally, the Soviets are taking the very real risks that increased tourism and exchanges will raise their own population's demands for goods and opportunities. Yet, to satisfy the West Europeans and to ensure that it will no longer be seen as the "black sheep" of Europe, the Soviet Union has made major concessions on who and what can be exchanged. In doing this the Soviets have paid their dues for Europe.

Long-term Directions

The days of the superpowers and their obedient allies have ended. For the superpowers the costs of "their" Europeans' obedience has been too great. They have turned to face each other head-on and, at the same time, to reach across to meet, but not draw in, the nations on the other side of what was once a curtain. The Europeans, East and West, have grown up and away from "their" superpowers. As nuclear weapons have become the order of the day, differences in governmental systems and ideologies have taken a backseat to Europeans' common fears and frustrations about being the battlefields for a nuclear conflict. As the German-Hungarian Obenhaussen Report reaffirms, the advent of the era of high technology means that the economic gap between the United States and Japan and the other industrial nations of the world will widen.[27] For these other nations (the Soviet Union and Eastern and Western Europe), this means they will be each other's best partners in trade.

On the other hand, the concessions the Soviets have made to Western Europe and the smaller steps the East Europeans have taken toward autonomy do not herald a neutral Europe or the collapse of ideologies and systemic differences between East and West. The leaders and the peoples of Eastern and Western Europe have vested interests in maintaining their systems. The Americans have long since recognized that movement toward independent action in the Soviet bloc does not mean a cutting of Soviet ties. The Soviets, in turn, acknowledge that capitalism and democracy are popular in Western Europe and that Western Europe's ties with the United States are looser but still there. The

Soviets need Western Europe as it is—technologically advanced, productive, and close to the United States—to survive economically while being able to challenge American arms control postures.

The long-term reality for superpowers and Europeans, then, is the emergence of active partnerships. Both superpowers' ability to move unilaterally has decreased, and will decrease still further. In the postsuperpower decades they not only need to consider but also to concede to the interests of their European allies. The power of European states vis-à-vis the superpowers frees them to fit policies to their own needs. It also allows them some room for maneuvering in efforts to cut the best deal possible with each superpower, on their own terms. Finally, it has allowed a return to the human and economic ties of the old Europe.

In the end, "superpower" will stand only as the symbol for two of the most powerful nations in the world. American and Soviet superiority in any one of a myriad of fields, ranging from economics to ideology, will be challenged by other powers like China, Japan, and some of the European nations. Even their negotiations with each other will no longer result in fiats for their allies but, rather, will be topics for discussion and challenge. As the image of unilateral decision making by the United States and the Soviet Union becomes a remnant of the past, Soviet and American allies in Europe will necessarily interact on the more complex and dynamic, and truly international, environment of a postsuperpower world.

Notes

[1] Ferenc Feher, "Eastern Europe's Long Revolution against Yalta," *Eastern European Politics and Societies* 2, no. 1 (1988).

[2] For a general and lively review of the shift in Moscow's relations with its allies see Ken Jowitt, "Moscow Center," ibid. 1, no. 3 (Fall 1987): 296–347.

[3] The classic discussion of the nature of bloc relations in a bipolar world is Hans Morgantheau, *Politics among Nations* (New York: Knopf, 1954). Other key theoretical discussions include Richard J. Rosecrance, "Bipolarity, Multipolarity and the Future," *International Politics and Foreign Policy* (New York: Free Press, 1969), pp. 325–35; and John Spanier, *Games Nations Play* (New York: Holt, Rinehart and Winston, 1984). See also Jeremy Azrael and Stephen Sestanovich, "The Superpower Balancing Act," *Foreign Affairs* 65, no. 4 (Spring 1987): 479–98.

[4] Zbigniew Brzezinski, *Soviet Bloc: Unity and Conflict* (Cambridge: Harvard University Press, 1967), chap. 1; Lawrence Kaplan, *The United States and NATO* (Lexington: University Press of Kentucky, 1984), pp. 121–86.

[5] Marcin Sar, "The Evolution of Centripetal Fraternalism: The Soviet Union and Eastern Europe," *Annals, Association for the Advancement of Political and Social Science* 481 (September 1985): 92–103; J. J. Servan-Schreiber, *The American Challenge* (New York: Atheneum, 1969). Both present articulate

statements on what has been a given, especially in Soviet-East European relations. In the American case, equality and superiority for Western Europe emerged
in the 1970s as American industry was going into a slump and West European
industry tended to produce better goods, cheaper. What this has added to the
equation is a periodically severe currency crisis.

[6]Brzezinski, *Soviet Bloc.*

[7]Jadwiga Staniszkis, "The Dynamics of Dependency," Woodrow Wilson
Center Occasional Paper, 1987.

[8]Daniel Chirot, *Social Change in the Modern Era* (New York: Harcourt,
Brace, 1986), p. 195. "The United States could produce enough to export huge
amounts of goods, but how would the rest of the world pay if they could not
produce exports to balance their imports from America? And how could they
produce such exports without making investments in their industrial plants? The
solution was the Marshall Plan."

[9]"U.S. Secretary of State Henry Kissinger Describes Gains by Anti-
Communist Forces in Portugal as 'Encouraging' for Ford Administration," *New
York Times*, September 10, 1975.

[10]Alfred Grosser, *The Western Alliance* (New York: Continuim, 1980), pp.
129–53.

[11]Ibid., pp. 209–60; Anthony Arnold, *Afghanistan: The Soviet Invasion in
Perspective* (Stanford: Hoover Institution Press, 1981).

[12]Hugh Seton-Watson, *The East European Revolution* (New York: Praeger,
1951), pp. 230–36.

[13]Valerie Bunce, "Neither Equality nor Efficiency: International and
Domestic Inequalities in the Soviet Bloc," in Daniel N. Nelson, ed., *Communism
and Politics of Inequalities* (Lexington, MA: Lexington Books, 1983), pp. 5–34.

[14]Karl Kaiser and Hans-Peter Schwartz, eds., *America and Western Europe*
(Lexington, MA: Lexington Books, 1977), pp. 19–96.

[15]Charles Gati, "Gorbachev and East Europe," William Luers, "The United
States and East Europe," both in *Foreign Affairs* 65, no. 5 (Summer 1987): 958–94.

[16]Christoph Bertram, "Europe's Security Dilemmas," ibid., pp. 942–57.

[17]Jackson-Vanick Amendment of 1972 coupled with President Carter's
policy of linking favorable trade policy with Soviet and East European human
rights observances.

[18]For influence by the Soviet Union on the Council of Mutual Economic
Assistance's view of LDC's and joint participation in economic ventures see
Horst Brezinski, "Economic Relations between European and the Less-Developed
CMEA Countries," U.S. Congress, Joint Economic Committee, *Selected Papers*,
vol. 2, March 28, 1986, pp. 302–28. See also Roger E. Kanet, "Eastern Europe and
the Third World: The Expanding Relationship," in *Foreign and Domestic Policy in
East Europe in the 1980's*, ed. Michael Sodaro and Sharon Wolchik (New York: St.
Martin's Press, 1983), pp. 234–59.

[19]Interview data from American bankers involved in Polish loan negotiations, 1981. Bankers universally reported to this researcher that they had assumed
the Soviets were good borrowers and would ensure that the East Europeans met
their debt obligations.

[20] "Bonn's Arms Stand Seen as Key in U.S.-Soviet Pact," *New York Times*, July 25, 1987; "Soviet Says Pershing Missiles Are Main Impediment to Pact," ibid., August 7, 1987; "Bonn Would Scrap A-Missiles in Reply to U.S.-Soviet Pact...Kohl Indicates He Wants to Help Remove Snag over the Pershings," ibid., August 27, 1987; "Moscow Welcomes Offer on Missiles; Hints Pact Is Near," ibid., August 28, 1987.

[21] Chirot, *Social Change*, pp. 201–02.

[22] "Her" political issues, then, have been the Alliance for Progress, Vietnam, Central America, and the Middle East. Virtually, Europe has never entered the campaign agenda.

[23] For a general survey of the changes in the traditional Soviet stance on foreign policy, human rights, and willingness to trade with Western Europe, especially under Gorbachev, see Timothy J. Colton, *The Dilemma of Reform in the Soviet Union* (New York: Council on Foreign Relations, 1986), pp. 177–228.

[24] F. Stephen Larrabee and Allen Lynch, "Gorbachev: The Road to Reykjavik," *Foreign Policy*, no. 65 (Winter 1986–87): 3–28.

[25] Anatoly Dobrynin is the most conspicuous example of such a preference for Western specialists.

[26] The classic cases of the Gorbachev era are Gorbachev's warm visit with Conservative Prime Minister Margaret Thatcher of Great Britain in 1986, and with conservatives in West Germany and France. In none of these visits have meetings with Communist party leaders played a part.

[27] *Obenhaussen Report*, 1986 (prepared by a West German-Hungarian study team).

Conclusion: To Change the Course of Soviet-American Relations

Daniel N. Nelson

Soviet-American relations must be recast fundamentally in light of enhanced mutual understanding and reciprocal conflict avoidance. But what should we understand? Where and how can confrontation or crises that might precipitate war be avoided? And, most important, why should these "lessons" instruct Soviet-American relations as the century draws to a close?

Understanding Differences

The contributors, through their own disciplines, have sought to evaluate Soviet-American relations. While some issues recur in several chapters—arms control, for example—each author has expressed concern about superpower interactions differently. Consequently, the insights offered form an interwoven, multifaceted portrait of what leaders and citizens of both the United States and the USSR should comprehend about each other.

It emerges from the Soviet Interview Project, as discussed by James Millar, that émigrés who resettled in the United States reveal substantial attitudinal differences across generations reinforced by educational cleavages. Generally, however, a large proportion of émigrés in the 1970s retained generally favorable impressions about their standard of living in the USSR and the socioeconomic provisions of such a system. Interestingly, the Soviet Union's "best and brightest" people are the "least satisfied members of that society," while certainly not qualifying as dissenters. Americans' misinformation and ignorance of the Soviet Union, coupled with "fear and loathing," are detailed by Jon Hurwitz and Mark Peffley. Here we find strongly negative beliefs about the Russians and communism based upon very little relevant information. Although their study reveals some benefit of doubt for Mikhail Gorbachev, Hurwitz and Peffley also have underscored Americans' expectations that the USSR, even more than other Communist states, is aggressive and untrustworthy. Furthermore, they find that other beliefs, such as religious fundamentalism, underlie vehement anti-Communist, anti-Soviet opinions.

Burns Weston takes up the theme of knowing each other by asking, rhetorically, "Who are the Soviets?" and argues that none of our common disparaging characterizations of the USSR—as the "evil empire," as a malevolent power culpable for political turmoil in the Third World, and as an untrustworthy negotiator—is accurate. The Soviet reality, in Weston's view, demands the attention of American policymakers and citizens in "the Age of Trident"—that is, a time in which nuclear first-strike weapons have become common to the arsenals of both superpowers. Weston identifies the Russian and Soviet historical ambivalence and insecurity vis-à-vis the West, and the continuities between authoritarian past and present in the USSR as facets of the Soviet condition that Americans must grasp. Only through such perspective, in Weston's assessment, can we escape a "distrustful competition" with the Soviets.

Soviets and Americans must understand about each other that both their societies confront similar problems of social policy. Bruce Rigdon, Mark Field, and David Powell have each probed a different aspect of citizens' well-being in the USSR, with some comparative references to the United States. From their respective disciplines, these contributors have pointed to the living conditions of Soviet citizens and their counterparts in the United States. The religiously faithful, the ill, and the aged are three social categories with which political systems must deal. In tangible respects, each can stand in the way of political authorities' goals because the beliefs of the religious and the infirmities of the aged or ill place burdens on the political system. These are people who must be accommodated or cared for. Regardless of the kind of political system, citizens' well-being is an affair of state. Social welfare and religion are treated differently in the Soviet Union than in the United States; that is, the policies differ while the issues confronting national leaders are often quite similar.

The severe deficiencies in Soviet health care documented by Field, for example, are exacerbated by long-term commitment to the military/industrial sector. The American health care dilemma to which he alludes differs greatly in that the United States spends a huge proportion of its GNP on medical services (12 percent or more)—and costs continue to escalate—while many Americans have inadequate access to even rudimentary preventative medicine. Both systems thus confront health care crises that threaten to undermine citizens' well-being and productivity— ironically derived from distributive imbalances of different kinds.

Americans often consider the USSR to be an atheistic state in which religions exist under severe duress. Rigdon finds that, notwithstanding the formal commitment to atheism of the Communist party, there is a thriving religious community within all republics of the USSR. This religious practice encompasses not only the largest Christian sect in the USSR, Russian Orthodoxy, but also Protestant Christianity, Islam, Buddhism, and other faiths. The relative "health" of religious faiths in the United States and the Soviet Union is impossible to assess. Yet, in an era when American Catholics have been wrestling with their own allegiance to the teachings of the Vatican, when American fundamentalists have had to confront the very public failings of television evangelists, and when the constitutional principle of separation of church and state has been assaulted by the Moral Majority and other groups, it may not be inaccurate to say that American religious convictions have been brought into the political realm as well. In the Soviet case the politicization arises from the Party's insistence that no other allegiance (for example, to a religious faith) preempts its authority, while in the United States the extension of religious fundamentalism into political life has been resisted by those who do not share those beliefs and wish to retain the long-standing principle of American democracy: separation of church and state.

The demographics of both Soviet and American societies also imply an inexorable aging of the populations—much more rapidly among some socioeconomic and national groups, but aging nonetheless. For the USSR, as Powell details, this challenges pensions, housing, health care, and other elements of social welfare. The drop in life span and the rise in morbidity indicate not only public health problems in the USSR but also an inability to provide the kind of care that can prolong life. The American dilemma of aging discussed by Powell intertwines spiraling health care costs, a declining Social Security fund, a reduced work force required to pay ever rising contributions to Social Security, and substantial disparities in the distribution of benefits to the elderly. The issues that both systems face in this regard are basic and unavoidable: When people no longer "produce," what is society's obligation to provide for them? And to what is that care for the elderly or the ill to be sought at the expense of other goals?

From these varied portraits of Soviet and American societies, what can we understand? What should we comprehend about these two systems? Several chapters in one volume cannot offer a comprehensive comparison, but Millar, Peffley, and Hurwitz alert us to mutual misperceptions and gaps in substantive knowledge that cannot be left untended (a point reinforced by Stephen White). Weston, Rigdon, Field, and Powell point toward the problems of social well-being and harmony that require attention in both societies. In other words, in the two superpowers reside both substantial ignorance about each other and the world, and festering problems of social policy.

Avoiding Conflicts

Stephen White, Jack Mendelsohn, Michael Klare, and Jane Curry each examine different arenas in which America encounters the Soviet Union. Most broadly, White considers the effect of Gorbachev's still young leadership on the West's relations with Moscow. Writing from the perspective of a European, White argues that the first several years of the Gorbachev era augured favorably for improved Soviet-American relations. Europeans, due perhaps to their centuries of contact with Russia, tend to place the military power of the Soviet Union in a different light and to evaluate with less suspicion every action of the USSR. White's criticisms of the Reagan administration's approach to relations with the USSR mirror those of Weston, Klare, Curry, and Mendelsohn. Although the Reagan administration was too reluctant to make meaningful concessions in arms control or other spheres, White holds out hope that people-to-people contacts would accelerate and provide an impetus for conciliatory steps at higher levels. From his perspective, then, greater comprehension of Soviet reality by Americans—and vice versa—would enhance the potential for progress in bilateral relations.

More specific discussions by Mendelsohn and Klare focus on arms control and Third World conflicts, respectively. In both essays, the authors see avenues for avoiding conflict between the superpowers. Reviewing arms control policies of both the United States and the USSR since the mid-1980s, Mendelsohn finds that the Soviet Union has taken the initiative and has moved aggressively to adopt positions that the United States had once proposed. Since the renewal of Geneva-based negotiations in 1985, it has been the USSR, in large part, that has offered concessions and suggested ways to break deadlocks. The United States, by contrast, has been reactive in its arms control behavior during the Reagan administration, vacillating in many of its positions and offering little in the way of substantively new proposals. Missed opportunities are noted by Mendelsohn, and he identifies the obstacles confronting a strategic arms accord in the near future. Mendelsohn concludes that the Soviet Union will continue to attempt to engage the United States in meaningful arms control and that the USSR will be a much more subtle and sophisticated adversary. Furthermore, he expects that Congress, our allies, and public opinion will enjoy a heightened role during the balance of the Reagan presidency.

In Klare's view, competition for the Third World has been a play performed with two "independent scripts," both written in response to domestic pressures more than in reaction to the other superpower. He contends that the United States and the USSR have been "out of sync" in the Third World, with interventionism rarely the consequence of the other's involvement. Of the two superpowers, the United States has long had, and continues to have, far greater force projection capacity. The USSR, of course, has employed its forces often at its periphery, and, when its ability to project forces expanded in the 1970s, Moscow used that capacity in Angola, Ethiopia, Yemen, and other regions. Yet, at the core of Klare's argument is the continuing danger that competition between the Soviet Union and the United States will arise in the Third World because of the failure to recognize purely indigenous causes for social and political turmoil. The danger also exists, even amid hopeful signs of superpower cooperation to limit conflicts, that the proclivity to intervene directly or through proxies mounts as force projection capabilities grow. The United States has been able to project power for decades. The USSR, when it began to obtain worldwide naval and airlift abilities, has exercised them in Africa and the Middle East.

Although Klare did not use these precise words, it may nevertheless be accurate to say that he regards the capability to project power in the Third World as an excellent predictor of intervention. The United States, particularly during the Reagan administration, has rationalized a commitment to strengthened conventional forces in large part by reference to Soviet activities and intentions in the Third World. This ignores both the indigenous sources of most regional or local conflicts and the substantially inferior Soviet force projection capabilities. It is a policy that precipitates a response from the other superpower, and the cycle of intervention and war by proxy is exacerbated.

In Curry's essay the postsuperpower era is discussed as a consequence of American and Soviet efforts to ensure that their respective "Europes" in the 1950s and 1960s serve and follow them. Neither side wants its European "allies" to move away from its leadership and the more or less tightly defined range of "loyal" behavior it has established. Ironically, the military security that both superpowers promise their European allies, in exchange for their loyalty, comes to be a disincentive to this loyalty. A security composed of nuclear weapons provided by the superpowers has become part of the impulse to find ways to pursue national interests. Curry also points to the economic strength of much of Europe relative to the United States and the USSR, and to the sociocultural distinctions of both Eastern and Western Europe vis-à-vis their large alliance partners. These factors, Curry argues, contribute to an increasingly strong European conviction that dependence on Washington or Moscow helps the super-powers more than Europe. By the 1970s there remained no rationale for dutiful obedience within either NATO or the Warsaw Pact. Avoiding conflict between the two alliances in Europe and reaching across what had been the barriers between the blocs to recreate a Europe of small and middle-sized states apart from the superpowers' politics, therefore, have become vital interests to all the countries of both Eastern and Western Europe.

Thus, avoiding Soviet-American conflict requires, at a minimum, the diminished involvement of the United States and the USSR in Third World conflicts—a process itself dependent on reducing the means by which superpowers intervene, that is, their force projection capabilities. Short of multilateral agreements designed to control such capabilities (which seem highly unlikely), international accords that involve a mutual and verifiable withdrawal of foreign troops and bases, an end to military training and aid, and Soviet and American support for negotiated settle-ments are requisite elements for defusing innumerable Third World "hot spots."

At the level of strategic negotiations between the superpowers, it may be necessary for the next American president to formulate a com-prehensive plan that can form the basis for renewed and constructive dialogue at Geneva. President Ronald Reagan's personal commitment to SDI has meant that, for his entire second term (most obviously at the Reykjavik summit), an insurmountable obstacle prevented movement in this most vital forum. It was the commitment to SDI that required the transparent "legal" reinterpretation of the 1972 ABM Treaty so that it could be construed to allow operational testing of space-based SDI kill systems. To a large extent, the possibility of using SDI in a "grand compromise" has been squandered; yet, avoiding Soviet-American con-flict necessitates accommodation on strategic offensive and defensive systems. The Soviets, at least during the latter part of the 1980s, have moved much more forcefully in seizing the "high ground," suggesting bases for combining limitations and reductions in both kinds of systems. The United States must renew its leadership role in strategic arms control. Were the next president to fail in that responsibility, the Soviets will have won the public diplomacy battle. At the same time, the USSR most certainly will not continue to make offers that are received coolly.

Finally, to avoid Soviet-American conflict, both superpowers, even in Europe among their erstwhile dependent and obedient allies, must step back from insistence on dominance. This will be far more difficult for the

USSR than for the United States because of Soviet insecurity and its record of unbridled repression in East Germany, Hungary, and Czechoslovakia. As Curry rightly points out, the Soviets have more to lose in their "empire." Yet, it may be that Gorbachev understands what he must do within the Warsaw Pact better than the Reagan administration understood what to do in NATO, notwithstanding the more limited nature of America's penetration of Western Europe. For the Soviet leaders there are deeply interwoven political, economic, and military interests with the six East European members of the Warsaw Pact. For the United States some political ties have been close (for instance, Margaret Thatcher and Reagan), but the European Economic Community (the Common Market) is surely a competitor, and European military concerns often extend outside Europe or deal with bilateral disputes—the French in central Africa, the British in the Falklands, and the Greeks and Turks against each other.

In short, what an American president can do in Europe to reduce the potential for East-West conflict must involve communicating with, and convincing, a large number of highly autonomous allies about politico-military policies. That the superpower role of the United States in Europe was no longer accepted by Europeans in the 1980s should have been clear to American leaders; yet, it was not until the debacle of trying to halt European participation in building a natural gas pipeline from the USSR to Western Europe—roundly rejected by NATO allies—that the autonomy of Western Europe was recognized by the Reagan administration.

For the Soviet Union to lessen the weight of control throughout Eastern Europe is another matter. None of the East European Communist party regimes has achieved a legitimacy that would ensure their long-term survival were Soviet troops to be withdrawn and political support reduced. There is, however, considerable impetus for a minimalist Soviet strategy in Eastern Europe, wherein more diversity is tolerated, more experimentation encouraged, and each ruling party is seen to be cultivating actively its own domestic support. Gorbachev wants to concentrate on Soviet problems, and the less there is of political turmoil in Eastern Europe the better it will be for *perestroika* (restructuring) in the Soviet context. There will be no effort, then, to enforce uniformity by insisting that Erich Honecker pay obeisance to *glasnost* (openness), or that Milos Jakes become an avid adherent to *demokratizatsia* (democratization).

Thus, minimized involvement in Third World conflicts, the aggressive pursuit of arms control proposals that combine limits in defensive systems with reductions in offensive systems, and a deemphasis on the dominant role of superpowers within Europe are vital processes. Each represents a critical first measure toward avoiding confrontations and crises between the United States and the USSR.

The Dilemma of Soviet-American Relations

Soviet-American relations, stated most bluntly, are the most important bilateral relations in the contemporary world or, perhaps, between any two nation-states at any time. Because nuclear annihilation would be the consequence of war between the superpowers, the USSR and the United States must avoid overt, direct conflict. At the same time, the two superpowers will never entirely reconcile their differences, at least not during our lifetime. Conflictual interactions (threats, name-calling, military provocations, or diplomatic harassments) can be reduced and cooperative actions (trade, cultural exchanges, or treaties including arms accords) can be increased. But the political and economic systems in these two states remain antipathetic, and the global interests of one will often be opposed by the other.

As the final decade of this century approaches, it is also clear that economic rationales for reducing the high level of tension between the United States and the Soviet Union, and thereby lessening the perceived need for continued expansion of armaments (especially strategic offensive and defensive systems), are becoming more stringent. In the United States the intense debate about SDI is as much a question of cost-effectiveness as it is a question of technological feasibility. In the USSR the interest in arms control measures is surely propelled by the need to rechannel resources into industrial modernization and technological development.

Thus, we cannot fight, and we will only damage our respective economies and societies by continuing to prepare to fight. At the same time, the United States and the Soviet Union cannot be sanguine about each other's intentions, and they both are certain to retain some degree of mistrust and suspicion about each country's foreign and military policies.

This is a strange state of affairs. World powers in earlier epochs, even in this century, eventually came to blows, and combat temporarily resolved the clash of interests. We, by contrast, are immersed in a condition of conflict without the "outlet" of war. Our wars, and Soviet wars, are wars of intervention, or wars by proxy, almost always to suppress or support insurgencies against governments supported, to one degree or another, by the other superpower. The record of such warfare over the last four decades, regardless of the superpower involved, has been decisive— and negative. By attempting to pursue their competition against each other globally, through intervention or proxy war, the United States and the USSR have lost far more than they have gained.

The Soviet-American relationship, then, cannot be played out through direct or indirect combat. We may not have seen the last of "low-intensity conflict" (LIC) supported by the United States, or "wars of national liberation" supported by the Soviet Union, but we will never see one in which a superpower winds up with a cost-effective victory, and certainly not a victory that is very certain or lasting. There is, therefore, a dilemma of worldwide proportions: two irreconcilable, militarily powerful nation-states that cannot beat or spend the other into submission, cannot eliminate the perceived threat of the other political system to its own values, and cannot ignore the competition posed by the other state around the world. Given this environment, what have we done?

The American response to such a fundamental dilemma— throughout the post-World War II decades, and especially in the last decade including the last two years of the Carter administration—has been to maintain a strategic "triad" to deter nuclear attack on the United States and to station land, air, and naval forces around the world at bases legitimized through alliances (NATO, ANZUS, and many bilateral ar-rangements). The ideas of deterrence and collective security have formed the cornerstones of U.S. military response to being stuck, as it were, in perpetual conflict with a strong adversary.

Times have changed, however. ANZUS has disintegrated, CENTO (once held in place by the shah of Iran) is no more, SEATO was a dead letter in 1975, and NATO is fraught with innumerable schisms (Greece and Turkey came perilously close to combat in March 1987 over oil exploration claims in the Aegean Sea, and Spain is seeking reductions in the U.S. presence). Meanwhile, $1-billion aircraft carriers and Trident submarines make a 600-ship navy unmaintainable, and procurement mistakes (DIVAD, for example) have cost hundreds of millions of dollars. Planes costing $100 million, such as the B-1, are only marginally capable of performing their mission since they have uncertain terrain-following capabilities and inadequate electronic warfare abilities.[1]

The Soviet response, on the one hand, has been, in the fashion of Russian empires, to seek security by erecting a *cordon sanitaire* in Eastern Europe, to extend buffer zones at each periphery, and to maintain a huge standing military, much larger than would be required to defend against one opponent alone. On the other hand, as opportunities have arisen and capabilities have increased, the USSR has also sought to weaken its adversary's alliances and political influence.

The socioeconomic malaise of the past several decades and especially the Brezhnev years, rooted in both the inefficiencies of central planning and massive defense spending, has created a dangerous domestic situation for the Communist party of the Soviet Union. In Eastern Europe, Solidarity has demonstrated the bankruptcy of Communist rule in Poland, and elsewhere there are varying degrees of disassociation from the USSR. The war in Afghanistan took on an almost endless character, and there is now public acknowledgment in the USSR about the gravity of losses. Soviet Third World clients—such as Yemen, Ethiopia, or Vietnam—are as poor as can be imagined and provide the Soviets with a cost-benefit problem of sizable proportions. Communist parties participating in electoral politics in multiparty democracies have suffered reversals throughout the 1980s, and moderate revolutions have fared better than Communist insurgencies. All in all, the world as viewed from Moscow at the beginning of the Gorbachev period is not reassuring.

The dilemma of Soviet-American relations—wherein the United States and the Soviet Union cannot reconcile their systems and cannot fight each other directly—has fostered two responses, both of which have become very brittle after more than forty years. The first response was a worldwide system of collective security and nuclear deterrence that, second, confronted a Eurasian land-power that had erected a defensive system of client states supported by massive military forces. That they came to confront each other globally, however, makes the dilemma of Soviet-American relations ever more palpable.

The Costs of Globalism

Prevented by their own perceptions and armaments from either reconciliation or conflict for almost fifty years, the USSR and the United States, particularly in the 1970s and 1980s, have broadened the scope of their competition. Enhanced Soviet military capabilities have heightened American anti-Communist sensitivities during the 1980s, and the complexities of an interdependent world have meant that the United States and the Soviet Union confront each other more often, and with more resources, than ever before. This widened competition is at once political and military, and leads to Soviet and American commitment of resources in many locales to seek advantageous outcomes or to avoid negative consequences. Not only is the geographic "spread" of Soviet-American competition wider but also the arenas in which that competition is undertaken have multiplied (for example, technology transfer). The costs, both literal and figurative, of such relations for both sides need to be assessed as we enter the final decade of the twentieth century.

The cost—or, perhaps, "burden" is a more appropriate term—of almost fifty years of superpower competition has been extraordinary to both the United States and the Soviet Union. It is impossible to relate this burden in a purely monetary sense, since much of what both countries has expended has been opportunity costs, not dollars or rubles. Americans and Soviets have "paid" an incalculable amount to defend and compete against each other, and both superpowers have caused innumerable other people to pay as well with their deaths and suffering.

Some of the consequences of being protagonists in the Cold War are painfully evident, however. In economic terms the choice was made by

Soviet leaders long ago that deprivation would be accepted indefinitely. A permanently depressed Soviet living standard was the sine qua non of military strength, a position unchallenged until now except for the abortive 1961 Party program that promised communism by 1980 and was ignored entirely after Nikita Khrushchev's ouster in 1964. That the USSR devotes an enormous proportion (perhaps 15 percent) of its GNP (about 55 percent of the U.S. GNP) to defense is unquestioned, although the precise percentage is debated among Western analysts. As a rough estimate, however, it is reasonable to presume that the Soviets consistently have invested in their military twice what the United States has, as a proportion of GNP.[2] Among all nation-states the USSR ranks in the highest tenth on measures of military expenditures, as a proportion of central government expenditures and as a proportion of GNP.[3] In other words, a significantly underdeveloped nation-state on many measures has sacrificed its socioeconomic development and modernization to create a strategic and conventional force equal or superior to that of the United States. Of course, the Communist party did not pose this choice to citizens as an issue for public discourse or decision.

Neither were the economics of defense burden raised for public view in the United States. Indeed, it was during the Reagan administration that military spending escalated sharply, while income taxes were cut. The consequence was a series of extremely large annual budget deficits (in the range of $200 billion), adding as much to the national debt in eight years as its previous total. The cost of global competition with the Soviets, given the Reagan administration's view of the competition particularly in military terms, thus was placed increasingly on future generations of Americans. At no time were Americans told by their presidents that a decline in their living standard through substantially higher taxes or deficits and debt was the stark alternative if military spending were to be raised greatly.

Thus, both superpowers have mortgaged their futures to the perceived military demands of their global competition. For the USSR it has meant, except for the military, the de facto status of a Third World country. For the United States it has meant an economy permeated by debt and deficits, one in which prosperity has a hollow ring for all except the already rich.

Defense burden is extracted in other ways, most notably by manpower demands that fall most heavily on the young male population. The Soviet Union, given its available pool of eighteen- to twenty-eight-year-olds, has maintained high levels of service through conscription; consequently, the USSR continues to have twice the number of active armed forces than the United States.[4] The United States, by contrast, has reverted to an all-volunteer force and allowed its active-duty forces to contract to between 2.1 and 2.3 million during the last decade, from a

Vietnam War high of more than 3.6 million.[5] Including U.S. Ready Reserve and National Guard formations, however, which arguably are closer to active-duty status than are the great majority (60 percent) of Soviet reserve divisions, it may be that American manpower demands do not differ substantially, particularly when the 10 percent larger Soviet population is considered. In any case, both superpowers must cope with issues of manpower quality—intelligence levels, educational backgrounds, social adjustment, and ethnic and national integration—that affect their recruits' abilities to operate complicated equipment and to understand commands in a combat environment, and with demographic trends that make it more difficult to ensure requisite numbers of qualified recruits.[6]

Finally, the long history of Soviet-American competition, now extended to include global confrontation, has imposed strenuous performance burdens on the military, socioeconomic, and political infrastructures of both states. The Soviet Red Army has fought in the streets of Budapest and in the mountain valleys of Afghanistan, while supplying and training forces for combat in places as diverse as Syria, Cuba, Vietnam, and Libya. In the decade-long fight against the Mujahidin the Soviets probably suffered 13,000 or more dead—a number too large to conceal.[7] These losses began to strain public acceptance of the Red Army's presence in Afghanistan, and Gorbachev himself in 1986 alluded to the need for a settlement and has now begun the process of a phased troop withdrawal and offered a cease-fire. But it is the reverberation of endless, bloody foreign interventions throughout the Soviet socioeconomic and political structures that may be the worst consequence of the "performance" burden that the United States and the USSR impose upon themselves.

Despite the possession of 25,000 or more nuclear weapons each, both superpowers have found themselves susceptible to deep immersion in guerrilla or nonconventional wars that, quite literally, bleed them over an extended period. The other superpower, of course, is quite willing to do whatever possible to support the insurgency or revolution that is inflicting casualties on its adversary. It is precisely this kind of involvement that maximizes socioeconomic and political burdens, even if the military cost per se can be contained (for example, by abandoning the countryside to the opposition and by using air power to attack guerrilla bases or formations). In such Third World conflicts the superpowers invariably oppose an indigenous force, the fighters of which are motivated largely by their own nationalism or belief system, and for whom death is but a sacrifice they are willing to make. Most often the side supported by the United States or the USSR through either superpower's intervention has been ill suited for gaining popular support.

Americans and Soviets have made sacrifices, but there is little sympathy in either society for senseless sacrifice. The globalism of late twentieth-century superpowers has called repeatedly for a military presence or aid, usually resulting in loss of lives and resources squandered. Meanwhile, the stockpiles of nuclear weapons have grown in number and accuracy. The senselessness of wars in Indochina or Afghanistan, then, becomes more poignant when juxtaposed with the amassed destructive power of American and Soviet nuclear deterrence.

Perhaps one might argue that, notwithstanding the enormous costs or burdens of Soviet-American confrontation, there was no choice: that as Alexis de Tocqueville had predicted, the United States and the Russian Empire were destined to compete for dominance. Furthermore, the same argument could emphasize national interests that inevitably clash, and realpolitik or *raison d'état* that would provide a justification for whatever policies were taken in pursuit of such interests. Ideologues would underscore this line of argument by citing the irreconcilable differences between a democratic republic with a capitalist economic system versus a Marxist-Leninist one-party state and its centrally planned Socialist economy.

Such a deterministic view in which global competition cannot be avoided—and burdens must be accepted and any sacrifice made—errs by assuming that worldwide superpower confrontation is the best way to preserve one's own system and its values. It fails to recognize the incremental weakening of one's own military, socioeconomic, and political institutions through the burdens of globalism. And, it wrongly attributes to a confrontational strategy the maintenance of alliances and preservation of friendly governments around the world. As argued above there are numerous and destructive costs to global superpower competition. Moreover, the demise, not the maintenance, of bilateral and multilateral politico-military alliances can be attributed to the pernicious effects of Soviet-American competition: the Soviets being ousted from Egypt after a twenty-year alliance or from Somalia after building a huge naval facility at Berbera, or the Americans being told to stay away from New Zealand and to reduce substantially military bases in Spain. These and other incidents reveal that smaller nations do not want, and do not need, U.S. or Soviet efforts to use them in their competition for influence and control. After almost fifty years of the Soviet-American Cold War, it seems that few nations prefer a close relationship with the United States or the USSR. Many seek aid from Moscow or Washington, but few desire the presence of Soviets or Americans since that presence is a correlate of destabilizing efforts by the other superpower or nationalistic reaction that may threaten the local government.

The costs of global competition in Soviet-American relations, in other words, cannot be dismissed because of the dictates of ideology or power since there is little evidence that the United States or the Soviet

Union has gained greater security through the vehicle of confrontation in ever wider arenas. The costs have been extreme for both sides, and the additions to the national security have been dubious at best.

Quite apart from the ledger sheet of costs and benefits, however, must be an evaluation of what a Soviet-American worldwide competition has meant for the psychological and moral condition of each society and other nations affected by superpower competition. Although this issue is far too complex for treatment here, we should not assume that the legacy of such a lengthy Cold War is immediately apparent in units of currency, in numbers of deaths, or forms of governments. Instead, two generations of Soviets and Americans have grown to maturity in an environment fraught with a misuse of humanitarianism and a deceitful application of goodwill. In earlier decades of the Soviet regime, it may be argued that Joseph Stalin turned law and morality on their heads to develop a totalitarian state. If we use Stalin as a standard by which to judge political morality, however, an evaluation becomes skewed by the extremes of the collectivization and purges at home or the brutal repression of political dissent in Eastern Europe.

For the Soviet Union of today, global competition with the United States has had anything but a salutary effect on Soviet norms. The perceived American threat has rationalized a deep commitment to secrecy, helped to maintain the pervasiveness of the KGB and GRU, and perpetuated the underdevelopment of most socioeconomic sectors in the Soviet Union. The combined effect of such conditions has been to create a normative environment in which the Russian words *blat* and *proteksia* convey the operational codes of society: one gets things done and gets ahead by under-the-table dealings and by knowing the right people. This does not mean, however, that such widespread corruption would not exist if Soviet-American confrontation vanished tomorrow. Instead, a "corrupt society" in the USSR was excused, justified, or its consequences ignored because the preeminent competition with the United States demanded unity and loyalty.

Although a competitive democracy may have insulated the United States from the worst correlates of the Cold War era, U.S. social and political morality has not been unscathed. In the course of America's anti-Communist policies the moral paradox in which we find ourselves has been revealed occasionally in succinct ways—for example, when a commanding general said that he had to destroy a village in Vietnam to "save it," or when we are told by a secretary on the National Security Council staff that, regarding the Iran-contra affair, "sometimes we must go beyond the law" to justify destroying evidence.

That moral issues and psychological dilemmas have arisen in the conduct of U.S. policy to oppose communism generally, or the USSR in particular, is not new. A world Communist movement, directed from Moscow, was thought to be penetrating the United States in the 1950s, and spawned the civil rights abuses of McCarthyism. In the late 1960s and early 1970s, Richard Nixon's White House directed the CIA to engage in clandestine activities against the American people within the United States, contrary to the law establishing the agency, and ultimately sanctioned break-ins, wiretaps, and harassment of legitimate political opposition within our country. In the 1980s the "president's men," if not Reagan himself, certainly violated laws in the pursuit of what included anti-Communist and anti-Soviet goals. In the minds of those who have pursued such policies, however, the Soviet Gulag, and its enslavement of dissidents or religious activists, receives exclusive emphasis. Repression in the Soviet Union or other Communist states thus obscures, and to some people even justifies, the abrogation of our own principles and the dilution of democratic processes.

A New Course for Soviet-American Relations

Facing the enormous burdens and corrupting effects of their confrontational relations, the United States and the Soviet Union nevertheless cannot ignore differences that lead them to oppose the interests of each other. The dilemma of Soviet-American relations is relentless, with each nation-state unable to eliminate the perceived threat of the other's political system to its own values, and each unable to ignore the competition posed by the other state around the world. The opportunity to sidestep this dilemma—not to act from naïveté and ignore it but, rather, to develop alternative planes on which the United States and the USSR can relate—may now be possible, however. There are several reasons for this optimism, the most obvious of which are leadership changes in both superpowers.

The mere fact of change, indeed, may be as important as the substance of the new leaders' policies. For the USSR an end to the incapacitation of leadership over at least a five-year period, during which Leonid Brezhnev was severely ill and Yuri Andropov and Konstantin Chernenko came and went in short succession, was enough to guarantee the image of vitality. That Gorbachev, since March 1985, also has attempted to inaugurate reforms gives a quasi-revolutionary aura to his regime. For the United States, Reagan's presidency meant, for at least six years, a particularly dogmatic opposition to communism, Marxism, socialism, or radical revolution. The Reagan administration faced a serious setback during its last two years because of the Iran-contra scandal and a faltering economy that created diminished confidence of investors and a huge deficit. No matter what one's views about the policies implicit to such events, there was a disruption in U.S. foreign policy and a heightened impression that Reagan's ability to lead in matters of world affairs was seriously impaired. Consequently, the inauguration of a new American president in 1989, coupled with continued Gorbachev leadership in the USSR, can put behind both superpowers the periods during which central political authority had been weakened. Thus, an opportunity for decisive movement may present itself.

There is more than leadership change, however, to suggest a potential breakthrough in Soviet-American relations. An INF agreement has now been ratified after a few last issues, such as the disposition of seventy-two old West German Pershing 1-A missiles and a precise verification regime, were surmounted. Such a treaty could presage other accords within Europe; for example, a reduction of conventional forces should follow the INF accord. Furthermore, as Stephen White has argued, people-to-people contacts are increasing between Americans and Soviets, and this process could have consequences for the level of information and accuracy of images held by citizens of both superpowers about each other. These conditions, together with the cumulative impact of the costs of global Soviet-American competition, should present new Soviet and American leaders with a strong rationale for reconsidering the bases of their relations.

The key to changing the course of Soviet-American relations is to establish new priorities for the national security of each superpower. Since the late 1940s, U.S. and Soviet national security policies have been articulated primarily in terms of threat from each other. Even if it were once warranted, such an equation is no longer viable. Instead, the best and principal determinant of national security may now be the health and vitality of domestic socioeconomic policies.

On February 16, 1987, at a Central Committee plenum, Gorbachev stated that Soviet "international policy is more than ever determined by domestic policy, by our interests in concentrating on constructive endeavors to improve our country." Others in the USSR do not concur; yet, to hear this from top officials in Moscow is an important development. Gorbachev's position is the view of a pragmatist and, perhaps, Russian nationalist: that the strength of the nation lies deep within itself. By 1985, when Gorbachev became general secretary, the weaknesses of the Soviet system had become too crippling to be avoided, and its socioeconomic malaise was not a very well-kept secret. It was this danger from within that posed the most imminent threat to Soviet security, and that led the then Moscow Party Chief Boris Yeltsin to note, at the 27th Party Congress, that the stability of the Soviet Union could not be taken for granted.

Americans are not accustomed to thinking of dangers to the political system, or about threats to the broad consensus represented by the two-party competitive democracy that has long existed. However, the accumulation of debt and the repeated assaults on political values through illegal and unconstitutional activities by government officials—all justified by claims of national security imperatives or anticommunism—cannot be dismissed as nonthreatening. The economic weaknesses of the United States, particularly as revealed in trade and budget deficits, cannot be addressed fully when the protection of national security is thought to reside in the Persian Gulf, in rebels led by Jonas Savimbi, or in the contras. Certainly, budget deficits, which each year give foreign banks and governments increasing leverage over the United States, cannot be addressed when a $1-trillion SDI program looms ahead.

Is national security, then, "secured" best in the arena of foreign policy, especially through the confrontation of superpowers? Alternatively, is national security generated from its bases at home, in social policy that speaks to maldistribution of resources and injustice, and in economic and labor policies that seek to revitalize technology and productivity? The choice is not as well defined as such rhetorical questions imply. Rather, in the 1990s the option will be available for the United States and the Soviet Union to make incremental changes in their relationship that, by reinforcing each other's confidence in their intentions, decouple superpower competition from a global perspective.

Adopting such an option will involve, in part, accepting judgments such as those made by the contributors to this volume. But, as the century enters its final decade, most of us can agree that it is time for a "new course" to be found. Such a new course does not necessitate an ambivalence toward the other political and economic system. To the contrary, we need only recognize that our security requires first the preservation of our own socioeconomic strength and second the defense of our own political principles. Rather than implying a new isolationism for the United States or a return to "socialism in one country" for the USSR, however, new priorities for national security suggest reorientation, not withdrawal.

Practical steps could be taken by both nations to moderate Third World conflicts, to implement strategic arms control, to proceed with European force reductions, and to engage in symbolic acts (joint space exploration, for example). Joint withdrawals of forces or aid from specific areas of conflict such as Afghanistan may be an initial step in this direction that includes bilateral verification, perhaps following on the heels of the INF accord. An American proposal to delay deployment of SDI while both sides accept deep reductions in strategic weapons would be a key ingredient in the entire scenario of effecting a new course in Soviet-American relations. Yet, beyond the specific instruments by which Soviet-American relations are to be recast fundamentally must be the recognition that we cannot continue indefinitely on our present course, a course on which both the United States and the Soviet Union have mortgaged their national wealth and endangered their security.

Notes

[1]See, for example, "The B-1B Aircraft Program: Statement of Frank C. Conahan, Assistant Comptroller General of the United States before the Committee on Armed Services, House of Representatives, Subcommittee on Research and Development," GAO Testimony (GAO/T-NSIAD-87-4A), February 25, 1987.

[2]U.S. Arms Control and Disarmament Agency, *World Military Expenditures and Arms Transfers, 1986* (Washington, DC: ACDA, 1987), pp. 93, 97.

[3]Daniel N. Nelson, *Alliance Behavior in the Warsaw Pact* (Boulder, CO: Westview, 1986), pp. 82, 86.

[4]ACDA, *World Military Expenditures*, p. 93.

[5]Ibid., p. 97.

[6]See Ellen Jones, *Red Army and Society* (Boston: Allen and Unwin, 1985), pp. 211–19.

[7]Alvin Z. Rubinstein, *Soviet Foreign Policy since World War II*, 2d ed. (Boston: Little Brown, 1986), p. 198. Rubinstein estimates that between 1,000 and 2,000 Soviets have been killed per year in Afghanistan.

Index